Temporary and Gig Economy Workers in China and Japan

Temporary and Gig Economy Workers in China and Japan

The Culture of Unequal Work

Edited by
Huiyan Fu

Great Clarendon Street, Oxford, OX2 6DP,
United Kingdom

Oxford University Press is a department of the University of Oxford.
It furthers the University's objective of excellence in research, scholarship,
and education by publishing worldwide. Oxford is a registered trade mark of
Oxford University Press in the UK and in certain other countries

© Oxford University Press 2023

The moral rights of the author have been asserted

All rights reserved. No part of this publication may be reproduced, stored in
a retrieval system, or transmitted, in any form or by any means, without the
prior permission in writing of Oxford University Press, or as expressly permitted
by law, by licence or under terms agreed with the appropriate reprographics
rights organization. Enquiries concerning reproduction outside the scope of the
above should be sent to the Rights Department, Oxford University Press, at the
address above

You must not circulate this work in any other form
and you must impose this same condition on any acquirer

Published in the United States of America by Oxford University Press
198 Madison Avenue, New York, NY 10016, United States of America

British Library Cataloguing in Publication Data

Data available

Library of Congress Control Number: 2022950802

ISBN 978–0–19–284969–4

DOI: 10.1093/oso/9780192849694.001.0001

Printed and bound by
CPI Group (UK) Ltd, Croydon, CR0 4YY

Links to third party websites are provided by Oxford in good faith and
for information only. Oxford disclaims any responsibility for the materials
contained in any third party website referenced in this work.

To my mentors

Foreword

Precarious work has emerged as a key challenge for workers, their families, and societies in the twenty-first century. This term denotes work that is uncertain, unstable, and insecure. Most importantly, it shifts the risks of work from employers and governments to individuals and their families, and so precarious workers typically have only limited social and legal protections. These risks have been exposed dramatically during the Covid-19 pandemic in the case of temporary and gig workers, many of whom provide essential services despite experiencing financial insecurity and being exposed to dangerous conditions. The realization that precarious work is central to addressing a myriad of social and economic problems—such as health, poverty and inequality, family formation, social integration, and individual well-being—has put this age-old topic on the front burner for social scientists and policymakers around the world.

The recent focus on precarious work reflects major economic shifts in the global economy. Macrostructural forces associated with globalization and technological change have created an increasingly competitive global economy, encouraging the spread of neoliberal economic and political policies to make labour markets and employers more flexible and reconfigure social welfare protections. This has shifted the balance of power in favour of employers against labour, and transferred the risks of work and responsibilities for social protections to workers and their families. Temporary and gig workers are especially vulnerable to these changes.

While precarious work is universal, it is cross-nationally variable, as the nature of this liberalization of work and social protections has differed, depending on a country's political situation and the collective power of workers. The character and consequences of precarious work also depend on a country's culture and history, which shape the institutions of work and how individuals come to understand and adapt to precarious work.

This book is a timely and welcome contribution to the current dialogue about precarious work and its outcomes. It is especially notable for advancing our understanding in several main areas that have been relatively neglected in previous research. First, it highlights the interplay between culture and political–economic forces, drawing on the anthropological notion of a 'total social phenomenon' that emphasizes society as an organic whole that provides the context within which individual lives unfold and take on meaning. In this view, culture serves to reinforce and interpret the structural changes induced by political–economic responses to neoliberalism. Second, several chapters illuminate how people cope with precarious jobs. These analyses show that individuals' responses to such jobs are not given, but that their expectations and the meanings they ascribe to their experiences and identities as precarious workers depend on cultural and institutional contexts. Third, the book illustrates ways in which workers seek to ameliorate some of the consequences of precarious work through collective forms of resistance. These collective actions range from unions to labour NGOs, depending on the possibilities provided by political and industrial relations systems.

Comparative studies are necessary to examine these kinds of questions, as they reveal the character of precarious work in different sociocultural and political–economic contexts. This enables understanding of similarities and differences in the roles of global and domestic factors in shaping precarious work and its consequences and suggests some generalizable conclusions. The comparison of China and Japan is apt for explicating precarious work as a total social phenomenon and shedding light on the interplay between institutions and cultures in influencing work arrangements and individuals' experiences.

The two countries are similar in some ways. Both are large and powerful economies, with China and Japan ranking as the second and third largest economies in the world in terms of GDP. Precarious work, in the form of non-regular work arrangements such as temporary and gig work, constitutes a large and growing component of work in each country. Both countries have common cultural influences, notably Confucianism, the system of thought and behaviour that emphasizes the importance of family, social harmony, hierarchy, and collectivism. These principles have influenced many of the features of work in these countries and guided the ways in which workers make sense of their lives.

China and Japan also differ in significant ways, allowing a comparative assessment of differences in precarious work produced by diverse political systems and domestic dynamics. While both countries exhibit forms of dualism in their labour forces, the bases of this dualism differ. In China, the basic dualism is between urban and rural workers, a divide reinforced by the *hukou* household registration system that provides various social and legal rights and benefits to urban but not rural citizens. In Japan, the dualism between regular and non-regular work is heavily gendered, with women being over-represented in precarious work. Dualism in both countries is supported by Confucian cultural traditions: the emphasis on a rigid hierarchy underlying the urban–rural divide in China; and the male breadwinner–female homemaker model defining family relationships in Japan.

Moreover, the political–economic systems of the two countries have patterned their responses to developments in the global economy. China's state-led economic model encouraged national and local governments to provide social protections to promote 'social harmony' and dampen worker unrest by rural migrants. Japan's employer-dominated enterprise unionism has encouraged the development of community unions, though these have not had much impact on public policy, which has been focused more on the interests of employers. In both countries, culture again sustains these industrial relations and social welfare systems.

Temporary and Gig Economy Workers in China and Japan advances our understanding of the dynamics of precarious work and helps to bridge the gap in research on precarious work between studies of institutions and cultures. In so doing, it draws our attention to important implications of the expansion of temporary and gig work in these countries for individuals and their families.

Arne L. Kalleberg
Kenan Distinguished Professor of Sociology
University of North Carolina at Chapel Hill, USA

Contents

List of Figures and Tables   x
List of Contributors   xi

    Introduction: The Culture of Unequal Work: Temps and Giggers in China and Japan   1
    Huiyan Fu

1. **Old and New Inequalities: Citizenly Discounting and Precarious Work in a Changing China**   24
   Huiyan Fu

2. **Gender, Precarious Labour, and Neoliberalism in Japan**   48
   Saori Shibata

3. **Teleworking in Pandemic Japan**   74
   Machiko Osawa and Jeff Kingston

4. **Organizing around Precarity in China**   93
   Jude Howell

5. **Precarious Work and Challenges Facing Japanese Unionism**   118
   Arjan Keizer

6. **Organizing Temporary Agency Workers in Japan: Two Types of Inclusive Union Responses**   137
   Akira Suzuki

7. **Negotiating Gender, Citizenship, and Precarity: Migrant Women in Contemporary China**   154
   Nana Zhang

8. **Hierarchies, Shadows, and Precarity: Cultural Production on Online Literature Platforms in China**   175
   Elaine Jing Zhao

9. **Making Sense of Inequalities at Work: The Micropolitics of Everyday Negotiation among Non-Regular Workers in Japan**   196
   Shinji Kojima

10. **'I'm Not a *Real* Freeter': Aspiration and Non-Regular Labour in Japan**   218
    Emma E. Cook

Index   248

List of Figures and Tables

Figures

1.1	Legal protection disparities between rural migrant workers and urban workers	28
1.2	Five-tiered hierarchical employment segmentation in the pre-reform era	32
1.3	Accepted cases by Labour Dispute Arbitration Committees (1994–2014)	37
2.1	Proportion of employees by type in Japan, 1984–2020	54
2.2	Wage index comparison, by country	56
2.3	Year-on-year rate of change in scheduled monthly earnings, 1977–2019	57
2.4	The number of the unemployed	66
2.5	Receipt of leave allowance, by employment type	67
5.1	Stylized representation of union voice fragmentation	131

Tables

2.1	Major policies and reforms in labour market, 1980s–2020	53
2.2	Employee by type (ten thousand persons)	55
5.1	Union membership data (x 1,000)	123
6.1	Two types of inclusive responses of unions to non-regular workers	148
9.1	Average lifetime earnings by gender and employment status	198
9.2	Employment categories and remuneration	199
9.3	List of interviewees	201

List of Contributors

Emma E. Cook, Associate Professor in Anthropology, Modern Japanese Studies, Hokkaido University, Japan.

Huiyan Fu, Senior Lecturer in International HRM, University of Essex, UK.

Jude Howell, Professor in International Development, LSE, UK.

Arne L. Kalleberg, Professor in Sociology, University of North Carolina, Chapel Hill, US.

Arjan Keizer, Senior Lecturer in Comparative HRM & IRs, University of Manchester, UK.

Jeff Kingston, Professor in Japanese & Asian Studies, Temple University, Japan.

Shinji Kojima, Associate Professor in Sociology, Ritsumeikan Asia Pacific University, Japan.

Machiko Osawa, Professor in Economics, Japan Women's University.

Saori Shibata, Lecturer in East Asian Studies, University of Sheffield, UK.

Akira Suzuki, Professor in Sociology, Hosei University, Japan.

Nana Zhang, Lecturer in Sociology, University of Southampton, UK.

Elaine Jing Zhao, Senior Lecturer in Digital Communication and Culture, University of New South Wales, Australia.

Introduction: The Culture of Unequal Work

Temps and Giggers in China and Japan

Huiyan Fu

> I'll take a paracetamol if I have a temperature and pull myself up because I don't have any other means of earning and this is my livelihood.—a 42-year-old Uber driver in London
>
> *The Guardian,* **17 March 2020**

> I feel like I'm in a really terrible lottery. I want to put food on my table. I want to pay a very large sum of bills.—A freelance writer in the US seeing her finances take a hit by coronavirus and struggling to access government aid
>
> *CNN,* **13 April 2020**

Coronavirus (Covid-19), an unprecedented and still-unfolding global pandemic, lays bare stark realities faced by workers in precarious forms of employment. Drivers, couriers, and carers are at heightened risk of contracting and transmitting coronavirus, but simply cannot afford to miss work. Freelancers and (in)dependent contractors see their work dry up and have to contend with its financial implications. While government emergency schemes provide temporary relief, they tend to discriminate against highly precarious employment categories, as well as imposing obstacles (such as onerous administrative burdens) to assessing benefits. The resulting increased health and financial vulnerability among precarious workers—many of whom have been designated as 'key workforces' during the pandemic—is a painful reminder of growing social polarization between the haves and the have-nots. As Fairwork researchers at the University of Oxford (2020a) point out, coronavirus brings to light a fundamental issue that 'unless those providing the care are protected, none of us are'. Indeed, the interconnected nature of society, sharpened by the global health crisis, makes it imperative that we delve deeper into the roots of precarious work that has accelerated across the world over the past three to four decades.

Precarious work can be best defined as the *uncertainty, instability*, and *insecurity* of work in which workers bear the risks of work (as opposed to businesses or the government) and receive limited social benefits and statutory protections (Hewison 2016; Kalleberg 2000; Kalleberg and Vallas 2018; Vosko 2010). Under neoliberal globalization, a proliferation of temporary jobs in various bewildering forms has spanned a wide range of employment categories across almost all economic sectors. In addition, the past decade has witnessed a rapidly swelling number of workers in a so-called 'gig economy' or 'online platform economy' characterized by new technology-enabled links of work (Prassl 2018). Being paid per gig or assignment, which can be anything from delivering and driving services to creative marketing and computerized tasks, gig-economy workers are commonly treated as self-employed. However, disguised or bogus self-employment has been rife, which involves employers' deliberate misclassification of workers as independent contractors for the purpose of cost reduction (Fairwork 2020b). The lure of flexibility, freedom, and interesting technology, touted prominently in political and popular discourses, appears to be an important driving force behind the development. Nevertheless, a great many new giggers and traditional temps share the aforementioned key characteristics of precarious work, which is starkly revealed by the coronavirus pandemic when they are deprived of the 'luxury' of self-isolating and working from home with social protection entitlements. As Kalleberg and Hewison (2013) remind us, the growth of precarious work constitutes a serious global challenge and has wide-ranging consequences affecting workers, their families, and the society at large. It is an all-encompassing social phenomenon that touches on many salient topics for social scientists, ranging from inequality, industrial relations, and labour market regulations to social welfare and sustainability.

Against this backdrop, this book sets out to explore precarious work and social inequalities in China and Japan, with a view to showing both nation-specific factors and generalizable insights that could inform other countries. It aims to contribute to theory and practice on three main fronts. First, while a large number of studies exist on political and economic explanations for precarious work, relatively few have focused on culture and its oft-hidden pervasive effects. In this respect, China and Japan offer a prime example, not least because their cultural traditions are intriguingly distinct from western ones, thereby forcing us to question our own oft-taken-for-granted (ethnocentric) assumptions. By foregrounding the cultural dimension and its intricate entanglement with political-economic institutions, the book conceptualizes precarious work as 'a total social phenomenon', a key notion in anthropology that emphasizes the plural and interconnected aspects of social realities. Secondly, comparing China and Japan, the second- and third-largest economies in the world, is a daunting yet worthwhile endeavour. Despite substantial differences in their contemporary political–economic systems—which seem to present impediments to comparative research—the two Confucianism-influenced East Asian powerhouses are culturally proximate, historically exerting considerable influence upon each other. Thirdly, the importance of structural-institutional forces notwithstanding, the book places special emphasis upon how real people in everyday life perceive and act upon precarious work. Admittedly, combining macro-structural scrutiny and micro-agency empiricism can go a long way towards a better understanding of complex social life, yet it remains oft-neglected or under-researched. In addressing these gaps, the book benefits from extensive interdisciplinary collaboration and cross-fertilization of knowledge and ideas from multiple fields including anthropology, sociology, business management, international development, and communication.

In China and Japan, precarious work is manifested predominantly in the form of non-regular employment (NRE), which include temporary, part-time, and fixed-term contracts and agency-mediated labour dispatch. In both countries, the size of NRE has enlarged twofold since the 1990s; around 60 per cent of the Chinese urban workforce and nearly 40 per cent of the Japanese national workforce are now engaged in NRE. As elsewhere, the rise of online labour platforms has been driving a shift from traditional temps—many of whom are classified as employees—towards self-employed giggers. The expansion of precarious work goes hand in hand with the intensification of pre-existing labour market dualism and inequalities. In China, rural migrants are the quintessential embodiment of precarious work; despite their enormous contribution to the country's economic growth, they have continued to be segregated from urban citizens in profound socio-economic terms because of their second-class citizenship status. In Japan, women, who have long been relegated to the margins of political-economic life as part-time wage workers and full-time family care-givers, bear the major brunt of precarious work. The contrasting demographic features in China and Japan lend credence to the importance of social stratification variables (such as gender, class, age, citizenship, ethnicity, and race) in building and shaping the contours of precarious work. Significantly, these variables are imbued with nation-specific, deep-seated cultural values and practices that often elude policymakers and popular perceptions. By adopting a culture-centred holistic approach, the book intends to bring a more integrated and nuanced understanding of precarious work in China, Japan, and beyond. Specifically, it explores the following interrelated sets of research questions:

1. In what ways have cultural values been involved or implicated in the formation of key political-economic institutions, such as government policies, social welfare, regulatory systems, and employment relations that have, as well demonstrated by existing studies, played an important role in the growth of precarious work?
2. What may be the role of emerging new institutional actors (such as community unions and civil society groups) in resisting and otherwise reacting to precarious work as a serious social problem, especially when traditional institutional actors, i.e. the state, employers, and labour unions, fail to protect precarious workers?
3. How is precarious work experienced by real people in everyday life? What may be the reasons behind the oft-observed gaps between social expectations and realities, especially among the most disadvantaged groups of workers?
4. Finally, in tackling the negative consequences of precarious work, what generalizable insights and lessons can be learned from China and Japan?

The rest of this introductory chapter is organized into four sections. A brief theoretical framework is first laid out, which focuses on culture's relationship with institutions and its analytical importance in unpacking precarious work. The second section turns to a comparative examination of major themes arising from the above research questions. This is followed by a summary of the book's structure and chapters in the third section. The concluding section outlines broad implications that aim to inform policy, practice, and future research.

Precarious work as a 'total social phenomenon': Culture and institutions

In this book, precarious work is identified as a simultaneously political, economic, and cultural phenomenon, what anthropologists refer to as a 'total social phenomenon'. Derived from Marcel Mauss's classic treatise on *The Gift* (1954), the notion is used to accentuate the wholeness and interconnectedness of all facets of human existence. Rather than being separated into discrete and disparate units, society is conceived of as a relatively 'seamless' and 'organic whole' (Ortner 1984: 148). This theoretical basis, along with its methodological companion ethnography, is known as anthropological holism, which defines a distinct style of inquiry. Holism necessitates, first and foremost, a deep and thorough understanding of context or life worlds in which to make sense of any forms of human lives. Its intellectual genealogy can be traced back to, and is entangled with, some of the major traditions in western thinking (Otto and Bubandt 2011). Early western anthropologists often employed holism to compare the kinds of wholes that they saw in the lives of others with life in their own world. The comparison in turn provides revealing insights into the ideological limits of individualism and its variations in the west, which are deeply entrenched in political, economic, religious, moral, and many other areas of life (Lukes 1973). As the archetypal western value, individualism idealizes the self as a solid, free entity, seemingly devoid of social ties (Dumont 1985, 1986). This separation between individual and society stands in marked contrast to many non-western cultural traditions; in both China and Japan, individual interests are closely connected with, and subordinated to, socially prescribed norms, albeit in different ways. In deciphering such contrasting and contradictory life worlds, holism lends itself to a distinct vantage point from which to transcend the situatedness of western knowledge and to reflect critically on the constitution of these worlds (Otto and Bubandt 2011: 11).

Despite its critical potential, holism is notoriously vague and problematic. This is primarily caused by a perplexing variety of interpretations and applications among scholars. For one thing, prevailing disciplinary boundaries tend to generate not only different emphases on the practice of 'doing it in context' but also varying weight given to a particular dimension of context. For another, even within anthropology, controversy has been a prominent feature of the historical development of holism. Until the early 1970s, anthropology was divided between the British school of 'social' anthropology and the American school of 'cultural' anthropology. Durkheim-influenced British anthropologists approached culture from a distinctive sociological angle with an emphasis on power struggles and asymmetrical social relations (see, for example, Cohen 1969, 1974). By contrast, American anthropologists leant towards individual autonomous interpretations of culture as 'a web of meanings' (Geertz 1973). The subsequent paradigm shift towards 'discourse analysis' or 'symbolic anthropology' (Parkin 1984; Bourdieu 1991) has brought together the two foci as a collective concern, and renewed the dialectical relationship between individual interpretive freedom and structural–institutional constraints. More specifically, the new paradigm accentuates the role of language—an element and reflection of culture—and power relations in constructing social realities. Since then, culture has been widely recognized as an ever-continuing discursive process in which a society's core values, beliefs, and norms are constructed, maintained, mediated, challenged, or changed, a process intricately intertwined with political and economic forces.

Such a holistic and processual view of culture can make a distinctive contribution to the understanding of precarious work, especially in terms of bridging the divide between institutional and cultural debates. As stated earlier, there exists a burgeoning body of literature that offers compelling macro-structural explanations of the causes and nature of precarious work. Many scholars have been at the forefront of expounding a series of drastic changes wrought by neoliberalism, a new political-economic orthodoxy that promotes free market, free trade, investment, financialization, deregulation, and privatization—see Burawoy (2015) for a relatively recent critique. Since the 1970s, neoliberal tenets, albeit composing inconsistent, controversial, and highly contested ideas, have created an impetus for the state and businesses to establish global production processes. To compete in such processes, cost reduction and deregulation have become a key strategic area where labour markets are made more flexible and precarious types of labour are increasingly utilized. A race to the bottom has ensued, with detrimental impacts on employment conditions, labour rights, social progress, and sustainability. In a nutshell, these and other structural changes result in a reconfiguration of the relationship between the state, capital, and labour, which systematically tilts the balance of power more firmly in favour of capital and against labour. The shift in the power dynamics has profound implications for organized resistance and the well-being of the working class (Lambert and Herod 2016). Harvey (2005: 168) is at pains to explain how the protective coverings provided for labour under the 'interventionist' state—which 'embedded liberalism' allowed and occasionally nurtured during the 1950s and 1960s—are stripped away:

> The powers of trade unions and other working-class institutions are curbed or dismantled within a particular state (by violence if necessary). Flexible labour markets are established. State withdrawal from social welfare provision and technologically induced shift in job structures that render large segments of the labour force redundant complete the domination of capital over labour in the market-place. The individualized and relatively powerless worker then confronts a labour market in which only short-term contracts are offered on a customized basis.

The institutional-structural forces alone, however, cannot fully grasp the normalization and expansion of precarious work. Herein lies the crucial yet oft-overlooked role of culture in the ascendency of neoliberalism as a hegemonic model of governance. As Hann (2006) rightly points out, individualism has been reconstructed so as to fit in with the neoliberal 'free-market' logic seen as a guide for all human action:

> If the ultimate value in classical liberal thought was the liberty of the individual citizen, then under neoliberalism it is the innovative capacity of each individual entrepreneur. Every human being is assumed to think and act as an entrepreneur, with the result that the impersonal laws of the market are drawn into all areas of human capacity.

According to neoliberal ideology, rational, self-interested individuals need to compete in the market. Competition is then conceptualized and regulated as individual workers, rather than as the collective power of labour markets (Kalleberg and Hewison 2013: 277). In tandem with the individualization process, popular terms such as 'flexibility', 'freedom', 'enterprising self', and 'personal responsibility' have emerged. Equipped with the explanatory power of tradition, these culture-derived discourses play an instrumental role in facilitating political consent and deflecting attention from the deleterious and debilitating effects on workers, especially those at the bottom end of the labour market with little security, low wages, and poor working conditions. To a great extent, the neoliberal assertion of new individualistic values is foisted upon the global precarious working class, rendering many workers disorganized, dispossessed, and powerless. Thus, culture as a powerful discursive tool is utilized by ruling elites for constructing what Harvey (2005) describes as a neoliberal 'accumulation-by-dispossession' class project wherein more and more wealth and power has been redistributed and consolidated in ever smaller fractions of the capitalist class.

Acknowledging the interconnectedness of culture and institutions not only contributes to a better understanding of precarious work, but also opens fresh avenues for exploration of social change. This is perhaps particularly pertinent to discussion of the 'non-western holism' in China and Japan, where the state and labour maintain their distinct local 'stickiness', despite both countries having been integrated into the global economy. As scholars contend, neoliberal capitalism provokes a way of organizing heterogeneity, intensifies ever-complex cultural processes, and heightens conflicts (see, for example, Appadurai 1990; Edelman and Haugerud 2005; Eriksen 2003; Giddens 1990; Hannerz 1992, 1996; Held et al. 1999; Mann 2013). To be sure, the increasing interaction and tension between indigenous cultural values and imported neoliberal ones constitute a key characteristic of today's globalization. This points to the centrality of culture in social dynamics as a symbolic, discursive, malleable, and contestable construct, thereby offering crucial clues to agency and its role in challenging the status quo.

A comparison of precarious work in China and Japan

Cultural hierarchy and social inequalities: Rural migrants versus women

China and Japan share a common cultural tradition of (broadly defined) Confucianism, which emphasizes, among other things, relational hierarchy, family-oriented ethos, harmony, and collectivism. In contradistinction to Christianity-informed individualism, Confucianism foregrounds an interconnected relationship between individual and society, with precedence given to the fulfilling of socially prescribed rules, norms, and expectations. These and other core cultural values, which permeate almost every realm of social life, have an important bearing on understanding the demographic features of precarious work and institutional structures surrounding them.

In China, the predominance of rural migrants in precarious work is created by the country's long-existing rural-urban divide known as *hukou* (household registration). For over half a century, *hukou* has institutionally legitimized two classes of citizenship based on people's residential status they attained at birth. Despite recent decades' reforms, it continues to function as a key social entitlement mechanism that confers public benefits and services on urban citizens while denying many of them to rural citizens. The persistence of *hukou* has much to do with Confucian hierarchical prejudices that are deeply entrenched in the Chinese cultural history. Since Deng's 'open-door' economic reforms, hundreds of millions of peasant workers known as *nongmin gong* have flocked to cities to take up jobs in manufacturing factories, construction sites, and increasingly service industries—the kind of jobs in typically informal or private sectors of economy with least autonomy, protection, and dignity. As the quintessential embodiment of precarious conditions of existence, rural migrants are disproportionally subject to employment insecurity, low pay and benefits, wage arrears, lack of training and upward mobility, alienation, discrimination, and violence (see, for example, Lee 1995, 1998; Pun 2005; Pun and Lu 2010a, 2010b; Huang and Yi 2015; Swider 2015). Their second-class citizenship is further endorsed by the state's neoliberal modernization discourses, which label rural masses 'backward-looking', 'burdensome', 'dangerous', and 'desperate for a modern revamp'. These discourses are often centred on *suzhi* (human quality), which has become a 'cultural fixation', frequently invoked by the state and the media to problematize the peasant body as having low quality and hindering development (Anagnost 1997). Responsibility is then adroitly placed on the individual, rather than on the historical and socio-structural conditions, for failing to become the state's ideal citizen. That the rural masses should be disciplined into a modern citizenry seems to justify just-in-time provision of a cheap and relatively docile labour force who have toiled at fuelling China's extraordinary transformation into a global industrial powerhouse. From Mao-era liberation 'heroes' to modernization 'losers', the drastic shift of the peasant image reveals the importance of culture in policymaking, economic reforms, and social stratification processes.

In Japan, labour market dualism is marked by gender. Despite having one of the highest rates of tertiary education and work participation in the developed world, Japanese women account for more than two-thirds of all non-regular workers. While gender-based segmentation in many industrialized nations takes place largely along occupational lines, in Japan it is located within occupations along the lines of precarious employment status. Since the late 1980s, increased use of non-regular workers has been the single most important change in the labour market. The gendered precarious work is most pronounced among small and medium-sized firms, by far the largest segment of Japan's national workforce, whose working, earning, and bargaining environment for the peripheral majority is profoundly different from that of core, male regular workers in large firms (see Chalmers 1989). Like the hukou-based segmentation in China, the gendered core-periphery dualism in Japan is underpinned by Confucianism-informed assumptions concerning women's familial roles as 'good wife wise mother' (*ryōsai kenbo*) and men's breadwinner responsibilities as 'a central supporting pillar' (*daikokubashira*) in the traditional household. This distinct 'reproductive bargain' (Gottfried 2015) has been a long-standing yet oft-hidden cultural pillar, which explains much of Japan's post-war economic 'miracle' and is indeed consequential for defining the contours of precarious work. Gender patriarchy is also a prominent feature of the Japanese corporate management, as evidenced by a customary division between women's 'auxiliary' employment track (*ippanshoku*) and men's 'comprehensive' career track (*sōgōshoku*) leading to management positions. Moreover, it is embedded in a range of family and welfare policies, regulatory frameworks, and industrial relations, which in effect excludes the majority of non-regular workers from the protection of the state and mainstream unions (Marshall 2017; Roberts 2011, 2016; Osawa et al. 2013; Yun 2010). For instance, Japan's spouse tax reduction system not only encourages employers to offer married women low-paid, non-regular jobs, but also creates a disincentive for women to pursue ambitious full-time careers (MacNaughtan 2015). The entrenched male-breadwinner female-dependent family model also lies behind a series of high-profile 'women-friendly' policies promoted by the state; a careful examination of these policies will show that these policies are largely geared towards tackling low fertility rates or labour shortages by persuading women of reproductive age to have children, boosting women's workplace participation (continuously as non-regular workers), and encouraging those who already work to put in longer hours.

Industrial relations: State-led model versus employer-dominated model

National industrial relations, which is centred on the institutional dynamics between the state, capital, and labour, serve as a focal point for debate on 'varieties of capitalism' (Hall and Soskice 2001). A comparison of this tripartite relationship and its entanglement with culture enables us to better grasp complex social conditions that drive precarious work. In China, the state exerts a powerful influence over the direction of economy directly through a gradually shrinking but highly concentrated state-owned enterprises (SOEs)—often used as 'instruments of macroeconomic policy and industry regulation' (Kroeber 2016: 89). Private domestic and foreign enterprises, under economic decentralization policies, have been granted more space and now contribute to the majority of economic output and employment. However, their meaningful autonomy can only materialize if 'remaining deeply integrated with local governments' (Friedman and Kuruvilla 2015: 182). The corollary is a distinct model of 'crony capitalism' (Pei 2016) where many local governments use their authority and *guanxi*—personal networks or connections, a key concept in Chinese culture—to forge close alliances with businesses, enforce market despotism, and suppress labour unrest. The relationship between local governments and businesses constitutes a major cause of the country's lax regulatory environment and has profound consequences for workers, especially rural migrants who are most vulnerable to employer exploitation. In response to growing social disparities and conflicts intensified by decades of unrelenting marketization, the central government has introduced 'harmonious society' (*he xie she hui*) as a major policy orientation since the early 2000s. The new policy is in effect a reinvention of the classical Confucian concept 'harmony', with the aim of reconciling social tensions, defusing class formation, and strengthening hierarchical solidarity. To realize the goal of 'harmonious society', the central government made a series of paternalistic concessions including a significant increase in social spending and the enactment of new pro-labour legislations (Gallagher et al. 2015). In addition to this development model based on the central–local government division, the absence of independent unions and collective bargaining rights is another salient feature of China's industrial relations. The All-China Federation of Trade Unions (ACFTU) is the only legitimate representative of organized labour, whose function is often derided as 'government agencies' (Friedman and Lee 2010), 'Leninist transmission-belt' (Zhu and Warner 2011), or 'benevolent mediators' serving to ensure political control at the workplace (Walder 1983, 1984). Compared to growing autonomy conferred upon private capita, the ACFTU remains firmly a part of the Party-led state; its bureaucratic hierarchy is cut off by Communist Party officials at every level in the personnel system (Chan and Chiu 2015: 159–160). Although state-sanctioned reforms have been implemented to improve labour-capital relations, they tend to be short-lived, confined to the enterprise level and marked by considerable local differences. Perhaps more strikingly, these reforms endorse 'individual'—rather than collective organizing—legal rights and are aimed at promoting 'harmonious society', maintaining stability and order, and facilitating economic growth.

In Japan, industrial relations is characterized by employer-dominated 'enterprise unionism' (*kigyo kumiai*) or decentralized bargaining at the enterprise level. Japanese employers are indeed a formidable force; they exert a powerful influence on state policy through a historically developed cosy relationship with government ministries—as exemplified by *amakudari* (descent from heaven), an institutionalized practice where senior government bureaucrats retire to managerial positions in private firms. The Japanese state, compared to the Chinese state's 'visible hand', is notoriously elusive, with party politicians, ministry bureaucrats, and employer associations composing a cohesive power triumvirate where no one seems to rule the roost—what Wolferen (1989) portrays as a 'truncated pyramid'. For Japanese workers, it is the employer, rather than the state, that provides main social protection; a good indicator is that Japan spent only 0.17 per cent of GDP on unemployment benefits, compared to an average of 0.68 per cent for all OECD countries (OECD 2020). The power of employers, however, goes far beyond this well-known 'welfare corporatism' (Lincoln and Kalleberg 1990) in a material sense. Cultural values, especially those derived from the traditional family (*ie*), figure importantly in Japan's post-war institution-building and management strategy; as Goodman (1998) explains, the Japanese 'firm-as-family' employment system was created by appealing to 'invented' traditions (Hobsbawm and Ranger 1983) in order to keep workers loyal to the firm, mask glaring inequalities, and boost profits. Under this culture-infused system, workers' struggles have been shepherded into the confines of a single firm. To ensure that the firm's performance is regarded as the most important determinant, employers have successfully cultivated a harmony-based, cooperative relationship with labour unions—aided by, for example, a personnel cross-posting practice whereby union officials are not only employees of the firm, but often become managers at later stages of their career after a temporary assignment in the union. This employer-dominated model, combined with deep-rooted cultural beliefs especially concerning the male breadwinner of the family, results in a kind of 'conservative corporatism' (Yun 2010) where employers, labour unions, and the state collude to protect employment security of a shrinking labour aristocracy of (male) regular workers. The burdens of job insecurity and cost reduction are then shifted to the expanding labour market periphery occupied by temps, giggers and, more insidiously, 'second-tier' regular (female) workers whose unfavourable terms of employment share much in common with those of long-term temps (Gordon 2017).

Resistance from below: Labour NGOs versus community unions

In China, relatively privileged workers in SOEs took the helm of collective protests against drastic restructuring layoffs during the late 1990s and early 2000s (Lee 2000, 2002). However, the past two decades witnessed relentless waves of labour unrest among long-exploited rural migrants. There had been a marked upswing in 'wildcat strikes' or unofficial industrial action, which could be ascribed to pervasive disaffection with the state-led unions and local governments who were unable or unwilling to protect workers at the point of production. Better-educated, younger generations of migrant workers were less tolerant of injustice and more eager to engage in all manner of resistance (Friedman and Lee 2010; Pun and Lu 2010a; Chan and Selden 2014). Scholars note that there was also a qualitative shift from legal rights-based struggles to interest-based struggles that demanded higher wages, better working conditions, and greater respect from employers than the legal minimum (Chan 2015; Elfstrom and Kuruvilla 2014; Chang and Brown 2013; Chan 2014). Against this background, labour NGOs had emerged since the mid-1990s as new institutional actors in economically well-developed regions with labour-intensive, export-oriented industries, such as Beijing, Pearl River Delta, and Yangtze River Delta where labour disputes frequently arose (Xu 2013). They represented a grassroots effort to organize and empower rural migrant workers and actively drew on expertise and support from Hong Kong-based labour activists, mainland pro-labour intellectuals and international advocacy networks. Their positive interventions notwithstanding, labour NGOs had yet to succeed in generating a labour movement due to a combination of internal and external structural obstacles—see Chapter 4. In particular, the state's shifting strategies, ranging from intermittent harassment and muted tolerance to outright repression and welfare co-option (Howell 2015), posed the most daunting impediment to developing collective actions, officially deemed 'mass incidents' (*quntixing shijian*) that would threaten the 'harmony' of society and 'ruling-by-law' policies. Consequently, workers' everyday resistance, despite its rising number and intensity, was scattered, alienated, and unable to participate in the policymaking at the class level (Friedman 2014).

In Japan, mainstream enterprise unions rarely organize confrontational demonstrations or strike actions, although the number of individual disputes administered by government agencies and judicial systems is on the rise (JILPT 2016). Established in the early 1980s, community unions or 'individually affiliated unions' (*kojin kamei kumiai*) are one of the very few institutional devices whereby precarious and vulnerable workers have their voice heard and seek justice. Benefiting from liberal legal recognition and political independence, they are famous for developing aggressive and innovative bargaining tactics and enabling a small yet resilient labour countermovement (Weathers 2010; Royle and Urano 2012). Nevertheless, the overweening dominance of employers and their 'firm-as-family' management ethos creates considerable difficulties in mobilizing workers across different firms, industries, and regions. The exclusion, or differential inclusion, of non-regular workers outside the firm continues to define Japan's labour market dualism and presents fundamental barriers to new organizing strategies among both mainstream enterprise unions and community unions. This is further compounded by enduring union factionalism and male-dominated leadership practices, which are underpinned by Japanese cultural norms concerning groupism, gender, and hierarchy (Fu 2021). Historically inherited ideological conflicts were a major contributor to recurrent inter- and intro-group fighting and splitting at organizational and union-affiliation levels, which prevented community unions engaging in meaningful networking and building robust 'labour associational power' (Kojima 2017). It is also worth noting that Japan's state-controlled civil society lacks advocacy power and is too weak and fragmented to offer a substantial partnership (see Pekkanen 2006). Perhaps more thought-provoking is widespread gender- and seniority-based hierarchical organizational practices among community unions' older-generation male leaders (Fu 2021). These practices presumably hinder their ability to attract a broad cross-section of workers, especially women and young people, who account for the bulk of precarious workers in Japan. It could be argued that the institutional constraints, especially those imposed by the stable and largely unchallenged industrial relations structure, combined with the underlying cultural influences, explain much of Japan's increasingly patchy and fragmented labour movement landscape. Even occasionally high-profile collective campaigns such as Hakenmura, led by community unions (Takasu 2012)—where an unwieldy jumble of unions, political parties, and civil society groups were temporarily connected together—exerted little impact on the policy-making.

Insight from the comparison

The above brief comparison reveals, first and foremost, the complexity of social conditions where precarious work and inequalities are situated. In particular, it throws into relief the intricate entanglement between culture and social institutions, i.e. 'a total social phenomenon', whose impact cannot be reduced to neatly arranged categories and thus merits careful analytical scrutiny. It is evident that the contrast between China's state-led and Japan's employer-dominated corporatism demonstrates the direct effects of national industrial relations systems on the expansion of precarious work, the entrenchment of labour market dualism, and the challenges faced by emerging countermovements. However, more implicit is the role of traditional culture in constructing, maintaining, and legitimizing the industrial relations and other key institutions, including economic policy social welfare, and legal and regulatory frameworks. As shown in both Chinese and Japanese contexts, Confucianism-informed age-old values (notably hierarchy, harmony, and the subordination of individual interests to collective requirements) permeate almost every aspect of society. Crucially, these values provide essential symbolic ingredients for the discursive play of political language among the ruling elites in the (re)production of 'authentic' or 'definitive' cultural translations, thereby impinging importantly on the way in which social reality is perceived by the general populace. Such 'creativity' embodies hegemonic elements, which shape and dominate others' wills, impose the spectre of justified norms of inclusion and exclusion, and normalize a social order serving the interests of the dominant class (Parkin 1984; Bourdieu 1991, 2001). In China, the 'harmonious society' rhetoric with its emphasis on (hierarchical) solidarity and social stability is overtly invoked, in tandem with the promotion of 'ruling-the-country-by-law' policies, as justification for the rural-urban citizenship divide and the use of authoritarian forces. Despite recent decades' growing levels of assertiveness, rural migrants' resistance was either brutally suppressed or adroitly channelled into the state-controlled legal and bureaucratic apparatus (Lee and Zhang 2013; Howell 2015). In a similar vein, the symbolic power of culture is integral to Japan's much-vaunted 'firm-as-family' management that draws instrumentally on traditional family (*ie*) values that emphasize, among other things, loyalty, patriarchy, and organizational continuity. The employer-dominated enterprise unionism not only fosters union–management harmonious coordination in support of firm-centred goals, but also perpetuates the iniquitous division between regular and non-regular workers that stems from Japan's sharply delineated male/breadwinner/public-female/housewife/private paradigm (Roberts 2016; Marshall 2017). For new institutional actors and change agents including community unions and labour NGOs, such core cultural values as *hukou-* or gender-based hierarchy appear to lie at the heart of their resistance struggles (Fu 2021).

Book structure and chapter summaries

As emphasized throughout this introductory chapter, bridging culture and social institutions goes a long way towards obtaining a more integrated and nuanced picture of precarious work, which in turn enables a better understanding of everyday realities confronting workers. In line with this approach, the book is structured in three main parts that combine both macro-structural explanations and micro-agency empiricism. The first part comprising Chapters 1–3 provides an overview of precarious work and associated social inequalities in China and Japan, which outlines both historical developments and current trends. The second part, which is made up of Chapters 4–6, is centred on industrial relations structures, detailing how organized labour and new institutional actors resist and otherwise react to precarious work. Against the broader institutional and structural backgrounds, the last four chapters in the third part, Chapters 7–10, are focused on empirical investigations of individuals in various forms of precarious work, whose everyday narratives and experiences offer revealing insights into existing challenges and future changes.

Chapter 1 explicates how the rural-urban migration and citizenship is of central importance to grappling with China's ever-shifting contours of precarious work and social inequalities. By delving into three key historical phases of transformation, the chapter underlines the role of culture in legitimizing China's major political-economic institutional transitions and in entrenching the rural-urban citizenship divide and other inequalities. Chapter 2 provides a historical perspective on Japan's distinctively gendered core-periphery labour dualism, and explores a range of issues and challenges arising from the state's neoliberal labour market reforms, the rise of the gig economy, and the Covid-19 pandemic. Chapter 3 focuses on how teleworking (remote working), a new phenomenon in Japan emerging from the Covid-19 pandemic, has amplified existing disparities by gender and its intersections with work status and firm size, which bears important implications for inequalities in work-life balance and flexible work.

The second part begins with Chapter 4's systematic tracing of the roles of workers, unions, and labour NGOs in improving the labour conditions of migrant informal workers from the Maoist decades to labour precarity in the post-Mao era, including the Hu-Wen period and the subsequent Xi period. The chapter also discusses how the gig economy posed new challenges to worker organizing and opened up forms of resistance through disrupting the digital flow of production. Chapter 5 compares strategies for organizing non-regular workers by two main Japanese union confederations, Rengo and Zenroren, with a view to highlighting different forms of dualism and fragmented union movements that have hindered mainstream unions' ability to contest precarity. Drawing on three case studies, Chapter 6 offers a useful view on Japanese non-mainstream unions whose organizing strategies among non-regular workers, especially temporary agency workers, are critically examined.

In the third part, the micro-level empirical investigations merit special attention, since they are indispensable for gaining an in-depth understanding of what it means to be a precarious worker in real-world settings. Based on an extensive qualitative study of 33 Chinese rural migrant women, Chapter 7 brings to the fore individual negotiations of gender, citizenship, and precarity in the vicissitudes of their everyday lives during the migration process, thereby illuminating the complex ways in which they construct and perform identities. This is followed by Chapter 8, which investigates the experience of aspiring writers in China's growing online literature platforms amid the rising gig economy. Drawing on rich empirical data, this chapter delineates key features of creative labour markets, highlights power asymmetry and multiple realities of precarity, and explains how individuals respond to the uneven process of platformization. The last two chapters turn to gendered precarity in Japan, where non-regular workers' everyday negotiations are indeed multifaceted and equivocal. Using data from interviews of female non-regular workers, Chapter 9 brings the concept of 'disaffected consent' to bear on the understanding of individual formal and informal struggles, especially between strong feelings of dissatisfaction about precarious employment on the one hand, and self-doubt in the legitimacy and practicality of demanding better treatment on the other. Chapter 10 features male *freeters* or freelancers whose oft-negative social portrayals can be ascribed to postwar gendered cultural norms of male adulthood and breadwinner family model linked to the *seishain* or regular labour market. Through the lens of labour aspiration and responsibility, this chapter explores how men drew variously on neoliberal ideas to frame their *freeter* positioning.

Concluding remarks

It goes without saying that precarious work tends to be associated with the most disadvantaged groups of people in society. The rapid expansion of temps and giggers, in all their bewildering diversity, has deepened existing inequalities that are structured along a society's specific intersecting axes of stratification. In China and Japan, rural migrants and women respectively are the predominant groups who are most susceptible to low levels of pay, benefits, and statuary rights, limited training and upward career development, workplace discrimination and harassment, and generally poor health, safety, and well-being provisions. Such unsavoury working conditions are responsible for workers' reduced commitment, job satisfaction, morale and productivity, which have profound implications for human capital and sustainable development amid looming labour and skill shortages facing both countries (Cooke and Brown 2015). Moreover, workers from other groups such as urban citizens in China and men in Japan—particularly of younger generations—have increasingly been shunted into the ever-swelling precarious periphery. Consequently, the prevalence of precarious work, despite being embellished with such catchy neoliberal trappings as 'freedom', 'flexibility', and 'entrepreneurial creativity' in popular discourses, renders secure full-time employment achievable only for a shrinking labour aristocracy. For many, this has far-reaching deleterious and debilitating effects, as demonstrated vividly and poignantly by the book's empirical case studies. Due to their distinct cultural origins, the ubiquitous gap between imposed expectations on the part of the state and employers and experienced realities among workers tends to be made more strikingly in China and Japan than in many western nations. While feeling empowered by imported neoliberal individualist values, precarious workers are circumscribed by their indigenous cultural beliefs and norms, as well as a host of institutional barriers.

Hence, culture holds the key to unravelling fundamental structural problems pertaining to precarious work and social inequalities in contemporary society. This should not be interpreted as undermining the prominence of social institutions, especially those hinging upon the state-capital-labour dynamics that have an immediate bearing on workers' life. Rather, the culture-centred holistic approach directs our attention to more pervasive and formidable yet elusive obstacles that hamper our efforts to advance social progress. Engaging with the non-western holism in China and Japan could serve as a catalyst for the interrogation of our own often taken-for-granted cultural assumptions, which justify or otherwise obfuscate pre-existing fault lines such as gender, class, age, citizenship, ethnicity, and race. Of specific importance is the role of neoliberal individualism in facilitating the proliferation of temps and gig-economy workers as 'self-responsible', 'free', or 'entrepreneurial' individuals, in adversely affecting collective representation and bargaining power, and in making it convenient for employers and the state to evade their responsibilities. As exposed painfully by the global Covid-19 pandemic, the reality experienced by real people flies in the face of seemingly emancipatory neoliberal discourses: far from being separated from or independent of each other, individuals and society are inexorably interconnected and mutually constitutive. In this connection, culture is a dangerous word, since it can be adroitly manipulated by the ruling elites to legitimize exploitative conditions, nurture spurious expectations, and create a diversion from unequal social structures and relations. To end on a positive note, crises such as the Covid-19 pandemic often open a window of opportunity for change. As challenging as they may be, the liminal periods of discontinuity and uncertainty during the crisis, according to Turner's famous theory of 'liminality' (1967), throw into doubt what is conceived of as 'normal' and thus pave the way for the emergence of new norms and institutions for a more equitable and sustainable future.

References

Anagnost, A. (1997) *National Past-Times: Narrative, Representation, and Power in Modern China*. London: Duke University Press.

Appadurai, A. (1990) 'Disjuncture and difference in the global cultural economy'. *Theory, Culture & Society*, 7(2): 295–310.

Bourdieu, P. (1991) *Languages and Symbolic Power*. Cambridge: Polity Press.

Bourdieu, P. (2001) *Masculine Domination*. Stanford, CA: Stanford University Press.

Burawoy, M. (2015) 'Facing an unequal world'. *Current Sociology*, 63(1): 5–34.

Chalmers, N. J. (1989) *Industrial Relations in Japan: The Peripheral Workforce*. London & New York: Routledge.

Chan, A. (2015) 'The fallacy of Chinese exceptionalism'. In A. Chan (ed.), *Chinese Workers in Comparative Perspective*. Ithaca and London: Cornell University, pp. 1–17.

Chan, C. K. (2014) 'Constrained labour agency and the changing regulatory regime in China'. *Development and Change*, 45(4): 685–709.

Chan, C. K. and Chiu, Y. (2015) 'Labour NGOs under state corporatism: Comparing China since the 1990s with Taiwan in the 1980s'. In A. Chan (ed.), *Chinese Workers in Comparative Perspective*. Ithaca and London: Cornell University, pp. 157–173.

Chan, J. and Selden, M. (2014) China's rural migrant workers, the state, and labor politics. *Critical Asian Studies*, 46(4): 599–620.

Chang, K. and Brown, W. (2013) 'The transition from individual to collective labour relations in China'. *Industrial Relations Journal*, 44(2): 102–121.

Cohen, A. (1969) 'Political anthropology: The analysis of the symbolism of power relations'. *Man*, 4(2): 215–235.

Cohen, A. (1974) *Two-Dimensional Man: An Essay on the Anthropology of Power and Symbolism in Complex Society*. Berkeley, CA: University of California Press.

Cooke, F. L. and Brown, R. (2015) 'The regulation of non-standard forms of employment in China, Japan and The Republic of Korea'. Conditions of Work and Employment Series No. 64, International Labour Organisation (ILO).

Dumont, L. (1985) 'A modified view of our origins: The Christian beginnings of modern individualism'. In M. Carrithers, S. Collins, and S. Lukes (eds.), *The Category of the Person: Anthropology, Philosophy, History*. Cambridge: Cambridge University Press, pp. 93–122.

Dumont, L. (1986) *Essays on Individualism: Modern Ideology in Anthropological Perspective*. Chicago & London: University of Chicago Press.

Edelman, M. and Haugerud, A. (2005) *The Anthropology of Development and Globalization: From Classical Political Economy to Contemporary Neoliberalism*. Oxford: Blackwell.

Elfstrom, M. and Kuruvilla, S. (2014) 'The changing nature of labor unrest in China'. *Industrial & Labor Relations Review*, 67(2): 453–480.

Eriksen, T. H. (2003) *Globalisation: Studies in Anthropology*. London: Pluto Press.

Fairwork (2020a) 'The untenable luxury of self-isolation'. 18 March, *New Internationalist*. Available at: https://newint.org/features/2020/03/18/untenable-luxury-self-isolation/.

Fairwork (2020b) 'The Gig Economy and Covid-19: Fairwork Report on Platform Policies'. Oxford Internet Institute, University of Oxford.

Friedman, E. (2014) 'Alienated politics: Labour insurgency and the paternalistic state in China'. *Development and Change*, 45(5): 1001–1018.

Friedman, E. and Kuruvilla, S. (2015) 'Experimentation and decentralization in China's labor relations'. *Human Relations*, 68(2): 181–195.

Friedman, E. and Lee, C. K. (2010) 'Remaking the world of Chinese labour: A 30-year retrospective'. *British Journal of Industrial Relations*, 48(3): 507–533.

Fu, H. (2021) 'Social action as "a total social phenomenon": Comparing leadership challenges facing community-based labour organisations in China and Japan'. *Human Relations*, 74(9): 1396–1420.

Gallagher, M., Giles, J., Park, A., and Wang, M. (2015) 'China's 2008 Labour Contract Law: Implementation and implications for China's workers'. *Human Relations*, 68(2): 197–235.

Geertz, C. (1973) *The Interpretation of Cultures: Selected Essays*. London: Fontana Press.

Giddens, A. (1990) *The Consequences of Modernity*. Stanford: Stanford University Press.

Goodman, R. (1998) 'Culture as ideology: Explanations for the development of the Japanese economic miracle'. In T. Skelton and T. Allen (eds.), *Culture and Global Change*. London: Routledge, pp. 127–136.

Gordon, A. (2017) 'New and enduring dual structures of employment in Japan: The rise of non-regular labour'. *Social Science Japan Journal*, 20(1): 9–36.

Gottfried, H. (2015) *The Reproductive Bargain: Deciphering the Enigma of Japanese Capitalism*. Leiden: Brill.

Hall, P. and Soskice, D. (eds.) (2001) *Varieties of Capitalism: The Institutional Foundations of Comparative Advantage*. Oxford: Oxford University Press.

Hann, C. (2006) *'Not the Horse We Wanted!': Postsocialism, Neoliberalism and Eurasia*. Münster: LIT.

Hannerz, U. (1992) *Cultural Complexity: Studies in the Social Organization of Meaning*. New York: Columbia University Press.

Hannerz, U. (1996) *Transnational Connections: Culture, People, Places*. London: Routledge.

Harvey, D. (2005) *A Brief History of Neoliberalism*. Oxford: Oxford University Press.

Held, D., McGrew, A., Goldblatt, D., and Perraton, J. (1999) *Global Transformations: Politics, Economics and Culture*. Cambridge: Polity Press.

Hewison, K. (2016) 'Precarious work'. In S. Edgell, H. Gottfried, and E. Granter (eds.), *The Sage Handbook of the Sociology of Work and Employment*. Thousand Oaks, CA: Sage, pp. 428–443.

Hobsbawm, E. and Ranger, T. (1983) *The Invention of Tradition*. Cambridge: Cambridge University Press.

Howell, J. (2015) 'Shall we dance? Welfarist incorporation and the politics of state-labour NGO relations in China'. *The China Quarterly*, 223: 702–723.

Huang, Y. and Yi, C. (2015) 'Invisible migrant enclaves in Chinese cities: Underground living in Beijing, China'. *Urban Studies*, 52(15): 2948–2973.

JILPT (Japan Institute for Labour Policy and Training) (2016) 'Labor situation in Japan and its analysis: General overview 2015/2016'. Available at: http://www.jil.go.jp/index.html/.

Kalleberg, A. (2000) 'Nonstandard employment relations: Part-time, temporary, and contract work'. *Annual Review of Sociology*, 26: 341–365.

Kalleberg, A. and Hewison, K. (2013) 'Precarious work and the challenge for Asia'. *American Behavioral Scientist*, 57(3): 271–288.

Kalleberg, A. and Vallas, S. (eds.) (2018) *Precarious Work*. Bingley, England: Emerald Publishing.

Kojima, S. (2017) 'Social movement unionism in contemporary Japan: Coalitions within and across political boundaries'. *Economic and Industrial Democracy*. Available at: https://journals.sagepub.com/doi/full/10.1177/0143831X17694242/.

Kroeber, A. R. (2016) *China's Economy: What Everyone Needs to Know*. Oxford: Oxford University Press.

Lambert, R. and Herod, A. (2016) *Neoliberal Capitalism and Precarious Work: Ethnographies of Accommodation and Resistance*. Cheltenham: Edward Elgar.

Lee, C. K. (1995) 'Engendering the worlds of labor: Women workers, labor markets, and production politics in the South China economic miracle'. *American Sociological Review*, 60(3): 378–397.

Lee, C. K. (1998) *Gender and the South China Miracle: Two Worlds of Factory Women*. Berkeley: University of California Press.

Lee, C. K. (2000) 'The "revenge of history": Collective memories and labor protests in north-eastern China'. *Ethnography*, 1(2): 217–237.

Lee, C. K. (2002) 'From the spectre of Mao to the spirit of the law: Labor insurgency in China'. *Theory and Society*, 31: 189–228.

Lee C. K. and Zhang, Y. (2013) 'The power of instability: Unraveling the microfoundations of bargained authoritarianism in China'. *American Journal of Sociology*, 118(6): 1475–1508.

Lincoln, J. and Kalleberg, A. (1990) *Culture, Control and Commitment: A Study of Work Organization and Work Attitudes in the United States and Japan*. Cambridge: Cambridge University Press.

Lukes, S. (1973). *Individualism*. Oxford: Basil Blackwell.
Macnaughtan, H. (2015) 'Womenomics for Japan: is the Abe policy for gendered employment viable in an era of precarity?'. *The Asia-Pacific Journal: Japan Focus*, 13(12): No. 1, March 30.
Mann, M. (2013) *The Sources of Social Power: Volume 4, Globalizations, 1945-2011*. Cambridge: Cambridge University Press.
Marshall, R. (2017) 'Gender inequality and family formation in Japan'. *Asian Anthropology*, 16(4): 261–278.
Mauss, M. (1954) *The Gift: Forms and Functions of Exchange in Archaic Societies*. London: Cohen & West.
OECD (2020) Public unemployment spending (indicator). doi: 10.1787/55557fd4-en (Accessed on 28 April 2020).
Ortner, S. B. (1984) 'Theory in anthropology since the sixties'. *Comparative Studies in Society and History*, 26: 126–166.
Osawa, M., Kim, M. J., and Kingston, J. (2013) 'Precarious work in Japan'. *American Behavioral Scientist*, 57(3): 309–334.
Otto, T. and Bubandt, N. (eds.) (2011) *Experiments in Holism: Theory and Practice in Contemporary Anthropology*. Oxford, UK: Wiley-Blackwell.
Parkin, D. (1984) 'Political language'. *Annual Review of Anthropology*, 29: 107–124.
Pei, M. (2016) *China's Crony Capitalism: The Dynamics of Regime Decay*. Cambridge, MA: Harvard University Press.
Pekkanen, R. (2006) *Japan's Dual Civil Society: Members without Advocates*. Stanford: Stanford University Press.
Prassl, J. (2018) *Humans as a Service: The Promise and Perils of Work in the Gig Economy*. Oxford: Oxford University Press.
Pun, N. (2005) *Made in China: Women Factory Workers in a Global Workplace*. Durham, NC: Duke University Press.
Pun, N. and Lu, H. (2010a) 'Unfinished proletarianization: Self, anger, and class action among the second generation of peasant-workers in present-day China'. *Modern China*, 36(5): 493–519.
Pun, N. and Lu, H. (2010b) 'A culture of violence: The labor subcontracting system and collective action by construction workers in post-socialist China'. *The China Journal*, 64: 143–158.
Roberts, G. (2016). *Japan's Evolving Family: Voices from Young Urban Adults Navigating Change*. Honolulu: East-West Centre.
Roberts, G. S. (2011) 'Salary women and family well-being in urban Japan'. *Marriage & Family Review*, 47(8): 571–589.
Royle, T. and Urano, E. (2012) 'A new form of union organizing in Japan? Community unions and the case of the McDonald's "McUnion"'. *Work, Employment and Society*, 26(4): 606–622.

Swider, S. (2015) 'Building China: Precarious employment among migrant construction workers'. *Work, Employment & Society*, 29(1): 41–59.

Takasu, H. (2012) 'The formation of a region-based amalgamated union movement and its future possibilities'. In A. Suzuki (ed.), *Cross-National Comparisons of Social Movement Unionism: Diversities of Labour Movement Revitalization in Japan, Korea and the United States*. Oxford & New York: Peter Lang, pp. 289–323.

Turner, V. (1967) *The Forest of Symbols: Aspects of Ndembu Ritual*. Ithaca, NY: Cornell University Press.

Vosko, L. (2010) *Managing the Margins: Gender, Citizenship, and the International Regulation of Precarious Employment*. Oxford: Oxford University Press.

Walder, A. G. (1983) 'Organized dependency and cultures of authority in Chinese industry'. *The Journal of Asian Studies*, 43(1): 51–76.

Walder, A. G. (1984) 'The remaking of the Chinese working class, 1949–1981'. *Modern China*, 10(1): 3–48.

Weathers, C. (2010) 'The rising voice of Japan's community unions'. In H. Vinken, Y. Nishimura, B. L. J. White, and M. Deguchi M (eds.), *Civic Engagement in Contemporary Japan: Established and Emerging Repertoires*. New York: Springer, pp. 67–83.

Wolferen, K. (1989) *The Enigma of Japanese Power: People and Politics in a Stateless Nation*. London: Macmillan.

Xu, Y. (2013) 'Labour non-governmental organizations in China: Mobilizing rural migrant workers'. *Journal of Industrial Relations*, 55(2): 243–259.

Yun, J. W. (2010) 'Unequal Japan: Conservative corporatism and labour market disparities'. *British Journal of Industrial Relations*, 48(1): 1–25.

Zhu, Y. and Warner, M. (2011) 'Employment relations "with Chinese characteristics": The role of trade unions in China'. *International Labour Review*, 150(1-2): 127–143.

1
Old and New Inequalities
Citizenly Discounting and Precarious Work in a Changing China

Huiyan Fu

Introduction

Precarious work can be defined by the *uncertainty, instability,* and *insecurity* of work in which workers bear the risks of work (as opposed to businesses or the government) and receive limited social benefits and statutory protections (Kalleberg 2000; Kalleberg and Vallas 2018; Hewison 2016; Vosko 2010). In China, it is most commonly experienced among those engaging in non-regular or informal employment (NRE), ranging from a bewildering variety of part-time and fixed-term contracts to agency-mediated labour dispatch and self-employment. It should be stressed that NRE and its concomitant social stratification has long been a defining feature of the Chinese labour landscape. Of particular significance is *hukou*, the country's long-existing rural-urban household registration, which plays a salient role in driving internal rural-urban migration processes, meting out institutional discrimination against rural citizens and entrenching social class divisions. Compared to distinctively gendered patterning in its neighbouring countries such as Japan and South Korea where women bear the major brunt of precarious employment, China is characterized by rural–urban migration and citizenship as a key structural axis for grappling with NRE and its ever-shifting forms and patterns.

Since China's 'open-door' reform in the late 1970s, millions of 'peasant workers' (*nongmingong*) have migrated en masse each year to cities in search of work and disproportionately clustered in the periphery of insecure, low-pay, and low-status jobs. In 2019, there were more than 290 million migrant workers, roughly 35 per cent of China's total labour force, the majority of whom left their hometowns without their families and worked in regions

Huiyan Fu, *Old and New Inequalities*. In: *Temporary and Gig Economy Workers in China and Japan*. Edited by Huiyan Fu, Oxford University Press. © Oxford University Press (2023). DOI: 10.1093/oso/9780192849694.003.0002 and urban cities far away—the number decreased slightly in 2020 due to the Covid-19 pandemic (Statista 2021). Rural migrants are referred to in common parlance as 'floating population' (*liudong renkou*), a somewhat pejorative term denoting a social malaise. Despite being the powerful engine that has propelled China's extraordinary transformation into the world's second-largest economy, they continue to be denied equal opportunities to settle in the city where they engage in income-generating activities—what Pun and Lu (2010a) aptly describe as 'unfinished process of proletarianisation' whereby a spatial chasm persists between production in the city and reproduction in the countryside. Rural *hukou* holders are rendered second-class citizens, institutionally and culturally, in an alluring yet oft-hostile urban environment that subjects them to an overarching system of exploitation, discrimination, and alienation. This 'citizenly discounting' (Fu et al. 2018) features prominently in China's changing contours of precarious work and therefore merits close scrutiny.

The saliency of *hukou* has been widely discussed among Chinese studies scholars, especially in relation to power dynamics between the state, capital, and labour that falls largely within the area of Marxist class relations. Notwithstanding valuable insights from existing studies, there is a distinct lack of careful probing into the role of deep-rooted traditional cultural values; in other words, how and why *hukou* and its associated citizenly discounting emerges, persists, and evolves has yet to be fully grasped. To bridge this gap, this chapter sets out to bring anthropological perspectives to bear on the elusive cultural domain and, perhaps more importantly, its connections with broader political-economic forces. In the next section, key characteristics of NRE in contemporary China are first outlined, with an emphasis on *hukou* and its intersections with fundamental economic structures and other inequality variables—drawing on insights from sociological research on 'intersectionality' (Collins 2015). This is followed by a brief navigation of historical trajectories of precarious work, which takes culture and tradition into careful consideration and is organized in three broadly defined phases: (1) the pre-reform era (1949–1978), (2) the reform era (1979–2007), and (3) the regulation era (2008–present). In so doing, the chapter aims to bring a more integrated, nuanced, and contextualized understanding of precarious work in a dynamic China. Theoretically, special attention is paid to the complex ways in which traditional norms and assumptions are embedded and/or appropriated in major transitional processes, with a view to casting light on the symbolic power of culture and its implications for social change.

Key characteristics of NRE in contemporary China

Although comprehensive and accurate official statistics are not available, it is estimated that well over half of China's total urban workforce are now engaged in NRE. In contrast to advanced economies where most workers tend to be absorbed into the formal sector, China's informal sector still commands a considerable proportion of urban employment (Xiao et al. 2022), where precarious and low-paid jobs are most concentrated, and rural migrants remain by far the largest group of workers. This is of particular interest given the country's centralized economy. Since the late 1990s, the size of NRE across all sectors has enlarged twofold, which corresponded with massive downsizing of state-owned and collective-owned enterprises (SOEs) and subsequent expansion of private-owned enterprises (POEs) and foreign-owned enterprises (FOEs). The retrenchment of the state sector saw many of the laid-off urban workers transformed into temps in POEs and FOEs. To help the once-privileged urban regular workers who lost their 'iron rice bowl' (*tie fanwan*)—a specific form of secure work in state-sector firms (Kuruvilla et al. 2011)—government re-employment services were quickly set up in the late 1990s. It was in this context that the official language *feizhenggui jiuye* (NRE), rhetorically designed as *linghuo yonggong* (flexible employment), emerged and has since been widely endorsed by both state and academic discourses as an effective means of absorbing urban unemployment and boosting economic competitiveness. By contrast, the long-standing and pervasive informality of rural migrants was until recently largely ignored by the state.

NRE in contemporary China is comprised mainly of temps on a wide range of temporary and fixed-term contracts and the self-employed working alone or for family-owned or small-scale firms that face little legal pressure to comply with labour standards. As the country's economic reforms proceed, employers have been emboldened to seek the economic advantages of utilizing a cheaper workforce—at the expense of such things as income security, health and safety protection, and welfare provision. As a consequence, the number and composition of temps have evolved drastically over the past two decades. New categories such as dispatched or agency-mediated workers and in-sourced contract workers have been widely used by large firms, especially SOEs, in order to bypass regulatory pressures and keep labour costs down. Among formal-sector firms, it has become a common practice that the burden of labour cost is increasingly transferred to the informal sector via subcontracting or outsourcing.

The resulting expansion of the informal economy is strengthened by the emergence of gig or platform economy (*linggong jingji*), which has generated a host of non-traditional self-employment opportunities. Situating in the wider context of precarious work, the gig economy is concerned predominantly with the use of third-party digital platforms or 'apps' in connecting (self-employed) workers and customers or client firms. Significantly, this technology-driven modernization involves a new mechanism of power in the organization of work whereby platform owners externalize risks and impose socio-technical control of workers through, for example, ownership and management of actionable data—such power asymmetries and class conflicts are well documented by Chan and Humphreys' study of Uber drivers' experiences (2018) and Wood and Lehdonvirta's thesis on structured antagonism inherent in platform labour relations (2019). In China, the gig economy has grown exponentially due to the country's remarkable technological advancement and flourishing informal sector. Recent years have witnessed a rising number of gig economy workers, estimated around 200 million, who subject themselves to the prerogatives of platform owners. For instance, Didi Chuxing, China's giant car-hailing business, claimed that it attracted more than 21 million registered drivers on its platform within one year (people.cn 2017). Perhaps more strikingly, the gig economy and its meteoric boom has been widely portrayed in official discourses as a new, 'inevitable' business model contributing to 'flexibility' (*linghuo*) and 'creativity' (*chuangxin*). Employers are encouraged to use state-endorsed 'multiple types of flexible employment' (*duoqudao linghuo jiuye*) (China Today 2021). According to the latest China Development on Flexible Employment (2022), 61 per cent of the firms actively used NRE in 2021, a further 5.5 per cent increase on 2020. Like elsewhere, the global Covid-19 pandemic has accelerated the trend towards a greater proliferation of short-term gig jobs, which particularly affects informal workers (Webb et al. 2020). During the pandemic, many rural migrants became disproportionately unemployed and were urged by the state to educate themselves about the gig economy and to seek gig jobs within close proximity to their homes.

The realties faced by the expanding legions of temps and giggers are further complicated by the ownership structure of firms, which is crucial to grasping the complexity of precarious work and its implications for social inequalities in China. Temps employed by SOEs—which are highly concentrated and remain the largest firms in almost every industry, despite their gradually shrinking number—are normally protected with a labour contract and a basic level of social insurance coverage. Moreover, they tend to be urban citizens whose *hukou* status and associated social capital play an important role in retaining them in the upper echelons of precarious workers. Most of labour rights' violations stem from POEs and FOEs—which contribute to the majority of economic output and total employment—in the private sector where rural migrants are concentrated. A 2007 national report estimated that only about 50 per cent of all firms signed contracts with their workers and that the rate among private-sector firms was only 20 per cent (Friedman and Lee 2010: 509). While there is a general consensus that the 2008 Labour Contract Law has produced moderate success in improving the share of workers having a labour contract and/or being covered by social insurance schemes, the difference in treatment between rural migrants and urban locals remains substantial. As shown in Figure 1.1, among employed rural migrants in 2010, 34 per cent signed labour contracts, 24 per cent enjoyed employer-provided pension, and 22 per cent had employer-provided health insurance, compared to 71 per cent, 89 per cent, and 86 per cent, respectively, for their urban counterparts (Gallagher et al. 2015: 206–207, 224). It is worth noting here that precarious workers' experiences are also mediated by regional differences, especially with respect to labour protection and law enforcement. Empowered by the state's decentralization policy, local governments, which are keen to foster economic growth and develop different strategies, have considerable discretion in the way they forge alliances with different ownership types of firms and enforce labour laws. This in turn has an important bearing on workers' interests and welfare, particularly for the most vulnerable.

On a macro level, the above key characteristics of NRE are closely related to China's reorganization of employment in a services-based economy. In contradistinction to the classic English industrialization, the Chinese development model features a relatively small percentage of employment in

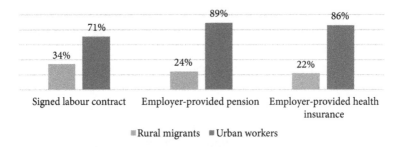

Figure 1.1 Legal protection disparities between rural migrant workers and urban workers

Source: Gallagher et al. 2015: 206–207, 224

manufacturing industries, which since the mid-1990s has been exceeded by growth in service industries. As China shifts away from manufacturing and investment towards services and consumption, the contribution of the service economy has risen rapidly, with its share of GDP reaching nearly 60 per cent in 2018 (China Statistical Yearbook 2019). The macro-structural change has certainly led to a growing proportion of affluent professional jobs, particularly in capital-intensive technology and financial services. However, the bulk of new service-sector employment gains emanate from weakly regulated, labour-intensive industries such as food and beverage, hospitality, entertainment, cleaning, and care work. Along with low-skilled construction sites and manufacturing factories, these service industries have most informal, precarious jobs filled by many rural migrants.

To summarize, the complex nature of NRE in China can be best captured by focusing on an intersecting set of key inequality variables, with rural-urban *hukou* as a central axis—whose cultural roots and implications in relation to the changing political economy will be explored in detail in the next section. As the largest and longest exploited group of the working class, rural migrants are disproportionately concentrated in the informal sector, the gig economy, private-sector POEs and FOEs, and labour-intensive service industries. Although not all traditional temps and new gig-economy workers are associated with precarious work, a great many are susceptible to the uncertainty, instability, and insecurity of work, low pay and benefits, poor working conditions, lack of training and upward mobility, and labour rights' infringement. In particular, discrimination against rural migrants is rife; the *hukou* system is widely used by employers to segment workers by different employment contracts and terms, even though they undertake similar tasks. Precariousness and employment informalization has also spread steadily among urban *hukou* householders; more and more are shunted to the periphery of labour markets, working as temps and giggers with or without a written contract or a formal worker status. Young graduates have become an increasingly important component of NRE, which is aggravated by China's new system of mass high education.[1] In its perhaps most disturbing form, employers' unrelenting search for cheap and flexible labour has extended to dual commodification of education and labour whereby vocational schools and employers, under the auspices of local governments, turn large numbers of teenage student interns into constrained factory workers (Selden, Chan, and Pun 2015; Smith and Chan 2015). Finally, gender in China appears to be a less pronounced variable in the patterning of NRE than observed in its neighbouring countries such as Japan and South Korea; yet far fewer women than men are employed as a secure worker in SOEs, still regarded as a more privileged employment status than its equivalent in private-sector POEs and FOEs.[2]

Hukou, culture, and the political economy of precarious work in a changing China

The Pre-Reform Era (1949–1978)

China after 1949 witnessed a distinct historical transformation of 'the working class' in Marxist terms that unfolded against the backdrop of a highly centralized planned economy. Under Mao's leadership, a period (1949–1957) of unprecedented industrial expansion in heavy industry attracted a new mass of workers—the bulk of whom had no skills and experience—into factories, and created the social basis for a new tradition of labour relations. The state itself took charge of the recruitment, job allocation, and remuneration of urban workers in SOEs or work units (*danwei*) that were then the main business and political institutions. To accumulate capital, it prescribed low agriculture prices and industry wages; centrally administered pay grids were implemented to emphasize seniority-based wage differentials while allowing for only small differences across firms, industries, and regions. The management, which was subject to strict political control, set up employment, wages, and conditions of work according to local governments' rulings. At the workplace, workers' political loyalty to the Communist Party, induced by a vast array of material rewards and punishments, was an essential prerequisite to the 'iron-rice-bowl' employment; the latter offered earnings, lifetime security, and a wide range of social benefits including housing, health insurance, and retirement. In this state-orchestrated labour system, workers were not allowed to move from their allocated firm without government approval; neither could they form independent organizations outside Party auspices that were deemed 'counter-revolutionary' (*fan geming*) and treated with consistent severity (Walder 1983). A crucial corollary to this regime was workers' personalized forms of dependency and managerial paternalism in shop-floor authority relations, which were derived from core values and beliefs of Confucianism, one of China's longest philosophical traditions. In particular, hierarchy—which is fundamental to the Confucian order of human relationships—became the defining characteristic of the new post-revolution working class. The iron rice bowl at SOEs was a privileged status conferred upon only a minority of workers with urban *hukou*; the rural majority, then accounting for between 70 per cent and 80 per cent of the national population, were excluded from jobs at SOEs and associated benefits.[3] A cultural orientation was, therefore, recreated in the making of new political-economic institutions.

The *hukou* system, which has been central to the structuring of NRE throughout contemporary China, was established in 1958 under severe demographic pressure. Indeed, no account of China's industrialization and working class after 1949 would be complete without a careful consideration of the demographic setting and its impact (Walder 1984). Unlike many Western nations, China in the early 1950s could not take the established path of industrialization-led urbanization, for it already had an extensive network of large cities, a massive rural population and very high rates of population growth, especially in rural areas. As a result, a growing labour surplus—which was greatly aggravated by the Great Leap Forward (1958–1960)—compelled the state to institute astringent control over rural exodus with the aim of reducing unemployment and improving the welfare of the existing urban population. By the early 1960s, an apartheid-style segregation was written into law. *Hukou* became a de facto internal passport system, which tied people to the residential status they attained at birth. It also functioned as a social entitlement mechanism whereby a dichotomy was created between the access to land for rural *hukou* holders and most state-provided social goods restricted to urban *hukou* holders. From this time forward, rural-urban mobility control was enforced vigorously; rural residents were prohibited not only from working in urban work units, but also from freely entering into cities without obtaining a temporary official permission. Throughout the pre-reform era, urban *huko* holders were given special ration cards for purchasing grocery and other necessities, while those rural *hukou* holders who were residing in urban areas received none of these benefits.

In his classic account (1984), Walder explicates cogently how Chinese industrial workers were split and immobilized by a five-tiered hierarchical pyramid (Figure 1.2) where there was little upward mobility among employment statuses. The top-tier workers comprised only 42 per cent of the total industrial workforce in 1981, with their average pay level 40 per cent higher than that of the second-tier workers, well over twice the average for workers in other lower tiers (Walder 1985: 37). At the bottom fifth tier were rural workers in rural small-scale, collectively owned industries, who worked on a mostly temporary basis to supplement their main agriculture-based household income and whose treatment was at the same level as average commune peasants. At the fourth tier were a diverse and shadowy group of rural temporary workers outside of state planning and regulation. They took short-term seasonal jobs in urban enterprises of all types and sizes while having periodic

32 Old and New Inequalities

Figure 1.2 Five-tiered hierarchical employment segmentation in the pre-reform era
Source: Walder 1984

obligations to work in rural agricultural communes that exercised management and control of all rural resources, including land and labour. Because of their rural *hukou* status, they were officially denied the opportunity to become permanent workers as well as any of the fringe benefits attached to such secure employment. The third, middle tier was occupied by urban temporary workers, who, compared to their rural counterparts, relied heavily on waged labour for their livelihood since they had no agricultural income to fall back on. While their position was not significantly dissimilar from rural temps in terms of regulatory protection, urban temps were far more likely to be integrated into the core factory production process, to have their employment periods extended indefinitely, and to be employed eventually as part of the permanent labour force. The second tier was composed of secure urban workers in collective enterprises administered by local and regional governments. The majority were women and young people, who did not enjoy the same pay scales and benefits as available to the top-tier workers in state enterprises; the latter were the only group who participated fully in the near-total iron-rice-bowl welfare benefits, which in large enterprises extended to workers' families and amounted to as much as above 80 per cent of their average earnings.

Such rural–urban divisions and segmentations were new hierarchies arising from China's reconstruction of society; they shattered fleeting historical processes of class consciousness and political unity that were well underway by the 1920s. To be sure, the post-1949 revolution ushered in institutional arrangements, especially with regard to *hukou* and five-tier employment statuses, which 'froze into place some rather striking sectoral inequalities within the working class itself' (Walder 1984: 14). Noteworthily, these newly formed institutions were reinforced, albeit implicitly, by age-old Confucian values, notably hierarchy and paternalism, which place an emphasis on social order based on prescribed status moral codes. This was despite that Confucianism was denounced, particularly during the Cultural Revolution (1966–1976), as a backward, feudal tradition, an impediment to modern development in Maoist China. For the new working class, life chances were dictated by not only residential and employment statuses but also a bureaucratic order at the workplace; the latter was infused with paternalistic reciprocity that demanded workers' personalized forms of dependency and political loyalty. Moreover, this evolution towards neo-traditional norms and practices militated against workers' collective participation and activism in factory decision-making processes, which were ironically at odds with images of Mao's 'mass line' (*qunzhong luxian*) Party principles. For rural masses, the change from class to status, coupled with its cultural underpinnings, spelt the beginning of an 'unfinished process of proletarianisation' (Pun and Lu 2010a)—an unusual route to the world-historical process of capitalism that turns agricultural labourers to industrial workers by deriving the former of their means of production and subsistence. Perhaps more strikingly, it was consequential in transforming rural citizens from once highly acclaimed 'revolutionary heroes' to 'modernisation losers' from the reform era onwards.

The Reform Era (1979–2007)

In December 1978, faced with dual pressures of political uncertainty and economic stagnation, the new leadership under Deng Xiaoping embarked upon an 'opening-door' reform that strove to bring market forces, albeit under strict centralized supervision, to bear on China's modernization processes. As the reform pushed forward with privatization and urbanization, a shift towards marked-oriented labour markets ensued. In 1984, in order to meet an increasing demand for flexible, cheap labour, the state introduced a system of temporary residence permits, equivalent to temporary work visas, which allowed peasants with rural *hukou* holders to work in urban areas. Around the same time, rural agricultural communes were dismantled and replaced by a household responsibility system. These measures, combined with widening economic gaps between rural and urban areas, unleashed a massive flow of rural migrants into cities during the first decade of their application. Mobility restrictions were further relaxed during the late 1990s and early 2000s, leading to exponential growth in the volume of rural-urban migration; the number of rural migrants rose from more than 60 million in the mid-1990s and 100 million in the early 2000s to 140 million in 2008.

For rural migrants who were called on to work, but deprived of fundamental rights to settle in the city, industrialization and urbanization were, as Smith and Pun (2018: 607) put it, 'highly disconnected processes'. The resulting quasi-peasant and quasi-worker identities inflicted a deep sense of incompleteness, inadequacy, and unworthiness, despite their decades of hardship and toil that led to China's meteoric rise to global economic superpower (Pun and Lu 2010a). This was further aggravated by the emergence of neoliberalism-informed discourses on '*suzhi*' (human quality) that reverberated throughout the reform era. The Chinese term *suzhi* is a multi-faceted and malleable cultural concept that has many indigenous connotations. It was appropriated by the state as a prominent development policy and a discursive tool to problematize rural masses as having low quality, lacking civility, and hindering development—a drastic change in the public representation of peasants who were once Mao-era revolutionary heroes contributing greatly to the establishment of New China (*xin zhongguo*). To a large extent, *suzhi* was akin to a 'quasi-eugenic' discourse and a 'cultural fixation' indispensable for China's modernization endeavours (Anagnost 1997). In line with the doctrines of neoliberal capitalism, government policies and media reports frequently invoked *suzhi* to adroitly place responsibility on individuals, rather than on existing social structures and conditions, for failing to acquire desirable qualities. That peasants needed to be disciplined into a modern citizenry and use migration to relieve rural poverty and backwardness seemed to justify just-in-time provision of a large, cheap, and relatively docile labour force. As the quintessential embodiment of precariousness existence, a great many rural migrants took up low-wage, low-skill, and low-status jobs in informal and private sectors of economy with least autonomy, protection, and dignity. Their life was marked by job insecurity, wage arrears, low pay and benefits, lack of training and upward mobility, alienation, and violence, as well documented by numerous scholars such as Choi (2016), Huang and Yi (2015), Lee (1995, 1998), Peng (2011), Pun (2005), Pun and Lu (2010a, 2010b), Pun and Smith (2007), Swider (2015), and Zhang (2014), to name but a few.

In addition to the unleashing of rural–urban migration, the state stepped up efforts to restructure SOEs in the late 1990s by 'grasping the large and releasing the small' (*zhuada fangxiao*), which helped a minority of large ones become modern, profit-making enterprises and turned small- and medium-sized ones into private-sector enterprises. Many urban workers, especially women, lost their secure iron rice bowls and were rehired as precarious temps with limited welfare benefits and legal protection in rapidly expanding private-sector POEs and FOEs. As mentioned earlier, the government was attentive to the needs of those former urban 'labour aristocrats' and quickly established re-employment service centres to help jobseekers make a smooth transition from 'relying on the state' to 'relying on the market' (Xu 2015). Since the 2000s, the use of agency-mediated dispatched workers, who received lower wages and much less social security protection than regular employees, had become widespread among large firms, particularly SOEs in service sectors (such as postal services, telecommunication and railways); as Lin (2015) points out, dispatched workers accounted for more than 60 per cent of the entire workforce in some SOEs. Fixed-term workers with direct labour contracts, who were not counted as NRE in China, either worked under renewable one-year contracts in SOEs or faced far more precarious employment in POEs and FOEs. As more and more workers were absorbed into labour market peripheries, the size and diversification of NRE had grown rapidly, which resulted in a greater division of the working class than previously existed.

Shaped by a confluence of state-driven marketization and global neoliberal forces,[4] the reform era was characterized by an emphatic shift towards highly precarious and commodified forms of employment relationship. While the unparalleled economic growth alleviated the poverty of many, a crucial corollary was that China changed from one of the poorest and most egalitarian societies to one of the most unequal societies. During the turbulent restructuring process, all manner of differences emerged; old inequalities transformed themselves into not only rural-urban citizenship divisions, but also disparities between social strata and regions. In the chaos of transition, government officials, Party cadres, enterprise managers, and other elites acquired considerable personal economic advantages via a combination of corruption, hidden ruses, and appropriation of public assets and rights, which in effect enclosed the commons—large numbers of dispossessed farmers, rural migrants, and urban workers—to the benefit of a few. They emerged as the Chinese new capitalist class who, in Marxist terms, gained different private rights over the means of production and accumulated much of their capital through the super-exploitation of labour power, particularly of rural migrants. In this reconstitution of class relations, some neoliberal cultural elements such as 'flexibility', 'personal responsibility', and 'entrepreneurship' were incorporated into the state's pro-growth policies, as evidenced by the aforementioned *suzhi* discourses and Deng's famous slogan of 'to get rich is glorious'. These transformations, albeit 'with distinctly Chinese characteristics' (see Harvey 2005: 121–151),[5] resonated with western neoliberal emphases on individual subjectivities and marked a break from Maoist redistributionist ethics in the pre-reform era. Co-existing with the Confucian tradition of hierarchical social relations that implicitly served to legitimize or deflect attention from the widening divisions, the imported western values were instrumental in forging a national consensus on the Chinese logic of 'market socialism'.

The ascendency of Chinese capitalism, however, cannot simply be subsumed under the global process of neoliberalism, which manifests itself differently in different countries. As asserted by Nonini (2008), China's distinct cultural contexts, especially *guanxi*, are of vital importance in understanding the specific reconfiguration of state-class-labour relations in the post-Maoist era. *Guanxi*, variously translated as 'connection', 'networking', or 'relationship', is grounded in Confucian thought, and can be briefly described as pervasive and intricate personal connections based on social exchange (in the form of, for example, gifts and favours). As a fundamental governing feature of hierarchically structured social relationships, it is infused with a complex and dynamic set of norms and values surrounding reciprocity, obligations, trust, face, emotions, and personhood, often depending on the nature and context of relationships (see, for example, Barbalet 2021; Fei 1992). During the reform era, the operations of *guanxi* allowed greater integration between the state and the market among the rising capitalist class, while marginalizing the dispossessed who lacked the resources to employ *guanxi* connections with the new elites, as expounded by Nonini (2008: 160):

> Government cadres and Party officials have been in the vanguard of those profiting by privatization and liberalization, while private entrepreneurs have also emerged... . In this environment, local cadres formed prosperous partnerships with business people, including foreign corporate investors. Cadres provided entrepreneurs with vital information and access to credit and to markets; they shielded their capitalist partners from exactions by other cadres and from official or irregular taxes; and they accorded their partners the political protection they have needed to evade labor, health, pension and other welfare regulations. In return, capitalists provided 'their' cadres with money (via fees) and gifts, integrated them into valuable social networks, mobilized overseas connections, and provided them with shares in the enterprises they formed.
>
> (So 2005: 487)

To be sure, the Chinese culture of *guanxi* personalism plays an important role in creating old and new asymmetries in power, status and hierarchy, in laying the foundation for what is dubbed 'crony capitalism' (Pei 2016), and in dictating workers' everyday lives.[6] It was, and still is an essential part of the Chinese capitalist class formation process, whose ramifications continue to reverberate throughout contemporary China.

The Regulation Era (2008–present)

Social tensions and conflicts had sharpened since the late 1990s, amid growing inequality, exploitation, and suffering that the reform era inflicted on the working class, especially rural migrants at the bottom end of the labour market. Recent decades witnessed a growing number of protests, rallies, and petitions, which also reflected workers' pervasive disaffection with and distrust of official Party-led unions and local governments, whose activities were often seen by workers as closely aligned with the interests of management.[7] Within the political ruling elite, factions also emerged with Maoist advocates railing against the market-based economy and its negative effects on the interests of the masses and social order (Nonini 2008). Figure 1.3 shows a massive increase in formally processed labour disputes from 19,098 in 1994 to 715,163 in 2014, with a precipitous jump from 2008 when a new Labour Contract Law came into effect. The rising number and intensity of labour

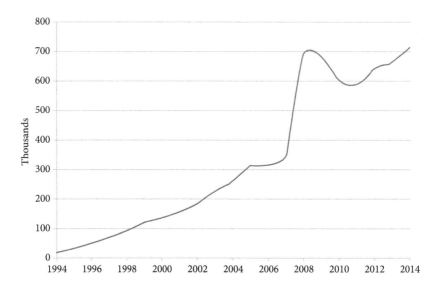

Figure 1.3 Accepted cases by Labour Dispute Arbitration Committees (1994–2014)

Source: *China Labour Statistical Yearbook,* various years, National Bureau of Statistics of the People's Republic China

unrest in China was fuelled in part by younger and better-educated migrant workers who were less tolerant of injustice and more eager to engage in all manner of resistance (Chan and Selden 2014).

It was against this tumultuous backdrop that the state introduced a series of laws and regulations, including Labour Contract Law (2008, amended in 2013), Labour Disputes Mediation and Arbitration Law (2008), Social Security Law (2011), Provisional Regulations on Labour Dispatch (2014), and Opinions on Building Harmonious Labour Relations (2015)—China would rank third in Employment Protection Legislation strictness among OECD countries (Gallagher et al. 2015). The 2008 Labour Contract Law, although being significantly watered down from its draft version as a result of employer associations' lobbying, was widely viewed as a vital step towards regulating NRE and safeguarding workers' interests. While there were some increases in contract-signing rates, the law produced only modest success in expanding social insurance coverage, as many rural migrant workers who were offered labour contracts remained uncovered by major social insurance programmes (Gallagher et al. 2015: 228, see Figure 1.1). In addition to the existing rural–urban citizenship divide, the new regulation regime proved to be more useful to socially advantageous groups of workers who occupied a relatively strong position in the labour market (Friedman and Lee 2010: 526–527); a large proportion of precarious workers including part-timers, insourced 'independent' contractors, and student interns fell largely outside of the protection of the labour laws (Cooke and Brown 2015: 31–32). Furthermore, the heightened regulatory restrictions provided employers with strong incentives to exploit legal loopholes or ambiguities and/or replace permanent or non-fixed-term workers with new sources of cheap labour; for example, the use of dispatched workers increased drastically shortly after the enactment of the Labour Contract Law. To ameliorate the situation, subsequent amendments imposed a 10 per cent cap on dispatched and independent contract workers. Nevertheless, it became evident that laws and regulations alone would not suffice to curb the widespread exploitation of precarious workers.

The limitations of the seemingly pro-labour regulatory approaches, to a great extent, could be ascribed to China's state-centric political economy and its intricate connections with cultural particularities. As the economic restructuring enabled capitalist enterprises to form and function freely, the state gradually pushed forward with its decentralization policies, which granted local governments more leeway to pursue their own economic goals (Friedman and Kuruvilla 2015). Under this efficiency-driven, pro-growth development model, local governments were keen on nurturing a pro-capital, competitive economic climate. The devolution of power enabled them to strengthen their alliance with businesses aided by the aforementioned *guanxi* personalism. It also allowed them to exert a considerable leverage over legal and judiciary systems—activities that constituted an essential element for China's lax enforcement and differential implementation of national laws and regulations at the local level. This central–local government division, coupled with official unions' subservience to the state and the absence of independent unions, had a profound impact on workers' everyday struggles (Friedman 2014). While there was mounting antagonism towards employers and local governments, the legitimacy of the central paternalistic state—who was expected to protect the masses against all evil aspects of capitalism—remained relatively intact. Rather than resorting to unionization or organized movements, aggrieved workers were urged by the state to use law as a tool for protecting labour rights and resolving disputes. It should be noted here that many disputes were collective in nature, but formal arbitration and civil courts' systems tended to break up collective actions into individual or small-scale cases. The new regulatory regime, therefore, played a key role in promoting individualized employment relations, cellularizing conflicts, and defusing working-class formation. As reported by Lee and Zhang (2013), despite its growing number and militancy, work insurgency, especially among rural migrants, was either brutally suppressed or channelled adroitly into the state-controlled legal and bureaucratic apparatus.

Central to the state's renewed enthusiasm for 'ruling the country by law' were concerns over social stability and economic growth, to which large-scale public protests were deemed serious threats. In tandem with the enactment of a series of new laws and regulations, 'harmonious society' (*hexie shehui*)' had been introduced by Hu's government since the early 2000s as a major policy orientation. Herein again lies the importance of traditional culture. 'Harmony' (*he*) is a fundamental principle of Confucianism that carries paternalistic and benevolent overtones and emphasizes co-prospering, complementarity, and hierarchical solidarity. While classical uses often denote loyal opposition and constructive disagreement, contemporary political interpretations focus predominantly on stability and order, which can be used as a convenient tool for suppressing dissent. Such an overt assertion of 'harmonious society' in regulation-era China reflected state-orchestrated efforts to contend with the problems and failures of modernization through the revision and reimagination of old traditions—a prevalent phenomenon in modern nation-building endeavours where the past is being '(re-)invented' to construct the present (Hobsbawm and Ranger 1983).[8] As a key governing political–cultural discourse, 'harmonious society' had apparent explanatory power; it was instrumental in reinforcing the state's stance on laws and regulations, masking glaring inequalities, and entrenching social status hierarchies.

More recently, the Chinese development model had been redefined with a new focus on domestic consumption that would require the improvement of rural migrants' earning power and economic security. In the context of increased inequalities, growing urbanization pressures and a reduced demographic dividend, reforming the *hukou* system had become a political and economic necessity. Since the 2000s, many provincial and municipal governments had been experimenting with *hukou* reforms including permanent *hukou* transfers. Those reforms, however, varied greatly across localities. For example, large so-called 'first-tier' cities such as Beijing and Shanghai, where rural migrants were highly concentrated, imposed much more stringent criteria for obtaining urban 'green cards' than small and medium cities. In addition, a high proportion of inter-provincial migrants found it considerably harder to convert *hukou* than those migrating within the same province. For the vast majority of rural migrants, the removal of barriers to job mobility had not been accompanied by adequate welfare and social security reforms that would address the coverage gap between rural and urban *hukou* holders and between different types of firms; for instance, the lack of *hukou* portability between regions is a contributing factor to the gap. More importantly, employers had a strong incentive to minimize social security contribution costs by reducing the number of regular workers on their payroll. This was further compounded by the practices of local governments, which often used social security laws as an economic strategy and administered them differently according to their *guanxi* relationships with firms, often depending on the latter's ownership and size. Consequently, the *hukou* reforms were fraught with important political, economic, and cultural issues. As discussed earlier, of particular salience were the reconfiguration of class relations that tilted the balance of power in favour of the new capitalist class, the lack of independent labour unions and bargaining power essential to advance workers' rights and interests, the weak enforcement and differing implementations of national legislations at the local level, and the complex and dynamic interplay of those political-economic structures with cultural traditions, noticeably *guanxi*, hierarchy, and harmony.

Conclusions

This chapter has shown how the rural–urban migration and citizenship is of central importance to grappling with China's ever-shifting contours of precarious work and social inequalities. Despite various reforms, *hukou* continues to function as a crucial feature of the social entitlements' system that confers many public benefits and services—ranging from health insurance and pension to education and housing—on urban local workers while denying them to rural migrant workers. This distinct citizenly discounting, combined with its intersections with other key inequality variables, including formal and informal sectors and firms' ownership structure, sets China apart from its neighbouring countries such as Japan and South Korea; the latter are characterized by predominately gendered patterns of stratification. To gain a deeper and more nuanced understanding, future research should pay careful attention to the intersection of rural-urban citizenship with other identity categories (such as gender, age, regionality, education, and family background) that engenders a specific 'matrix of domination' (Collins 1990) in the Chinese context. In this regard, empirical studies are particularly needed to reveal the perceptions and experiences of real people in concrete social worlds, thereby offering qualitative insight for agency and social change.[9]

Perhaps more importantly, by delving into—albeit cursorily—the three well-known historical phases of transformation, the chapter has thrown into relief the role of culture in China's major political–economic transitions. Traditional Confucian beliefs and values permeated the historical processes, from the pre-reform institutional establishment of *hukou* and its rural–urban mobility control, workers' personalized forms of dependency and managerial paternalism in *danwei* or work units and the five-tiered hierarchical employment segmentation, through the reform-era's discursive emphasis on *suzhi* or human quality and appropriations of *guanxi* network, not least during the tumultuous entry into neoliberalism-informed market modernization, to the ubiquitous evocation of *hexie shehui* or 'harmonious society' in the regulation era. Throughout those prominent development trajectories, culture provided an underlying basis, and was immensely powerful, for legitimizing and reinforcing the institutional changes.

Such interconnectedness of culture with institutions merits special attention. Compared to institutions, traditional culture, as a system of malleable and inherently contestable symbols (Turner 1967; Cohen 1969, 1974), is an elusive and enigmatic domain and yet possesses apparent explanatory power. The so-called 'linguistic turn' in many social sciences highlights a renewed focus on the importance of culture, especially language use, and power relations in the (re-)construction of social reality (Bourdieu 1991; Parkin 1984). This is particularly true when it comes to those deep-seated beliefs and values rooted in remote antiquity, which are often taken for granted, hidden, internalized, and difficult to contest. As demonstrated in the Chinese context, Confucian doctrines concerning hierarchical status and harmony were influential in entrenching rural-urban citizenship inequalities and reconciling social tensions. Moreover, they played an important role in deflecting attention away from working-class struggles and collective actions geared towards confronting the structural subordination of labour to capital and exploitation against the backdrop of growing social disparities and conflicts intensified by decades of unrelenting marketization.[10] For example, labour NGOs' activism, a well-trodden field of research in the Chinese studies, focused mainly on the resolution of individual disputes within state-proved regulatory frameworks and rarely connected labour rights' violations with *hukou*'s socio-cultural exclusion of rural migrants (Fu 2021; Howell 2015). Thus, the prism of Marxist class relations, which is indeed an indispensable tool (Smith and Pun 2017),[11] needs to be combined with a cultural lens. This in turn can go a long way towards tackling the root causes of precariousness and casting fresh light on social change in China and beyond.

Notes

1. There had been a massive increase in the number of bachelor's graduates, which rose from 600,000 in 1990, doubled to 1.2 million in 2002 and then leapt by over fivefold to 7 million in 2013 (Freeman 2015). The role of education in improving social mobility was waning on the whole, although it remained an important factor in future job prospects and upward mobility.
2. In addition, women in China have to retire, as stipulated by official guidelines, at 55 (50 for blue-collar workers), five to ten years earlier than their male counterparts.
3. From a historical comparative perspective, the iron rice bowl at SOEs was not the result of a de facto compromise between capital and labour that came to normalize the post-war standard employment across many Western countries (Xu 2015).
4. China's tortuous path of internal transformations coincided with the gathering strength of neoliberalism in the advanced capitalist world; the latter indeed opened up a space for China's tumultuous entry and spectacular emergence as a global economic power after 1980 (Harvey 2005: 121).
5. China's key development strategies during the reform era were characterized by heavy reliance upon foreign direct investment and keeping the power of state ownership structures intact, which seemed to fit with the aim of inhibiting the formation of any coherent capitalist class power bloc (see Harvey 2005: 121–151).
6. *Guanxi* or personal connections with government and workplace authorities can have a profound impact on people's major life events. For example, workers may reply on *guanxi* help from family, relatives, former classmates, and friends to find new employment or

move to more desirable jobs. This is particularly effective when it comes to strong *guanxi* ties of obligation, trust and intimacy.
7. In contrast to growing autonomy conferred upon private capital and rising power of employer associations, the All-China Federation of Trade Unions (ACFTU), as the only legitimate representative of organized labour, continues to be a vital component of political centralization, functioning as government agencies or benevolent mediators. Despite that ACFTU and its local branches played a facilitating role in introducing a series of pro-labour laws and experiments, they were unable or unwilling to protect workers' rights and interests at the point of production. For example, Hui and Chan's study (2015) shows how a post-2010 wave of democratic union elections in the Pearl River Delta region, driven by workers' wildcat strikes, turned out to be 'indirect' and 'quasi-democratic' as the Party-state, the high-level unions, and management exercised far greater organizational and institutional power than the workers.
8. Perhaps not surprisingly, the regulation era also saw a broad political and intellectual movement towards Confucian renaissance, as demonstrated vividly by the 2008 Beijing Olympic Opening Ceremony (see Worsman 2012).
9. It is striking that we know very little about NRE in China's rural areas where farmers and other types of informal-sector workers comprise a substantial share of precarious workers at the lowest end of labour markets with little protection and few rights.
10. The Marxist concept of 'class' is not invoked in China as the discursive frame to constitute workers' collective experiences. Rather, the Maoist social model continues to assume importance, which emphasizes 'harmonious' interests between people in different social statuses, including workers, peasants, the intelligentsia, and the bourgeoisie (see Wang 2021).
11. Among others, Smith and Pun's work (2017) offers trenchant criticism of Standing's conceptualization of 'the precariat' as a new class in the making (2011), which rejects or misunderstands Marxist notions of class and class struggles in changing capitalism, strengthens cleavages among workers and, therefore, undermines the importance of working-class formation processes. To be sure, precariousness is not evidence of a separate class with different interests, but rather a fundamental feature of working class, which has become exacerbated and more prevalent across different employment statuses under neoliberalism.

References

Anagnost, A. (1997) *National Past-Times: Narrative, Representation, and Power in Modern China*. London: Duke University Press.
Barbalet, J. (2021) 'The analysis of Chinese rural society: Fei Xiaotong revisited'. *Modern China*, 47(4): 355–382.
Bourdieu, P. (1991) *Languages and Symbolic Power*. Cambridge: Polity Press.
Chan, J. and Selden, M. (2014) China's rural migrant workers, the state, and labor politics. *Critical Asian Studies*, 46(4): 599–620.

Chan, N. K. and Humphreys, L. (2018) 'Mediatization of social space and the case of Uber drivers'. *Media and Communication*, 6(2): 29–38.

China Development on Flexible Employment (2022) Available at: https://www.pishu.com.cn/skwx_ps/bookdetail?SiteID=14&ID=13625846/ (Accessed at: 18 May 2022).

China Statistical Yearbook (2019) 中国统计年鉴 (2019). Available at: http://www.tjcn.org (Accessed at: 18 May 2022).

China Today (2021) 'The advent of gig-economy era' ("零工经济"时代已来). Available at: http://www.chinatoday.com.cn/zw2018/bktg/202104/t20210401_800242258.html/ (Accessed at: 18 May 2022).

Choi, A. Y. P. (2016) 'Gendered pragmatism and subaltern masculinity in China: Peasant men's responses to their wives labor migration'. *American Behavioural Scientist*, 60(5-6): 565–582.

Cohen, A. (1969) 'Political anthropology: The analysis of the symbolism of power relations'. *Man*, 4(2): 215–235.

Cohen, A. (1974) *Two-Dimensional Man: An Essay on the Anthropology of Power and Symbolism in Complex Society*. Berkeley, CA: University of California Press.

Collins, P. H. (1990) *Black Feminist Thought: Knowledge, Consciousness, and the Politics of Empowerment*. Boston: Unwin Hyman.

Collins, P. H. (2015) 'Intersectionality's definitional dilemmas'. *The Annual Review of Sociology*, 41: 1–20.

Cooke, F. L. and Brown, R. (2015) 'The regulation of non-standard forms of employment in China, Japan and The Republic of Korea'. Conditions of Work and Employment Series No. 64, International Labour Organization (ILO).

Fei, X. (1992) *From the Soil: The Foundations of Chinese Society* (Translated by Gary G. Hamilton and Wang Zheng). Berkeley: University of California Press.

Freeman, R. (2015) 'A labor market with Chinese characteristics'. In G. C. Chow and D. H. Perkins (eds.), *Routledge Handbook of the Chinese Economy*. London: Routledge, pp. 103–120.

Friedman, E. (2014) 'Alienated politics: Labour insurgency and the paternalistic state in China'. *Development and Change*, 45(5): 1001–1018.

Friedman, E. and Kuruvilla, S. (2015) 'Experimentation and decentralization in China's labor relations'. *Human Relations*, 68(2): 181–195.

Friedman, E. and Lee, C. K. (2010) 'Remaking the world of Chinese labour: A 30-year retrospective'. *British Journal of Industrial Relations*, 48(3): 507–533.

Fu, H. (2021) 'Social action as "a total social phenomenon": Comparing leadership challenges facing community-based labour organisations in China and Japan'. *Human Relations*, 74(9): 1396–1420.

Fu, H., Su, Y., and Ni, A. (2018) 'Selling motherhood: Gendered emotional labour, citizenly discounting, and alienation among China's migrant domestic workers'. *Gender & Society*, 32(6): 814–836.

Gallagher, M., Giles, J., Park, A., and Wang, M. (2015) 'China's 2008 Labour Contract Law: Implementation and implications for China's workers'. *Human Relations*, 68(2): 197–235.

Harvey, D. (2005) *A Brief History of Neoliberalism*. Oxford: Oxford University Press.

Hewison, K. (2016) 'Precarious work'. In S. Edgell, H. Gottfried, and E. Granter (eds.), *The Sage Handbook of the Sociology of Work and Employment*. Thousand Oaks, CA: Sage, pp. 428–443.

Hobsbawm, E. and Ranger, T. (1983) *The Invention of Tradition*. Cambridge: Cambridge University Press.

Howell, J. (2015) 'Shall we dance? Welfarist incorporation and the politics of state-labour NGO relations in China'. *The China Quarterly*, 223: 702–723.

Huang, Y. and Yi, C. (2015). 'Invisible migrant enclaves in Chinese cities: Underground living in Beijing, China'. *Urban Studies*, 52(15): 2948–2473.

Hui. E. S. and Chan, C. K. (2015). 'Beyond the union-centred approach: A critical evaluation of recent trade union elections in China'. *British Journal of Industrial Relations*, 53(3): 601–627.

Kalleberg, A. (2000) 'Nonstandard employment relations: Part-time, temporary, and contract work'. *Annual Review of Sociology*, 26: 341–365.

Kalleberg, A. and Vallas, S. (eds.) (2018) *Precarious Work*. Bingley, England: Emerald Publishing.

Kuruvilla, S., Lee, C. K., and Gallagher, M. E. (2011) *From Iron Rice Bowl to Informalization: Markets, Workers, and the State in a Changing China*. Ithaca, NY: ILR Press.

Lee, C. K. (1995) 'Engendering the worlds of labor: Women workers, labor markets, and production politics in the South China economic miracle'. *American Sociological Review*, 60(3): 378–397.

Lee, C. K. (1998) *Gender and the South China Miracle: Two Worlds of Factory Women*. Berkeley: University of California Press.

Lee, C. K. and Zhang, Y. (2013) 'The power of instability: Unraveling the microfoundations of bargained authoritarianism in China'. *American Journal of Sociology*, 118(6): 1475–1508.

Lin, K. (2015) 'Recomposing Chinese migrant and state-sector workers'. In A. Chan (ed.), *Chinese Workers in Comparative Perspective*. Ithaca and London: Cornell University, pp. 69–84.

Nonini, D. M. (2008) 'Is China Becoming Neoliberal?' *Critique of Anthropology*, 28(2): 145–176.

Parkin, D. (1984) 'Political language'. *Annual Review of Anthropology*, 29: 107–124.

Pei, M. (2016) *China's Crony Capitalism: The Dynamics of Regime Decay*. Cambridge, MA: Harvard University Press.

Peng, T. (2011) 'The impact of citizenship on labour process: State, capital and labour control in South China'. *Work, Employment and Society*, 25(4): 726–741.

people.cn (2017) 'Didi Employment Report indicates more than 21 million people gained income from its platform' (滴滴就业报告显示 最近一年2100多万人在平台获得收入). Available at: http://industry.people.com.cn/n1/2017/1013/c413883-29586704.html/ (Accessed at: 18 May 2022).

Pun, N. (2005). *Made in China: Women Factory Workers in a Global Workplace*. Durham, NC: Duke University Press.

Pun, N. and Lu, H. (2010a) 'Unfinished proletarianization: Self, anger, and class action among the second generation of peasant-workers in present-day China'. *Modern China*, 36(5): 493–519.

Pun, N. and Lu, H. (2010b) 'A culture of violence: The labor subcontracting system and collective action by construction workers in post-socialist China'. *The China Journal*, 64: 143–158.

Pun, N. and Smith, C. (2007) 'Putting transnational labour process in its place: The dormitory labour regime in post-socialist China'. *Work, Employment and Society*, 21(1): 27–45.

Selden, M., Chan, J., and Pun, N. (2015) 'Interns or workers? China's student labor regime'. *Asian Studies*, 1(1): 69–98.

Smith, C. and Chan, J. (2015) 'Working for two bosses: Student interns as constrained labour in China'. *Human Relations*, 68(2): 305–326.

Smith, C. and Pun, N. (2018) 'Class and precarity: An unhappy coupling in China's working class formation'. *Work, Employment and Society*, 32(3): 599–615.

So, A. Y. (2005) 'Beyond the logic of capital and the polarization model: The state, market reforms, and the plurality of class conflict in China'. *Critical Asian Studies*, 37(3): 481–494.

Standing. G. (2011) *The Precariat: The New Dangerous Class*. London: Bloomsbury Academic.

Statista (2021) 'Number of migrant workers in China from 2010 to 2020'. Available at: https://www.statista.com/statistics/234578/share-of-migrant-workers-in-china-by-age/ (Accessed at: 18 May 2022).

Swider, S. (2015) 'Building China: Precarious employment among migrant construction workers'. *Work, Employment & Society*, 29(1): 41–59.

Turner, V. (1967) *The Forest of Symbols: Aspects of Ndembu Ritual*. Ithaca, NY: Cornell University Press.

Vosko, L. (2010) *Managing the Margins: Gender, Citizenship, and the International Regulation of Precarious Employment*. Oxford: Oxford University Press.

Walder, A. G. (1983). 'Organized dependency and cultures of authority in Chinese industry'. *The Journal of Asian Studies*, 43(1): 51–76.

Walder, A. G. (1984) 'The remaking of the Chinese working class, 1949-1981'. *Modern China*, 10(1): 3–48.

Wang, M. (2021) 'The influence of the Confucian notion of "Great Harmony" on Mao Zedong's design of the social model'. In *The History and Logic of Modern Chinese Politics*. Singapore: Springer, pp. 165–177.

Webb, A., McQuaid, R., and Rand, S. (2020) 'Employment in the informal economy: Implications of the COVID-19 pandemic'. *International Journal of Sociology and Social Policy*, 40(9/10): 1005–1019.

Wood, A. J. and Lehdonvirta, V. (2019) 'Platform labour and structured antagonism: Understanding the origins of protest in the gig economy'. Presented at Oxford Internet Institute, University of Oxford.

Worsman, R. (2012) 'Tradition, modernity, and the Confucian revival: An introduction and literature review of new Confucian activism'. *History Honors Papers*, Paper 14.

Xiao, M., Chen, H., Li, F., and Guo, Y. (2022) 'The dynamics of social assistance in the informal economy: Empirical evidence from urban China'. *Journal of Social Policy*, 1–24 (published online by Cambridge University Press).

Xu, F. (2015) 'Regulating precarious labor for economic growth and social stability in China'. In H. M. Hsiao, A. L. Kalleberg, and K. Hewison (eds.), *Policy Responses to Precarious Work in Asia*, Taipei, Taiwan: Institute of Sociology, Academia Sinica, pp. 135–178.

Zhang, N. (2014) 'Performing identities: Women in rural-urban migration in contemporary China'. *Geoforum*, 54: 17–27.

2
Gender, Precarious Labour, and Neoliberalism in Japan

Saori Shibata

Introduction

Prior to the 1990s, Japan's employment relations were typically considered to be characterized by social compromise between capital and labour, but with divergent dual employment practices between men and women, with job security for core male workers and a tax–welfare system that prioritized women's reproductive role. This social compromise saw wage–labour relations in which employers promoted skills and training, innovation, and employment security, creating a situation in which Japan was perceived, according to some accounts, to be more egalitarian than the Scandinavian countries (Lechevalier 2014: 86–87). This compromise reduced the potential for social conflict and achieved stable economic growth between the 1960s and 1980s. However, significant changes have taken place since the 1990s. The government and business managers have gradually introduced neoliberal policies and practices which emphasize, among other things, labour market flexibility. This trend of neoliberalization has increased precarity for non-regular and women workers and reinforced gender roles in the workplace and household. These processes of neoliberalization have not, however, gone unchallenged, and different forms of opposition have seen the government face pressure to address the disaffection it has prompted. Nevertheless, the government's commitment to a flexible workforce remains in place, with a strong focus on promoting competitiveness for Japanese business.

The labour market and gender policies introduced by the Abe administration between 2012 and 2020 have largely failed to improve the status of non-regular workers and women workers. There has also been an increase in the number of women and non-regular workers who lost their jobs during the coronavirus crisis, something which was compounded by the difficulties

Saori Shibata, *Gender, Precarious Labour, and Neoliberalism in Japan*. In: *Temporary and Gig Economy Workers in China and Japan*. Edited by Huiyan Fu, Oxford University Press. © Oxford University Press (2023).
DOI: 10.1093/oso/9780192849694.003.0003

faced in accessing allowances to which they were entitled. Precarity among non-regular and female workers thus continues to exist.

The Japanese government and business elites promote gig work, a new form of work which is organized through the allocation of tasks through online platforms, and which has seen a large numbers of workers willing to carry out paid tasks (Valenduc and Vendramin 2016: 38). This gig work has, in turn, led to much work becoming increasingly precarious and further reinforced women's reproductive role, whilst also further locking women into a peripheral position within the workforce.

This chapter presents a historical overview of the characteristics of the Japanese post-war labour market, including dualism, a compromise between employers and employees, women's role as a peripheral section of the workforce, and a persistent prioritization of women's reproductive role in both the household and society. The chapter illustrates the change, continuity, and new challenges that neoliberalization has generated from the early 1990s onwards, and how the government has responded to the disaffection and dissatisfaction which emerged during the 2000s. It also introduces the emergence of gig work, which the government has promoted in an attempt to solve a number of labour market challenges, despite the ongoing problems of precarity and gender inequality.

Dualism and compromise in the labour market until the late 1980s

The Japanese labour market in the immediate post-war period experienced considerable unrest. This saw a rapid increase in the number of union members and the emergence of militant workers and strikes, especially in the mining industry. In an attempt to regain control over Japanese society following the rise of worker militancy, the US-led Occupation government and the Japanese government with the support of the Nikkeiren (Japan Federation of Employers' Association) responded by introducing a number of measures that successfully reduced the power of labour unions (Shibata 2020a: 41). As a product of this repression, a shift towards more moderate unions and organized labour occurred (Jeong and Aguilera 2008: 115).

The model of Japanese capitalism that emerged from this period of turmoil and repression, up until the 1980s, has been described as a coordinated and stable, consensus-based model of capitalism and is largely considered successful in terms of achieving sustained economic growth between the

1960s and 1980s (Hall and Soskice 2001). The labour market during this period also took on the characteristics of stability, compromise, consensus, and coordination. Long-term employment relations, the seniority wage system, enterprise unionism, training, and skill acquisition within firms were each enabling conditions of this model of capitalism. At the same time, the Japanese state failed to develop a substantial welfare system, and instead relied largely on firms' long-term employment relations to secure citizens' welfare. Firms developed production/supply business networks (*keiretsu*), which enabled efficient production as well as a built-in labour adjustment mechanism which flexibly absorbed abundant employees within the *keiretsu* groups and avoided dismissals (Vogel 2006: 125). This configuration of (and coordination between) socio-economic institutions, therefore, facilitated the stability witnessed in Japan's model of capitalism during this period.

Coordination also existed between employees in large companies and in small and medium-sized companies in the *keiretsu* groups, as well as between regular and non-regular workers. Small- and medium-sized enterprises in the same *keiretsu* network (business network) provided a buffer to absorb excess labour from large companies when necessary, thereby consolidating employment security and contributing to long-term employment (Mizuno 2018: 267). Similarly, non-regular workers acted as a protective shield for core regular workers in terms of employment security, as employers could flexibly adjust employment by hiring and firing non-regular workers according to demand. This represented a built-in form of labour market stabilization (Mizuno 2018: 268; Osawa and Kingston 2021).

The role of non-regular workers, and especially female non-regular workers, has always been important in the post-war Japanese labour market when the demand for labour increased (Gottfried 2015; Osawa and Kingston 2021; Nagamatsu 2021: 3). This constituted a dual employment mechanism between the 1950s and 1970s. In the manufacturing sector, outside workers (*shagaiko*) who worked in subcontracting firms were flexibly sent to work for their client (parent) firms in the same *keiretsu* network (Mizuno 2018: 268). Large firms with links to subcontracting firms in their *keiretsu* network could rely on such outside workers whenever they needed to. At the same time, a shortage of labour led companies to hire female workers who had become housewives with low wages, as temporary workers for short time periods. As a result, we witnessed an increased amount of female part-time employment in the service, wholesale, and retail sectors. We also saw the rapid spread of outsourced contracting services in the 1980s, particularly for white-collar jobs. This aimed to reduce labour costs and also saw the introduction of the Worker Dispatch Law in 1985 (Mizuno 2018: 268).

As women were integrated in the labour market as a temporary labour force when needed, their role in the Japanese economy during this period was essential (despite the fact that they were often marginalized and placed on the periphery of the labour market). Women's reproductive role, unpaid family care work, and part-time employment all enabled Japan's economic growth. Further, the gendered labour market not only contributed to the stability of employment relations but also institutionalized male-centred work practices and the gender gap (Osawa 2015). The ratio of women working part time was over 12 per cent in 1955, growing to 15 per cent in 1974 (Shibata 2017: 29).

In 1986 the Equal Employment Opportunity Law sought to improve women's rights within the workplace. This further increased the level of women's participation in the labour market. Nevertheless, women's non-standard employment functioned as a cheap buffer to manage high labour costs associated with long-term male employment (Gottfried 2015: 12–13, 25).

In addition to labour market practices, the welfare–tax system in post-war Japan institutionalized women's reproductive role by establishing a tax reduction for housewives who limited their work hours per month, thereby incentivizing women to prioritize their reproductive role and childcare duties. Women entered wage labour when demand was high, but this was constrained to part-time work, as annual wages were limited by the tax threshold of 1.03 million yen introduced in the 1960s. This gendered tax mechanism constrained female workers to non-regular employment status. It also discriminated against single working women who did not benefit from the tax reduction. The tax-welfare system has been closely linked to the M-shaped curve which shows the characteristics of the female labour participation in Japan: female labour force participation declines during the years of marriage and childbirth, and rises again as children grow older and more independent (although the valley of the curve has recently become shallower) (Gender Equality Bureau Cabinet Office 2020a: 103–104).

The features of Japan's society and working culture—including a male-centred workplace and 'firm-as-family' ethos (Clark 1979; Fruin 1980), prejudice against women, a prioritization of 'family values', and women as housemaker who are restricted to the periphery of the labour market—permeate many of the country's institutions. The culture of gender bias in Japanese society has placed constraints upon women in the workplace and their role in both the labour market and within households. The norm of a 'good wife and wise mother' (*ryousai kenbo*) has limited women to the role of housewife, whilst freeing men from household responsibilities so that they can focus on their role as salarymen (Gottfried 2015: 37). Furthermore, the culture of gender bias has enhanced male workers' commitment to their employers and firms whilst relying on women to take care of the household. This has enabled men to work as core workers, for longer hours, as well as benefiting from long-term employment security and a seniority wage system; all of which has reinforced a core–periphery divide in the labour market where women play a peripheral role. This gendered division, together with cultural assumptions surrounding women, has been central to Japan's post-war economic growth (Fu 2020: 267, 269; Gottfried 2015; Osawa et al. 2013; Osawa and Kingstone 1996).

The precarization of labour and the breakdown of social compromise

Japan's stable post-war economic growth has faced recession and then ongoing difficulties since the late 1980s. The economy became overheated due to the expansionary monetary and fiscal policies introduced under the Plaza accord in the mid-1980s, which saw the Japanese government shift the focus of its economic policies to a stimulation of domestic consumption. Money supply was increased, which led to an increase in the price of assets, including stocks and land, resulting in the bubble economy in the late 1980s. This bubble burst in the early 1990s, and the Japanese economy experienced a prolonged period of recessions and slow growth. The sluggish growth prompted a restructuring of Japan's model of capitalism. Since the 1990s, as globalization increased uncertainty about the economy, companies sought more flexible employment strategies, including part-time employment that would allow firms to respond quickly to changes in the business environment (Mizuno 2018: 257). This saw the majority of companies, regardless of their size, starting to use flexible employees (Imai 2021: 107).

The government also acted to facilitate this process of expanding the proportion of non-regular workers through the introduction of a number of neoliberal policies (see Table 2.1). This included measures to flexibilize and deregulate the labour market (Imai 2021: 82), particularly after the 1997–1998 Asian Financial Crisis (AFC). In the post-AFC period, many firms reduced labour costs by dismissing employees, breaking links with *keiretsu*-group subcontractors, regulating overtime work, and laying off non-regular workers (Mouer and Kawanishi 2005: 106). The Koizumi government (2001–2006) actively sought to extend those practices (Shibata 2020a: 29; Imai 2021: 106; Osawa and Kingston 2021). This also saw a shift in Japan's model of labour adjustment, which had previously adopted the practice of transferring

Table 2.1 Major policies and reforms in labour market, 1980s–2020

	Neoliberal reforms	Main effect
1980s	1983 Employment insurance reforms	Welfare retrenchment
	1984 Reduction of state subsidies in employment insurance	Welfare retrenchment
	1986 Worker Dispatch Law (WDL)	Labour market liberalization
	1987 Designated work system	Labour market liberalization
	1987 Variable workweek system	Labour market liberalization
1990s	1993 Labour Standard Law	Labour market liberalization
	1993 Act on Improvement of Employment Management for Part-Time Workers	Labour market liberalization
	1996 Amendment to the WDL	Labour market liberalization
	1999 Amendment to the WDL	Labour market liberalization
2000s	2004 Amendment to the WDL	Labour market liberalization
	2000 Employment Labour Insurance Law	Heightened precarity for non-regular workers
	2007 Amendment to the WDL	Labour market liberalization (enabled three years for the maximum dispatch in the manufacturing sector)
2010s	2012 Amendment to the WDL	Labour market liberalization + re-regulation of the labour market
	2015 Amendment to the WDL	Labour market liberalization + re-regulation of the labour market
	2018 Work-Style Reforms	Labour market liberalization + re-regulation of the labour market
2020s	2020 Part-time/Fixed-term Employment Labour Law	Re-regulation of the labour market
	2020 Equal pay for equal work	Re-regulation of the labour market
	2020 High Professional System	Labour market liberalization

employees between group firms within a single *keiretsu* (Vogel 2006: 117). Some policies, such as the amendment to Worker Dispatch Law (WDL) in 1999 and 2004, directly triggered the flexible usage of non-regular workers in favour of employers, and increased the precarity of workers (Table 2.1).

One especially impactful reform was the 1999 amendment of the WDL. This resulted in a steady increase in the proportion of non-regular workers in the Japanese labour force, from 24 per cent in 1999 to nearly 40 per cent between 2013 and 2020 (Figure 2.1). The proportion of female non-regular workers also significantly increased from 32 per cent in 1985, to 52 per cent in 2005, and 56 per cent in 2020 (Table 2.2), exacerbating the gendered core–periphery division within the labour market between male and female workers. Table 2.2 also shows how the number of non-regular workers in both men and women increased between 1985 and 2020. This process of labour

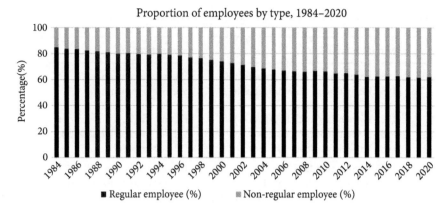

Figure 2.1 Proportion of employees by type in Japan, 1984–2020
Source: Statistics Bureau of Japan (2020), Figure 9(1)

market liberalization allowed firms to increasingly rely on non-regular workers with flexible contracts. A weakening of Japanese organized labour in the 1990s further enhanced this trend (Imai 2021, 2017; Watanabe 2018). Trade unions' ability and willingness to demand wage rises declined. Many unions chose to protect job security, rather than making wage demands. In addition, adverse economic conditions in the 1990s and most of the 2000s prompted employers to seek to weaken the influence of unions.

The internationalization of the Japanese economy in the 1990s also pressured Japanese firms to stay competitive by maintaining low labour costs (Uni 2000: 68). Junichiro Koizumi, the prime minister between 2001 and 2006, accelerated the introduction of neoliberal labour market reforms in an attempt to create a business-friendly environment. The reforms included a further amendment to the WDL in 2003, which expanded the employment of temp agency workers in the manufacturing sector. The amendment contributed to the increased number of precarious day labourers during the 2000s (Figure 2.1, Shibata 2020a:37).

Prior to the bursting of Japan's bubble in the early 1990s, Japanese firms had provided long-term employment security for their employees. In a context where the Japanese state was unable (or refused) to commit to substantial welfare spending, this role of Japanese firms acted as a form of a quasi-welfare state. The move by a majority of Japanese firms following the early 1990s, to restructure in the aftermath of the bursting of Japan's bubble economy, including the adoption of a performance-based wage system and stockholder-oriented corporate structures, therefore represented a significant change to Japan's welfare model.

Table 2.2 Employee by type (ten thousand persons)

		Employee	Employee, excluding executive of company	Regular employee	Non-regular employee	Part-time worker, Arbeit	Dispatched worker from temp agency	Contract employee, entrusted employee and other	Regular employee (%)	Non-regular employee (%)
1985	men	2749	2536	2349	187	83	–	104	92.6	7.4
	women	1509	1463	994	470	417	–	53	67.9	32.1
1990	men	2925	2674	2438	235	126	–	109	91.2	8.8
	women	1765	1695	1050	646	584	–	62	61.9	38.1
1995	men	3176	2876	2620	256	150	–	106	91.1	8.9
	women	1994	1904	1159	745	675	–	70	60.9	39.1
2000	men	3180	2892	2553	338	232	9	98	88.3	11.7
	women	2087	2011	1077	934	846	25	64	53.6	46.4
2005	men	3125	2824	2320	503	249	35	219	82.2	17.8
	women	2198	2100	1013	1087	845	60	182	48.2	51.8
2010	men	3140	2850	2331	518	246	34	241	81.8	18.2
	women	2337	2246	1050	1196	909	66	223	46.8	53.2
2013	men	3130	2869	2266	601	290	51	258	79.0	21.0
	women	2375	2295	1021	1272	998	73	202	44.5	55.5
2015	men	3157	2899	2260	638	316	48	274	78.0	22.0
	women	2450	2365	1018	1347	1048	73	226	43.0	57.0
2017	men	3204	2942	2302	639	327	53	260	78.3	21.7
	women	2545	2460	1083	1377	1089	76	211	44.0	56.0
2018	men	3238	2991	2322	670	347	50	274	77.6	22.4
	women	2629	2548	1101	1447	1132	89	226	43.2	56.8
2019	men	3259	3014	2340	674	347	52	276	77.6	22.4
	women	2687	2606	1118	1488	1166	91	233	42.9	57.1
2020	men	3286	3022	2348	674	356	54	264	77.7	22.3
	women	2722	2639	1161	1478	1167	89	222	44.0	56.0

Source: Statistics Bureau of Japan (2020), Figure 9(1)

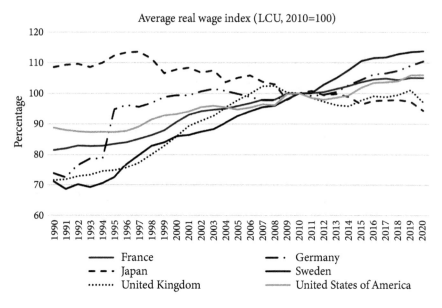

Figure 2.2 Wage index comparison, by country
Source: The Economist Intelligence Unit (n.d.)

Neoliberal policies and practices increased the precarity of workers. This can be witnessed in terms of stagnant wage growth. Figure 2.2 shows that Japan has shifted from one of the countries with the highest wages in comparison with other high-income countries in the 1990s, to one of the lowest by 2020. The Japanese labour market witnessed a steady decline in wages, whereas other countries such as the US, Germany, and Sweden saw stable wage increases. This is partly explained by the increased proportion of non-regular workers in Japan's labour market.

This trend of wage decline is clearly visible in the year-on-year comparison displayed in Figure 2.3. Figure 2.3 demonstrates how monthly earnings for both men and women experienced sluggish growth, particularly after the bursting of the bubble economy in the early 1990s and following the implementation of neoliberal labour market policies in the 2000s.

Alongside declining wages, Japan's flexibilized labour market has also resulted in a growing trend of indirect employment (*kansetsu koyou*), in which a third party mediates the relationship between the worker and the employer (MHLW 2020). Dispatch work (temp agency work) is a typical example of this form of employment. The dispatch work system creates an absence of responsibility for providing workplace-related welfare on the side of employers. Workers' rights have also been diminished, placing workers in a weaker position (Mizuno 2018: 274–275). This is especially the case for

Figure 2.3 Year-on-year rate of change in scheduled monthly earnings, 1977–2019
Source: Basic Wage Structure Survey (2020)

the registered type of dispatch work (*touroku gata haken*), which work on zero-hour contracts. In the case of registered dispatch work, the employment contract is concluded for each job, and when the job contract ends, dispatch workers are not guaranteed another contract, leading to highly unstable and precarious employment conditions (Fu 2011; Shibata 2020a: 37).

Japan's already gendered and dualized labour market, in which female workers tend to take up non-regular employment, has therefore worsened since the 1990s (Gottfried 2015; Osawa et al. 2013). The increase in the number of female workers has also affected the caring services sector. In particular, facilities for childcare and elderly care have increased over recent decades, as the state has sought to provide caring services. This has enabled many women to take up non-regular employment (Gottfried 2015: 95). This is oftentimes an involuntary long-term option for women workers, especially in taking up new caring service-sector jobs. Many female workers, therefore, continue to be relegated to the peripheral workforce in the labour market, often on a long-term basis (Kurokawa 2020: 3, 8).

To summarize, neoliberalism advanced in Japan in the 1990s and the 2000s. This saw the steady erosion of the established social compromise in the country and in turn has acted to destabilize employment relations. Non-regular and female workers have disproportionately and increasingly experienced precarity, including in the form of low wages and unstable employment. Perhaps unsurprisingly, this experience of precarity has subsequently generated increased levels of discontent among workers, which we now turn to consider.

Contested precarity

The flexibilization of the labour market and precarization of workers are closely related to the decline in union movements in Japan. The fact that most unions in post-war Japan have tended to be enterprise unions, as well as their willingness to compromise with management, and their unwillingness to represent non-regular workers, have all contributed to the weakening position of labour vis-à-vis capital in Japan (Imai 2021). Nevertheless, it would be misleading to portray a complete defeat of labour unions. As many unions lost members and faced weakening negotiating power, we have also witnessed the emergence of newer independent or community unions representing precarious workers and leading the grass-roots union movement in Japan. This is in contrast to enterprise unions, which have continued to focus predominantly on the representation of male regular workers, and when they have successfully organized non-regular workers, this has tended to be only in a limited way (Keizer 2019). As such, community unions have tended to represent non-regular workers and female and foreign workers, who have typically been excluded from union representation. In addition, non-regular workers acting independently, citizens' groups, and non-profit organizations (NPOs), have all gradually developed initiatives to proactively support unrepresented precarious workers (Shibata 2020a).

These newer community unions and non-regular workers' unions have provided a means by which discontented and disaffected non-regular workers are able to express their opposition to neoliberal labour market policies and practices in Japan. This has included opposition to the practice of terminating contracts early, the increased numbers of dismissals, the unfair treatment of employees, unpaid wages and lack of overtime payment, and austerity policies (Shibata 2020a). The acts of contestation through which opposition is expressed has also taken various forms, and is normally outside of the traditional institutionalized forms of May Day protest events.

There are a range of these newer unions. For instance, Freeter Zenpan Roudou Kumiai (Unions for Casual Workers), the Women's Union Tokyo, Cabacula Union, and Nanohana Union have each sought to organize typically unrepresented precarious women workers. The Women's Union Tokyo support female workers who have experienced sexual harassment (whereas male-centred enterprise unions have often been unwilling to handle sexual harassment cases) (Zacharias-Walsh 2016). The Women's Union Tokyo, since its establishment in 1995, has sought to represent the large number of female workers who have suffered from unfair dismissals in connection to their caring responsibilities and pregnancy.

The Cabacula Union supports female non-regular workers who work in bars or nightclubs where female workers serve mainly male customers (Shibata 2020a: 83). These women workers tend to lack employment insurance and suffer from bias and social stigma due to the nature of their work. They often face considerable ambiguity in terms of their work schedule, contract, wage entitlement, who their employers are, and sometimes even face the sudden closure of the bars in which they work and disappearance of their employers and managers without the appropriate payment. These precarious female workers tend to be excluded from mainstream unions, prompting the Cabacula Union to represent these female workers through a variety of tactics. These tactics often depend upon using the support from public authorities to engage in direct negotiation with managers and owners of bars, as well as conducting protest in front of bars, and using publicity-generating tactics (Shibata 2020a: 83–85).

As the gendered divide between core workers and peripheral workers in Japan's labour market has developed, women's caring duties have also been commodified, with women workers facing new challenges. Independent unions have also emerged to address these challenges.

Overall, through their efforts to draw attention to a range of injustices within the Japanese labour market, community unions have acted to put pressure on the government and employers to adopt more conciliatory policies. This was an especially notable trend during the period of the Abe administration (Bailey and Shibata 2019).

A return to social compromise under the Abe administration?

The former Abe government (2012–2020) ostensibly sought to address both the growing inequality between regular and non-regular workers, and the associated dissatisfaction of non-regular workers. This saw the Abe administration adopt a range of measures to alleviate labour market discontent, in what appeared to be an attempt to partly re-regulate Japan's labour market (see Table 2.1). Nevertheless, these reforms remained largely at the level of rhetoric and occurred alongside a weakening of regular workers' status.

The Abe government introduced a number of deregulatory labour market policy measures in order to ensure that regular workers could be hired more flexibly in the late 2010s. First, it introduced the deregulation of working-time rules. Second, the administration made it easier to fire regular workers by allowing fiduciary compensation in cases of unfair dismissal (Watanabe

2018: 590). Finally, the Abe government promoted the use of semi-regular work and sought to reduce the number of regular workers operating in a system guaranteeing lifetime employment. This final reform saw an expansion of semi-regular employment, which has existed in Japan as a status for employment practices since the early 1990s (Gordon 2017: 21, 27). The status was created as a choice for workers who prefer to avoid transfer to remote offices; although in reality it has been reserved for female workers (Imai 2021: 268–269). The semi-regular track, promoted by the Abe government in the late 2010s, claims to reinforce individual choice, forward ability and competency, and to amount to more inclusive employment practices. The effect of the semi-regular track, however, is to create a situation whereby individual workers are more beholden to the demands of their companies. As such, it amounts to a way of creating less privileged employment conditions for regular employees.

Women workers also experienced no substantial improvement in their working conditions under the Abe administration. Despite the Abe government's emphasis on women's advancement and its proclaimed efforts to increase work opportunities, many women still end up with non-regular employment status as a result of their expected household duties. According to the Comprehensive Survey on Diversified Forms of Employment in 2019, undertaken by the Ministry of Health, Labour and Welfare (MHLW) (2019a: 24), over 40 per cent of female non-regular workers chose non-regular employment in order to be able to manage their work alongside child care, elderly care, and household duties. In contrast, only 7.7 per cent of male non-regular workers chose non-regular employment for the same reason. Instead, more than 34 per cent of male non-regular workers chose this employment status in order to make the most of their qualifications and skills. In contrast, only 18 per cent of female workers chose non-regular employment for the same reason. This highlights how the choice of non-regular employment is much more often due to cultural expectations and institutional constraints, including women's roles in households, and the tax and insurance mechanisms which consolidate women's peripheral status within the workforce; and as such exposing the inaccurate nature of neoliberal emancipatory discourses regarding the 'choice' offered by flexible working.

Given that the measures introduced by the Abe government to tackle gender inequality in the workplace were largely cosmetic, it is perhaps unsurprising that disparities between regular and non-regular workers remained unresolved. As a result, discontent and opposition continued, especially voiced by non-regular workers, and focusing around a call for equal pay for equal work (Shibata 2021: 168).

Many of the government responses to these expressions of dissent, however, have sought to consolidate (rather than reverse) efforts to liberalize the Japanese labour market. For instance, the semi-regular employment status (mentioned earlier) was heralded by the Abe administration as a means to provide non-regular workers with an opportunity for more stable status and better wages (albeit with limited responsibilities). This was despite the fact that semi-regular status/nominally regular status represents a deterioration of regular workers' status (Watanabe 2018: 591). As such, the Abe government has sought to respond to disgruntlement arising from the neoliberalization of Japan's model of capitalism by aggravating the existing inequalities in the labour market. It therefore seems unlikely that workers' concerns will be genuinely assuaged.

Similarly, the Work-Style Reforms introduced by the Abe government in the late 2010s saw tighter regulations proposed alongside deregulation measures. For instance, the government advocated 'equal pay for equal work', at the same time as seeking to maintain Japan's flexible employment system by revising the Worker Dispatch Law (WDL) to increase the hiring of dispatch (temp agency) workers.

Likewise, the Abe administration sought to address long working hours, at the same time as introducing a new rule which allows unpaid overtime. *Karoushi* (death from overwork) has been a long-standing problem in Japan, and unions and workers have consistently called for the government to curb long working hours. To address this problem, the Abe government implemented a new regulation to limit overtime. This specifies that, as a general rule, the upper limit for overtime work (not including holiday work) is 45 hours per month and 360 hours per year (MHLW 2019b). At the same time, the Abe government implemented what it termed a High Professional System from April 2019. This system enables employers to avoid paying overtime for workers whose annual salary is above 1.1 million yen. Under this system, the provisions of the Labour Standards Law relating to premium wages for working hours, rest periods, holidays, and late nights do not apply (MHLW 2019c). This system only applies to workers who have a high level of specialized knowledge and requires management to consult with its labour union and receive consent from workers themselves; nevertheless, it enables employers to require certain workers to work for long hours without the obligation of overtime and holiday pay. It therefore has the clear potential to exacerbate working conditions or normalize precarious working conditions for concerned employees. As such, the Work-Style Reforms are contradictory in that one policy acts to tighten the regulation of long working hours, while the other deregulates the rule on overtime/holiday work and removes working hour regulations under the guise of performance-based pay.

Other (largely cosmetic) reforms introduced by the Abe administration in the field of gender inequality include a commitment to promote women's career advancement as part of its growth strategy (Womenomics) adopted in 2013 (MacNaughtan 2015), part of which included a promise to increase the proportion of women in management/leadership positions to 30 per cent by 2020. This saw a number of pieces of legislation introduced. The Act on the Promotion of Female Participation and Career Advancement in the Workplace in 2015 was adopted to advance women's careers. The Act on Promotion of Gender Equality in the Political Field (2018) was also adopted in an attempt to ensure equal opportunities for women to participate in planning and policymaking. Further, the Promotion of Female Participation and Career Advancement in the Workplace (2019) sought to encourage large companies to employ more women and make their business environments more female-worker friendly (MHLW 2019d). Despite these efforts, the Abe government carefully avoided directly addressing gender inequality. Instead, the policies introduced were designed to ensure flexibility and increase the number of female workers (Horie 2017: 40). As such, it is more accurate to consider the gender policies adopted by the Abe government as economic policies aimed at improving economic growth, rather than policies that will promote gender equality (Horie 2017: 2).

The incorporation of women as a measure designed primarily to improve economic growth is also in line with the intentions of the business community, such as Keidanren's 2014 action plan on the advancement of women (Keidanren 2014). This was reflected in the Abe government's decision to review the spousal deduction in the tax system in an attempt to address the declining birth rate and labour shortage and to integrate women into the labour market (Horie 2017: 41). This was also introduced alongside a commitment by the Abe government to keep labour flexibilization while maintaining 'conservative' family and gender values (Horie 2017: 41).

Gender policies under the Abe government are fundamentally economic policies. In essence, they have sought to maintain a culture whereby women's social reproduction role is prioritized and their role within the labour market is to serve as a source of flexible labour supply on the periphery of the labour market and in the context of an ever more severe labour shortage. Indeed, under the Abe government, the proportion of female non-regular workers reached over 57 per cent in 2019 (Table 2.2). Rather than addressing the barriers that women face in the workplace, the Abe government's contradictory policies have consolidated the predominantly flexible conditions available to female workers.

Policies claiming to advance gender equality have merely set and revised numerical targets, and have so far been inadequate and ineffective. The Gender Equality Bureau announced numerical targets in July 2020 in the Fourth Basic Plan for Gender Equality. According to this announcement, the target of time spent on housework by husbands with child(ren) aged under 6 is 2.5 hours, while 83 minutes per day was only achieved in 2016. The proportion of male workers who take childcare leave is only 6.16 per cent at private companies, 5.6 per cent at local civil service, and 12.4 per cent at national civil service, as opposed to the target of 13 per cent (Gender Equality Bureau 2020b). The percentage of men taking childcare leave immediately after their spouse has given birth is still 58.7 per cent in 2019 compared with an 80 per cent target by 2020. These numerical indicators have improved since 2016, yet progress is slow, and the government has not achieved the majority of its targets. At the same time, women's career advancement in private companies and the local civil service sector remain slow.

The persistent culture of gender bias permeates many institutions and prevents women's advancement in society. Assumptions, expectations, and norms associated with women and their roles in both the workplace, and the family and household, are deeply rooted in Japanese society. Gender bias remains strong under the Suga government (2020–2021). Indeed, the Suga administration faced considerable criticism from the public concerning a number of sexist, misogynistic, and prejudiced comments against women made by political elites from the ruling Liberal Democratic Party of Japan (LDP), including expressing opposition to gender equality. This became most evident when Mori Yoshiro, the former prime minister and the former chair of the Olympic Committee in Japan, commented that women talk too long and as a result should not be invited to meetings. As Miura (2021) notes, attitudes such as this routinely act to undermine women in decision-making positions, affecting their ability to speak up, and forcing them to remain silent (2021). In addition, Miura shows how Mori's statement attempted to divide women into two groups: those who do not care (*wakimaenai onna*) and those who do care (*wakimaeru onna*). This sought to consolidate the norm whereby women are expected to play a traditional supporting role and stand up for men. As such, Mori's statement reveals a prejudiced attitude against women and an underlying set of values that support a male-centred decision-making culture, in which men decide behind closed doors and structurally exclude women.

There are many other cases that illustrate a fundamental unwillingness on the part of Japan's political elite to achieve gender equality, reflecting a deep-rooted bias against women. Sugita Mio, Lower House member of the LDP, commented that women tend to lie when it comes to sexual assault (Tokyo Shinbun 2020a). She also commented that gender equality would never be achieved, and that LGBT people are unproductive since they cannot have babies (Tokyo Shinbun 2020a). Despite such inappropriate remarks, she remains a parliamentary member and has never resigned. The language and narratives uttered by the ruling LDP's political leaders, therefore, illustrate a biased view of women and the absence of a willingness to seek equal treatment for women, continuing the culture of gender bias and acting as a barrier to gender equality.

In summary, the contradictory nature of the Abe and Suga administrations' labour market and gender policies are not accidental outcomes. Rather, such policy choices reflect a prioritization of the economic problems and challenges faced. This is despite ongoing claims made by the government regarding its commitment to addressing societal problems such as precarious employment, inequality, and discontent among precarious workers. The Abe government's Work-Style Reforms introduced re-regulation policies as a concession that would seek to legitimate and promote crucial *deregulatory* policies being introduced, acting to conceal a more general intention to maintain (and promote) a flexible labour market. The attempt, therefore, has been to adopt the Work-Style Reforms initiative in such a way that it gives a particular impression to the public, that the government seeks to address some of the labour market problems, while at the same time increasing the degree to which Japan's labour market becomes increasingly flexible and precarious for a growing section of the population. The women-friendly policies advocated by the Abe government and the current Suga government may appear to be driven by the goal of gender equality, but in practice they have acted to maintain the division of labour between men and women.

The emergence of gig work and the continuity of flexible labour

The intention of the ruling LDP to maintain traditional gender roles has also become increasingly apparent in its response to the country's developing gig economy. The Abe government's promotion of more autonomous work for people excluded from the traditional labour market resonates well with their underlying expectation of women's gender roles. Moreover, the new trend is closely associated with Japan's ongoing labour shortage as well as its problem of low productivity and the need to improve firms' competitiveness. Significantly, the emergence of the gig economy in Japan needs to be understood alongside the culture of gender bias.

The Japanese government has sought to provide a solution to the country's labour shortage problem by increasing labour market participation by women, the elderly, and young people (Shibata 2020). This saw the government promote a new form of work—gig work—as part of the rise of the digital economy, and as one of the solutions to address challenges in Japan's contemporary economy. Gig work is a form of contracted labour, whereby workers choose each gig (contracted task) through an online platform (Valenduc and Vendramin 2016: 38). It includes online-based tasks and physical tasks, including delivery services and caregiver services.

Gig work comes with a number of concerning side effects. It deskills workers as each gig tends to be fragmented as workers perform repetitive tasks for low wages (Huws 2014: 87; Kenny and Zysman 2016: 66–67; Shibata 2020b). While 'gigs' do sometimes include tasks that require high professionalism and creativity, the majority of gigs available tend to be low paid and fragmented tasks in Japan. In addition, gig work does not provide employment status for workers; and instead provides a contractor status for each gig. This can lead to more precarious employment practices in which workers are not entitled to employment security, paid holiday, bonuses, overtime pay, or skill-training. As such, gig employment is flexible rather than stable, and represents a new form of flexibilization of employment relations.

One of the distinctive features of gig work is the fact that it has the capacity to reinforce the primacy of women's reproductive role. The Japanese government promotes gig work for female workers who face challenges in participating in employment relations due to their domestic roles (Shibata 2020b). The Ministry of Health, Labour and Welfare (MHLW) has undertaken a number of initiatives designed to make gig work both more accessible and attractive. This includes initiatives such as the 'Home Workers Web', which provides guidelines for online-based gig workers so that they can make the most of their work practices, and organizes seminars which advertise the benefits of autonomous working that gig work can provide. The MHLW also seeks to promote the benefits of gig work by highlighting how 'female workers can take advantage of gig work and earn extra money' (MHLW 2018, author's translation). In doing so, however, a number of key problems associated with gig work are largely concealed from view. Female gig workers with household duties who tend to take up fragmented gigs are not likely to upgrade their skills. This further locks women into non-regular work and precarious employment conditions, consolidating the primacy of the reproductive role for women and their peripheral status within the workforce. As such, gig work seems likely to reinforce the gender bias prevalent across Japan's society and economy.

Precarity and inequality under the era of Covid-19

This chapter has so far illustrated how Japan's labour market has been increasingly flexibilized, and women and non-regular workers have experienced inequality and precarity since the late 1990s. What follows is an account of how this flexibilized labour market acted to exacerbate vulnerabilities in the context of an economic crisis.

The Covid-19 crisis prompted the large-scale dismissal of workers in a way which echoed the aftermath of the 2008 Global Financial Crisis (see Figure 2.4). According to the Ministry of Internal Affairs and Communications (MIC), the average unemployment rate for 2020 was 2.8 per cent, 0.5 percentage points higher than in 2018 (Statistics Bureau of Japan 2021a). This is the first time the rate has worsened since 2009. According to the summary of the labour force survey of January 2021, the number of people in employment fell by 500,000 to 66.37 million. This is the tenth consecutive month of decline (Statistics Bureau of Japan 2021b: 1). In particular, the number of non-regular workers fell to 20,580,000. This is the eleventh consecutive month of decline, down 910,000 on the same month last year. Amongst those 910,000, the decline of male non-regular workers was 220,000, whereas the number of female non-regular workers was 680,000 (Statistics Bureau of

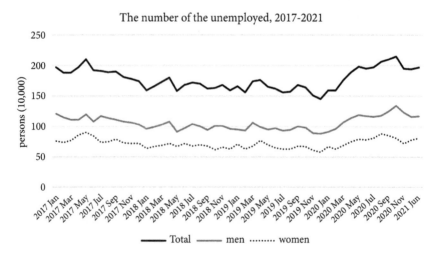

Figure 2.4 The number of the unemployed

Source: The Japan Institute for Labour Policy and Training (2021), compiled from kanzen shitugyousyasuu toukei hyou

Japan 2021b: 2). As such, the Covid-19 crisis has disproportionately affected female non-regular workers, whose jobs were the first to be shed in the context of the pandemic, and which is a direct result of women being locked in the peripheral workforce.

Many non-regular workers have also been unable to access benefits that they are entitled to, especially when compared with regular workers. For instance, the percentage of those who were forced to take time off work but received less than half of their benefits was 11.9 per cent for non-regular employees, compared with only 3.6 per cent for regular employees (Takahashi 2021: 23). Practices such as these also produced a growing anxiety and concern over work conditions, living costs, and physical and mental health. Unfair dismissals were also reported, with employers dismissing workers without meeting any of the adequate criteria nor condition for dismissals.

Similarly, the government placed the requirement upon employers during the pandemic, that they would provide employees with 60 per cent of their average salary earned over the past three months (if it became necessary to suspend the business). Yet some employers instead dismissed their workers to avoid this payment; a move which especially hit non-regular workers (Tokyo Shinbun 2020b). This also affected women disproportionately. According to the Nomura Research Institute survey, 70 per cent of part-time women who had to take time off work due to the spread of the coronavirus have not received the leave benefits to which they are entitled (Umeya and Takeda 2020: 4) (see Figure 2.5). Unsurprisingly, this causes high levels of anxiety,

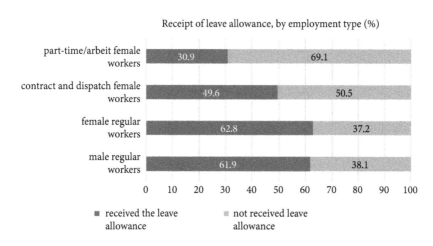

Figure 2.5 Receipt of leave allowance, by employment type*

Source: Umeya and Takeda (2020: 27)
*Note: The data is based on workers who experienced a decrease in actual working hours by 10% or more during the absence.

with one in two part-time women on leave reporting being worried about losing their job in the future. One in four also reported being concerned about the difficulty in maintaining their work–life balance and facing difficulties in maintaining their physical and mental health. In comparison with those who obtained leave benefits, a higher proportion of those without leave benefits were worried about losing their jobs and experienced difficulty maintaining their physical and mental health (Umeya and Takeda 2020: 2–5).

Conclusion

Japan's labour market has experienced a significant transformation over the last three decades. Prior to the 1990s, gender inequality and the associated core–periphery labour market divide formed a part of, and served to underpin, the socio-economic compromise, and male-centred stability in employment relations. The welfare–tax system in post-war Japan institutionalized women's reproductive role by establishing a tax reduction for housewives and reinforced gendered employment relations, in which women workers were the full-time caregivers as well as being part-time workers.

From the 1990s, a gradual yet steady process of neoliberalization has seen flexibilized employment relations and the commodification of women's caregiving role. The gendered core–peripheral labour dualism has remained. Non-regular, especially female, workers have experienced more precarity, including a higher proportion of low-wages, low-status, instability, and dismissals, than regular (male) workers. In this process, we saw the steady erosion of the established social compromise, which in turn has acted to destabilize employment relations. The dualized labour market has prompted a rise in workers' discontent. While the Abe government has ostensibly sought to respond to this discontent by introducing labour market reforms, including a policy package of re-regulation and liberalization, these have been either largely insubstantial, rhetorical and contradictory, or served to worsen the conditions of those who they were claimed to be benefiting.

The reforms introduced have so far reinforced or expanded flexible and precarious employment for women and non-regular workers. There has been a persistent lack of willingness to achieve gender equality and continued bias against women among political elites under both the Abe and Suga governments, reflecting the obstacles to Japanese labour market reform that advocates of greater gender equality face. The policy package introduced by the Abe administration was contradictory. On the one hand, it claimed to improve labour market problems stemming from dualism and gender inequality, but on the other hand, it reinforced flexibilization and further institutionalized and consolidated women's reproductive role. In addition, the emergence of gig work has exacerbated precarity for low-skilled workers, particularly for female non-regular workers. In both traditional and new forms of employment, women have experienced a higher proportion of dismissals, unemployment, a lack of sufficient support, fewer opportunities, resultant mental strain, and health risks in the Covid-19 pandemic era. Overall, therefore, there is far more to do in order to achieve a more gender-equal society and labour market in Japan.

References

Bailey, D. J. and Shibata, S. (2019) 'Austerity and anti-austerity: The political economy of refusal in "low resistance" models of capitalism'. *British Journal of Political Science*, 54(3): 496–521.

Basic Wage Structure Survey (2020) 'Shoteinai kyuugyo gaku no suii [Changes in salaries and wages]'. Dai san pyo (Figure 3). Available at: https://www.e-stat.go.jp/stat-search/files?page=1&layout=datalist&toukei=00450091&tstat=000001011429&cycle=0&tclass1=000001020466&tclass2=000001020468&cycle_facet=cycle&tclass3val=0/.

Clark, R. (1979) *The Japanese Firm*. New Haven: Yale University Press.

Fruin, W. M. (1980) 'The firm as a family and the family as a firm in Japan'. *Journal of Family History*, 5(4): 432–449.

Fu, H. (2011) *An Emerging Non-Regular Labour Force in Japan: The Dignity of Dispatched Workers*. London & New York: Routledge.

Fu, H. (2022) 'The culture of unequal work: Temps and giggers in China and Japan'. In H. Fu (ed.), *Temporary and Gig Economy Workers in China and Japan: The Culture of Unequal Work*. Oxford: Oxford University Press.

Gender Equality Bureau (2020a) Gender Equality White Paper 2020 (as of October 8). https://www.gender.go.jp/about_danjo/whitepaper/r02/zentai/index.html#pdf.

Gender Equality Bureau (2020b) 'Numerical targets and updated figures of the Fourth Basic Plan for Gender Equality (as of 31 July 2020)'. Available at: chrome-extension://efaidnbmnnnibpcajpcglclefindmkaj/https://www.gender.go.jp/about_danjo/seika_shihyo/pdf/numerical_targets_r030611.pdf.

Gordon, A. (2017) 'New and enduring dual structures of employment in Japan: The rise of non-regular labour'. *Social Science Japan Journal*, 20(1): 9–36.

Gottfried, H. (2015) *The Reproductive Bargain: Deciphering the Enigma of Japanese Capitalism*. Leiden: Brill.

Hall, P. A. and Soskice, D. (2001) 'An introduction to varieties of capitalism'. In P. A. Hall and D. Soskice (eds.), *Varieties of Capitalism: The Institutional Foundations of Comparative Advantage*. Oxford: Oxford University Press. Chapter 1: 1–70.

Horie, T. (2017) 'Abe seiken no jyosei seisaku' [Women's policy under the Abe government]. *Oohara Shakai Mondai Kenkyusho Zassi [Journal of Oohara Institute of Social Problems]*, pp. 38–44. Available at: http://doi.org/10.15002/00013638/.

Huws, U. (2014) *Labour in the Global Digital Economy: The Cybertariat Comes of Age*. New York: Monthly Review Press.

Imai, J. (2017) 'Are labour union movements capable of solving the problems of the "gap society"?'. In D. Chiavacci and C. Hommerich (eds.), *Social Inequality in Post-Growth Japan: Transformation during Economic and Demographic Transformation*. London: Routledge, Chapter 6: 89–104.

Imai, J. (2021) *Koyoukankei to Syakaiteki Fubyoudou: Sangyouteki Shitizunshippu keisei/tenkaito shiteno kouzou hendou [Employment Relations and Social Inequality: Structural Change as Industrial Citizenship Formation and Development]*. Tokyo:Yugaikaku.

Jeong, D. Y. and Aguilera, R. V. (2008) 'The evolution of enterprise unionism in Japan: Socio-political perspective'. *British Journal of Industrial Relations*, 46(1): 98–132.

Keidanren (2014) 'Jyosei katsuyaku akushon pulan' [Action plan for women's advancement]. Available at: https://www.keidanren.or.jp/policy/2014/029.html/.

Keizer, A. B. (2019) 'Inclusion of "outsiders" by Japanese unions? The organizing of non-regular workers in retail'. *Work, Employment and Society*, 33(2): 226–243.

Kenny, M. and Zysman, J. (2016) 'The rise of the platform economy'. *Issues in Science and Technology*, 32(3): 61–69.

Kurokawa, S. (2020) 'Jyosei katuyaku suishin to fuhonin hiseikiroudou' [Promotion of women's advancement and involuntary non-regular employment]. Tokyo Jyoshi Daigaku Syakaigaku Nenpou no.8 東京女子大学社会学年報 第8号.

Lechavalier, S. (2014) 'What is the nature of the Japanese social compromise today?'. In S. Lechevalier (ed.), *The Great Transformation of Japanese Capitalism*. London: Routledge, pp. 85–105.

Macnaughtan, H. (2015) 'Womenomics for Japan: Is the Abe policy for gendered employment viable in an era of precarity?'. *The Asia-Pacific Journal: Japan Focus*, 13(12): No. 1, March 30.

Ministry of Health, Labour and Welfare (MHLW) (2018) 'Yokuaru Shitsumon (FAQ): Jieigata Telewaakaa (Zaitaku Waakaa) Hen [Frequently Asked Questions]' HOME WORKERS WEB: All support site for gig workers. Available at: http://homeworkers.mhlw.go.jp/faq/faq.html#beginner8/.

Ministry of Health, Labour, and Welfare (MHLW) (2019a) 'Reiwa gannen shugyou keitaino tayoukani kansuru sougou jittai chousa no gaikyo' [2019 Comprehensive survey on diversified forms of employment]. Available at: https://www.mhlw.go.jp/toukei/itiran/roudou/koyou/keitai/19//.

Ministry of Health, Labour, and Welfare (MHLW) (2019b) 'Jikangai Roudouno Jyougen Kisei: wakariyasui kaisetsu' [Overtime limits: A simple explanation]. Available at: https://www.mhlw.go.jp/hatarakikata/img/overtime/000463185.pdf/.

Ministry of Health, Labour, and Welfare (MHLW) (2019c) 'Koudo Professionaru Seido: wakariyasui kaisetsu' [High professional system: An easy-to-understand explanation]. Available at: https://www.mhlw.go.jp/content/000497408.pdf/.

Ministry of Health, Labour, and Welfare (MHLW) (2019d) 'Ippan Jigyounushi Joudou Keikakuno Kaisei Naiyou' [Amendments to the general business owner action plan]. Available at: https://www.mhlw.go.jp/content/11900000/000594316.pdf/.

Ministry of Health, Labour, and Welfare (MHLW) (2020) 'Paato Taimu/ Yuukikoyou Roudouhou: Taiouno tameno torikumi tejyunsyo' [Part-time and fixed-term employment law: Procedures for dealing with the situation]. Available at: https://www.mhlw.go.jp/hatarakikata/img/same/000467476.pdf/.

Miura, M. (2021) 'Mori Yoshiro no jyoseisabetu hatsugenkara kangaeru daisei chushin syakai nihon~watashitachi ha dou kaete ikubekika~' [Japan as a male-centric society in the light of Yoshiro Mori's discriminatory remarks against women—how should we change it]. *imidas*, Opinion. 25 March 2021. Available at: https://imidas.jp/jijikaitai/f-40-219-21-03-g644/.

Mizuno, Y. (2018) 'Jyouhouka Syakaini okeru roudou no henyou: hiseikikoyouka to kansetsu koyoukano siten kara' [Transformation of labour in the information society: From the perspective of casualization of labour and indirect employment]. *Nagoya Keizai daigaku kyousyoku shien shitsu hou [Departmental Bulletin Paper]*. 名古屋経済大学教職課程委員会. pp. 267–276. Available at: https://nue.repo.nii.ac.jp/?action=pages_view_main&active_action=repository_view_main_item_detail&item_id=346&item_no=1&page_id=32&block_id=39/.

Mouer, R. and Kawanishi, H. (2005). *Sociology of Work in Japan*. Cambridge: Cambridge University Press.

Nagamatsu, N. (2021) 'Japanese labor studies: Women and non-standard workers'. *International Sociology Review*, 1–12. Available at: https://journals.sagepub.com/doi/10.1177/02685809211005350/.

Osawa, M. and Kingston, J. (2021) 'Precaritization of work in Japan'. In J. Kingston. (ed.), *Japan in the Heisei Era (1989–2019): Multidisciplinary Perspectives*. London: Routledge. Chapter 10: 127–139.

Osawa, M. (2015) *Josei ha Naze Katsuyaku Dekinainoka [What's Holding Back Japanese Women?]*. Tokyo: Toyo Keizai Shimposha.

Osawa, M., Kim, M. J., and Kingston, J. (2013) 'Precarious work in Japan'. *American Behavioral Scientist*, 57(3): 309–334.

Osawa, M. and Kingston, J. (1996) 'Flexibility and inspiration: Restructuring and the Japanese labour market'. *Japan Labour Bulletin*, 35(1) (January): 6–14.

Shibata, H. (2017) 'Nihonno hiseiki roudousya mondai: Jyosei paato wo chuushin ni' [A study of non-regular employees in Japan—Focusing on female part-timers]. *Senshu Ningen Kagakuron Shu*, 7(2): 25–42.

Shibata, S. (2020a) *Contesting Precarity in Japan: The Rise of Nonregular Workers and Policy Dissensus*. Ithaca: Cornell University Press.

Shibata, S. (2020b) 'Gig work and the discourse of autonomy: Fictitious freedom in Japan's digital economy'. *New Political Economy*, 25(4): 535–551.

Shibata, S. (2021) 'Contradiction and discontent in Japan: Abenomics and the failing politics of economic reform'. In S. Maslow and C. Wirth (eds.), *Crisis Narratives, Institutional Change and the Transformation of the Japanese State*. New York: State University of New York Press, pp. 161–187.

Statistics Bureau of Japan (2020) 'Roudouryoku Chyousa: Chouki Jikeiretsu Deita' [Labour force survey: Long-term time series data]. Hyou 9(1) Nenrei kaikyuu(10 sai kaikyuu) betu shugyousyasuu oyobi nenreikaikyuu (10sai kaikyuu), koyou keitaibetu koyousyasuu [Figure 9(1) Employed person by age group (ten-year group) and Employee by age group (ten-year group) and type of employ]. Available at: https://www.stat.go.jp/data/roudou/longtime/03roudou.html/.

Statistics Bureau of Japan (2021a) 'Labour force survey (basic tally)'. Results for February 2021. Available at: https://www.stat.go.jp/data/roudou/sokuhou/tsuki/index.html/.

Statistics Bureau of Japan (2021b) 'Labour force survey (basic tally)'. Summary of February 2021. Available at: https://www.stat.go.jp/data/roudou/sokuhou/tsuki/pdf/gaiyou.pdf/.

Takahashi, K. (2021) 'Corona shyokku to hiseiki koyousya [Corona Shock and non-regular employment]. JILPT Discussion Paper 21–04. March 2021. Available at: https://www.jil.go.jp/institute/discussion/2021/documents/DP21-04.pdf/.

The Economist Intelligence Unit (n.d.) Country Data, Japan.

The Japan Institute for Labour Policy and Training (2021) 'Kanzen shitsugyousya toukeihyo' [Statistics on the number of totally unemployed persons]. *Statistical tables*. Available at: https://www.jil.go.jp/kokunai/statistics/covid-19/c03.html#c03-10/.

Tokyo Shinbun (2020a) 'Sugita giinn no bougen: Jimintou no sekinin mo jyuudai da [MP Sugita's abuse: LDP is also to be blamed]'. Tokyo Shinbun. 5 October 2020. Available at: https://www.tokyo-np.co.jp/article/59719/.

Tokyo Shinbun (2020b) 'Kyugyo teate rokuwari ijyo nanoni jissaiha yonwari 70nen maeno seifutsuutatsu ga eikyou mo' [More than 60% leave allowance but 40% in reality, influenced by a government notice 70 years ago]. Tokyo Web. 23 September 2020. Available at: https://www.tokyo-np.co.jp/article/57079/.

Umeya, S. and Takeda, K. (2020) 'Kyugyousya no jittai ya ishiki no henka wo tekikakuni torae, shinni hitsuyouna koyouseisaku no kentou/jitsugenwo' [Towards a consideration and realization of truly necessary employment policies based on an accurate understanding of the actual situation of those on leave and changes in their awareness]. *Nomura Research Institute*. No. 299 NRI Media Forum. 10 December 2022. Available at: https://www.nri.com/-/media/Corporate/jp/Files/PDF/knowledge/report/cc/mediaforum/2020/forum299.pdf?la=ja-JP&hash=B3A860B0FEE528874DF562E127D510CB3904D2F4/.

Uni, Hiroyuki. (2000) 'Disproportionate productivity growth and accumulation regimes'. In B. Robert and T. Yamada (eds.), *Japanese Capitalism in Crisis: A Regulationist Interpretation*. New York: Routledge, pp. 54–70.

Valenduc, G. and Vendramin, P. (2016) 'Work in the digital economy: Sorting the old from the new'. Working Paper 2016.03, *etui*.

Vogel, S. K. (2006) *Japan Remodeled: How Government and Industry Are Reforming Japanese Capitalism*. Ithaca. NY: Cornell University Press.

Watanabe, H. R. (2018) 'Labour market dualism and diversification in Japan'. *British Journal of Industrial Relations*, 56(3): 579–602. doi: 10.1111/bjir.12258.

Zacharias-Walsh, A. (2016) *Our Unions, Our Selves: The Rise of Feminist Labor Unions in Japan*. Ithaca: Cornell University Press.

3
Teleworking in Pandemic Japan

Machiko Osawa and Jeff Kingston

Introduction

The Covid-19 pandemic has caused less devastation in Japan than in the US and EU, but the impact on the labour market has been considerable, accentuating the gender gap and existing divides between regular and non-regular workers, large and small firms, and various sectors of the economy. The government's countermeasures have relied chiefly on voluntary compliance, requesting shortened hours and early closing at bars and restaurants, and encouraging firms to expand teleworking (remote working) for staff as much as possible with a notional target of 70 per cent of employees. Politicians have also admonished the public to avoid the '3 C's'—closed spaces, crowded places, and close-contact settings—with implications for travel, commuting, and workplaces.

The pandemic recession has battered the most vulnerable segments of the labour market as many non-regular workers have lost their jobs. By June 2020 the number of employees on temporary leave was nearly 6 million, the highest since December 1967 (Zhou 2021). The 2020 figure is about 9 per cent of total employed persons and about 3.4 times the number of unemployed workers (1.78 million). Women are much more likely than men to be furloughed and mothers with small children are especially at risk. About 1.6 per cent of male workers were furloughed compared to 4.7 per cent of women overall, 7.1 per cent of women with minor children, and 8.7 per cent of single mothers. Due to school closures in March 2020, many working women 'voluntarily' stayed at home until the end of May to take care of their children. Typically, grandparents provide some childcare help but due to the higher risk for the elderly this was not an option. Subsequently, when schools reopened, furloughed women nonregular workers found it difficult to resume working in the midst of a deep recession.

Teleworking was not introduced due to the pandemic but has gained some impetus from employers trying to manage risk and abide by government

Machiko Osawa and Jeff Kingston, *Teleworking in Pandemic Japan*. In: *Temporary and Gig Economy Workers in China and Japan*. Edited by Huiyan Fu, Oxford University Press. © Oxford University Press (2023).
DOI: 10.1093/oso/9780192849694.003.0004

advisories. Prior to the 2020 outbreak in Japan, some major firms like Hitachi had announced plans to expand teleworking and reported that there was strong interest from employees, such that the number of those applying to join the programme far exceeded the original target of 100,000 workers (Nikkei 2018). It appears that the possibility of achieving a better work–life balance drew strong employee interest, especially in young households juggling childcare responsibilities; no commuting frees up time for household duties, child-rearing, and relaxing. Hitachi sees benefits from introducing flexibility in terms of recruiting and retention, and lucrative business consulting opportunities in sharing lessons about what it learns from its experience of promoting teleworking, an area that appears poised to become a growth sector.

Teleworking in Japan

Before the pandemic, Okubo Toshiro found that Japan had, 'the lowest use of telework among developed countries. Despite strong promotion by government and companies in recent years, the utilisation rate of telework has remained low' (Okubo 2020a). Overall, large urban areas had higher rates of telework because of the greater concentration of white-collar workers whose tasks are suitable to remote work.

In 2019, fewer than 10 per cent of Japanese firms adopted teleworking, but this figure increased dramatically during 2020 in response to government directives (Morikawa 2020). Zhou (2021) found that teleworking rapidly expanded after a state of emergency was declared in April 2020, doubling to 28 per cent in the space of a month. The government encouraged businesses to allow 70 per cent of employees to work from home as a pandemic countermeasure but this target was overly ambitious. As of May 2020, the overall rate of teleworking stood at 31.5 per cent, declining to about 20 per cent in July 2020 (Mainichi 2021). However, more recent data suggests higher rates of teleworking.

A March 2022 government report that draws on a survey of 40,000 workers provides the most comprehensive assessment of telework in Japan (MLIT 2022). According to this report, the overall rate of telework increased from 13.3% of workers in 2016 to 27.3% in 2021. The rate in Tokyo alone surged from 16.9% in 2016 to 42.1% by 2021. In terms of firm size, those with over 1,000 employees reported the highest rate of teleworking at 40.1% of workers compared to 19.2% in 2016 while for firms with 300–999 employees the rate rose from 14.7% in 2016 to 29.1% of workers in 2021. These are massive shifts in the employment paradigm in just five years.

The expansion of teleworking has navigated various problems, including difficulty in communications between employees, disruption to the flow of information, inadequate ICT skills and training, and a sense of unfairness among those who cannot work remotely. Additionally, many firms were unprepared for teleworking, lacking the digital infrastructure essential to the transition, and having employees at dispersed locations not under direct oversight of managers runs counter to a corporate culture emphasizing teamwork, collective effort, visible sacrifice, and rigid hierarchies. Teleworking is also not an option for many whose jobs require a physical presence such as face-to-face services and manual labour. Rather quickly, however, teleworking did expand on a hybrid basis to include some 18 million workers, digital capacities were ramped up, and at least at some firms' work is becoming more task oriented rather than requiring long hours at the office where managers can monitor effort.

The digital divide favours larger firms and regular employees as smaller firms have limited resources to upgrade IT and cybersecurity, while many companies don't allow non-regular workers to work remotely. Work practices may be changing but old ways linger, and some managers are leery of teleworking and the greater leeway it affords employees. Japan Inc. is known for its emphasis on face-to face communications and tight control of the work environment, inclinations that will weather the pandemic: there is no vaccine against old habits. But there is also no going back for many who suddenly discovered the advantages of work and life outside the office. Remote working may help recruit and retain workers, especially those with small children, while firms welcome not having to pay high rents for city office space.

Telework is one piece in a larger mosaic of gradually changing attitudes and incremental adjustments amid enduring values, norms, and inclinations. Covid-19 will leave a powerful legacy of disruption and transformation, but the scope will be uneven and there will be powerful continuities and institutional inertia. One key impediment to telecommuting is Japanese workplace culture and the emphasis on face-to-face interactions and careful monitoring of employees' commitment and diligence by managers. The office is seen as a space to build teamwork and nurture loyalty supportive of corporate goals while reinforcing corporate values. Another impediment is that many firms were ill-prepared to make the transition due to limitations of their ICT capacity, including software, hardware, cybersecurity, and employees' skills. This problem was less pronounced at larger firms, and they also had deeper pockets to upgrade and provide subsidies to workers enhancing their home-working environments, including better connectivity. This accentuated the existing digital divide with smaller and medium-sized enterprises (SMEs). The government stepped in to provide subsidies to these firms, but this programme was not a panacea because Japan suffers a shortage of IT specialists to assist in making the transition to teleworking (*Asahi* 2020a). Moreover, many households lack high-speed internet connections, an issue that was critical enough for PM Suga to establish a digitalization agency (Mukoyama 2021). This new agency is tasked with enhancing the nation's cyber infrastructure and promoting digital innovation as growth strategies, but much will depend on nurturing relevant human resources as Japan suffers shortages of IT specialists. It is hard to reconcile Japan's image as a cutting-edge high-tech economy with its significant digital limitations, but this is a reality that currently constrains the potential of telecommuting.

Fujitsu, Japan's leading provider of IT systems, has adopted teleworking for all staff except those in manufacturing and will slash office space by half (Uchiyama 2020). About 80 per cent of some 80,000 employees were telecommuting as of mid-2020 and the company has expanded flexible working hours for all employees and no longer specifies core working hours when staff are required to work at the office. The goal is to have only 25 per cent of all employees, except those working at factories, coming to the office. To address concerns about the lack of interaction and smooth flow of information, Fujitsu is establishing satellite offices equipped with communication technologies, and hubs where workers can meet each other and clients. Monthly one-on-one meetings between staff and managers are also required.

Remote work is rippling across corporate Japan and becoming the standard work style at other major companies like Hitachi and food giant Calbee. This required significant investments to upgrade IT systems and equip employees with smartphones and laptops and more flexible work rules. A cascade of similar reports suggests that concerns about Japan's face-to-face rigid business culture preventing extensive teleworking may be exaggerated as firms adapt to new circumstances and modify established working practices (Ono 2022). Mizuho Research is upbeat about the prospects for expanding teleworking and its positive impact on boosting gross domestic product, while noting that it can also be a boon to job prospects for disabled people (Horiuchi 2020).

Employers appear keen on telework. In November 2020, the *Asahi* interviewed 100 companies that had introduced teleworking due to the declaration of a national emergency and found that 68 had maintained or expanded teleworking since introducing it, while 21 had scaled back or stopped it

(*Asahi* 2020b). Just nine said that teleworking reduced productivity, while the same number expressed concerns about a decline in internal office communication.

Regular workers are also relatively positive about telework, with just 32 per cent of male and 27.2 per cent of women opposed to it and 37.6 per cent and 45.2 per cent respectively in favour (Cabinet Office 2021). Among non-regular workers, 44.9 per cent of men and 37.6 per cent of women do not want to telecommute, while 22.8 per cent and 27.1 per cent respectively are in favour. Alas, the survey data doesn't differentiate between those who have and have not telecommuted, or by sector, or if the work is suitable to telecommuting, so the findings of clear differences in preferences by gender and work status are only indicative. In contrast, a 2020 union survey provided a far more positive take on teleworking, finding that 81.8 per cent of workers overall wanted to continue teleworking (Rengo 2020).

Productivity?

Opinion is divided over the impact of teleworking on productivity and there is uncertainty whether it is too soon to assess, given the unusual circumstances of adoption during a pandemic. Even before the pandemic, researchers were not certain about why Japan's productivity lagged behind other OECD nations. Morikawa (2019) expressed scepticism about enhancing productivity by promotion of work-style reforms such as boosting work–life balance, reducing working hours, and enacting equal pay for equal work. Based on self-reporting from a limited sample during the lockdown, Morikawa (2020) found that teleworking lowers productivity, but was guardedly optimistic about a gradual convergence of home-based productivity towards office-based norms as the kinks of remote work are resolved.

The OECD speculates that teleworking will remain a permanent feature of the future working environment and suggests that this will require the attention of policymakers to ensure it is adopted in ways that promote innovation and workers' satisfaction (OECD 2020). While the impact on productivity is unclear, the OECD notes that it has been crucial to sustaining production during the pandemic. Findings from China and the US cited by the OECD provide a positive assessment of teleworking and productivity. Indeed, Ozimek (2020) reports short-term productivity gains. The OECD also warns against jumping to hasty conclusions due to the exceptional conditions in which telework was implemented, with little preparation in spaces shared with family. It expresses optimism that productivity could improve longer term 'to the extent that the crisis catalyzes wider and smarter adoption of efficient telework practices' (OECD 2020: 3). However, potential gains in productivity may be offset to some degree by loss of the more intensive and informal communication in office settings, and worker dissatisfaction with the fading of boundaries between work and family life in addition to hidden overtime.

Managerial practices, the digital infrastructure, ICT skill endowments, and the age structure of workforces are significant factors influencing the diffusion of teleworking and possible productivity gains. Teleworking also involves a range of options, including some office days, and is more suitable to knowledge-intensive services and less so for jobs that require a physical presence such as manufacturing, healthcare, social work, or hospitality. Ongoing digitalization of work is expanding the range of tasks that can be performed remotely, but the potential for increasing disparities with less knowledge-intensive occupations is apparent.

The OECD (2020) notes that Germany features trust-based working-time arrangements (TBW) that have facilitated adoption of telework because workers are assessed by output and granted considerable discretion over working time. TBW has recalibrated employee–employer relationships in ways that have lessened the importance of observed input and eased concerns about shirking. The German experience suggests that telework and high productivity are compatible, but this depends on managers ceding control over working time and forgoing direct supervision, a big ask for corporate Japan.

Telework can affect firm performance by influencing knowledge creation, motivation, and efficiency, and by cutting costs that enables firms to reallocate resources for innovation and reorganization. However, while workers gain significant time by not commuting, isolation, solitude, more sustained family interactions, and the blurring of work and private life can undermine worker satisfaction with telework.

There is a long-standing consensus that Japan's competitive strength depends less on superior business strategies than on their operational effectiveness. Operational effectiveness depends on continuous improvement that depends on close coordination and regular adjustments of work practices based on teamwork (Abegglen 2006). Employers will do what remaining competitive requires regardless of employees' desires, but white-collar work is not uniformly suitable to telework, and firms will balance what is gained from lower fixed costs such as rents against what may be lost in terms of efficiency and innovation.

Implications

Signs of change are gathering. It is worth bearing in mind that business culture is not set in stone, and successful firms are those that can adapt to change and make it work for them. Before the crisis, teleworking was not very common, but during the pandemic it spread out of necessity. Suntory has consolidated operations since mid-2020 and shut down satellite offices while signalling that in the post-pandemic era it will sustain a hybrid work model with 30 per cent of employees on premises and 70 per cent working remotely (interview Suntory manager May 2021). Aside from a similar shift towards remote work, Fujitsu has also terminated its seniority-based personnel system, provides employees with a monthly subsidy to help cover internet and related costs, and no longer mandates the *tanshinfunin* system of transferring employees to distant branch offices where they live apart from their families. The pandemic has thus not only accelerated ongoing changes but has also been invoked to further chip away at Japan's employment paradigm because some firms believe that change is necessary and beneficial.

These various disruptive changes are eroding some of the prevailing assumptions and norms that have shaped the Japanese employment system. This is one facet of Japan's ongoing transformation that is changing how people work and live, how employees, colleagues, managers, and employers interact, and how and where families are raised. The potential repercussions are tectonic, opening up new possibilities as Japan navigates the uncharted waters of its demographic dilemmas and people rethink their *ikigai* (purpose in life).

The pandemic has been like a pause button, as many people made significant changes in how they work and live as sensible precautions to avoid infection. There has been no mandatory lockdown in Japan, but officials encouraged people to stay at home, and bars and restaurants to curtail hours in exchange for modest subsidies for doing so. The three Cs of avoiding closed spaces, crowded places, and close contact (*sanmitsu*) were not mandated but widely embraced as people sacrificed their social life and reduced commuting to prevent transmission. In doing so many gained time to reconsider their lifestyles and priorities as they adjusted to the new normal of remote working. A Cabinet Office survey in 2020 found that 64 per cent of those who teleworked had come to value private life over work in contrast to just 34 per cent of those who did not telework, but remote work is not a panacea (Cabinet Office 2020b).

The upside for firms is less need for office space and equipment, freeing up resources to upgrade ICT capacities and boost productivity. Moreover, remote working gives firms access to a larger pool of skilled workers unconstrained by commuting distance. Digital nomads can work from appealing rural locations featuring lower costs of living, while firms in remote areas can use remote working to recruit workers who might otherwise balk at relocation to the boondocks. On the downside, reduction of in-person interactions can undermine communication and managerial supervision and lead to disengagement from the firm's stakeholders, while impeding information flows and teamwork. Since firm innovation and performance relies on sharing knowledge, telework requires rethinking the organization and how to enhance virtual interactions and the flow of information. Easier said than done!

In considering the future of remote work, it is important to acknowledge that most people are social animals and need some interaction with others and the sense of belonging that gives them. For all the problems of the office, it does create a group identity that many people desire. Workers with families often appreciate time away from their home situation and now understand that less can be more. Remote-only working seems to have little appeal and many workers seem to favour a hybrid combination of remote and office-based work. Moreover, it is difficult to train new hires relying solely on remote methods. Remote work also confronts a resistance to change, both among workers and managers. Management is accustomed to a certain system of supervision and evaluation, and is often hesitant to embrace radical change.

The government has issued guidelines about how firms assess workers and suggested not counting remote working against them. Telework thus raises questions about employment regulations which currently are based on the assumption that the worksite is the place where managers supervise and offer instructions to workers. Who is supervising employees, and how they are doing so, is key to the rules defining the employment relationship. The ramifications are significant and extend to how direct employment relationships (and the costs entailed) are avoided through outsourcing, gig working, and temp staff dispatch arrangements. It is also uncertain how regulations will adapt to the new norm of telecommuting and how far the regulations will intrude into employees' homes. Firms are keeping tabs on employees through monitoring programmes that enable them to track what employees are doing online and whether they are adhering to submitted work plans, raising privacy concerns.

By eliminating or reducing often lengthy commutes for many workers that can be three or more hours a day in Japan, teleworking can have a major impact on workers' well-being and ability to focus energy on work. This enhances the possibilities of improving work–life balance and makes it easier for couples to share in raising families and household chores. If remote working becomes common, this might have an impact on fertility, especially because teleworking opens access to more reasonably priced housing and underutilized childcare facilities distant from city centres. Day care shortages are primarily an urban problem. Young couples may also be rethinking their living arrangements as they discover the space they imagined to be adequate has become overcrowded and overutilized with too little privacy. Urban real estate is quite expensive so younger couples may have bought or rented smaller apartments that now seem inadequate for combining telework and family life. Resizing dwelling arrangements is expensive, but one can imagine that teleworking from home has made many households desperate for more space and privacy, and that may entail relocating to suburban or ex-urban areas. The appeal is larger living spaces for cheaper rent.

The pandemic has spawned numerous anecdotal, upbeat stories about the prospects of office workers relocating from large metropolises to the countryside or provincial towns (Ueda 2020). No more rush hours? As people adjusted to teleworking, it dawned on some that they could live anywhere because the internet suddenly opened up new options. Cheaper rents, uncrowded trains and roads, clean air, and natural surroundings are part of the appeal. Local areas are eagerly promoting their virtues online and offering enticements, while there are also migration assistance sites and support groups. The outbreak also sparked renewed interest in the so-called U-turn phenomenon, of returning to one's hometown from the big city. Familiarity, relatives and old friends, and the cosy relations in small towns make this a relatively easier move for returnees than it is for those with no such connections.

There is little analysis about the extent and impact of remote working in rural areas, but there is much speculation about the potential benefits associated with teleworking. In mid-2020, a Cabinet Office survey reported that one in four workers who had engaged in telework during the pandemic were contemplating ditching big city living and moving to a rural area (Yamamoto 2020). In Tokyo, the figure was 35.4 per cent. In this sense the pandemic sparked a shift in attitudes that had been impervious to sustained government efforts to stem rural depopulation and encourage rural migration. It also appears that two-thirds of these workers seek to prioritize their personal life over work, questioning one of the hallowed shibboleths of the Japan, Inc. system. What this apparent shift in mindsets portends is uncertain, but it does indicate that many workers seek a work–life balance and are open to change.

The potential impact of telecommuting on consumption patterns and real estate may prove substantial. Large urban areas depend on spending by working and commuting populations to sustain a range of businesses and public transport systems. This generates pressure to get workers to return to their pre-pandemic workplaces rather than continue telecommuting. Some firms have announced significant reductions in urban office space, but if this becomes an exodus there could be a significant drop in land prices and rents, especially if workers follow suit. There are likely to be significant continuities, however, in workplace location and work styles, perhaps with some hybrid mix of telework, due to inertia, and because firms and employees are locked in to some extent by, inter alia, loans, mortgages, a preference for urban amenities, better schools, and the convenience of public transport. Moreover, urban areas are massive markets where customers are clustered, and centres of innovation and entrepreneurship that no amount of broadband can replicate. So remote working may be feasible, and in some respects desirable, but there are significant trade-offs.

Digital nomads, a small and young demographic, may prefer working in beachside Okinawa, the mountains of Nagano, or sunny Bali, but once they start families, priorities may shift. For the majority of already employed workers, they will mostly comply with corporate directives on telecommuting, and certainly many will welcome the spare time no longer devoted to commuting, but relocating from familiar settings to small towns will probably be limited. There are busybodies everywhere, but urban life provides a degree of anonymity and privacy that is rare in rural areas, and few will willingly relinquish that freedom. So telecommuting is not a panacea for rural depopulation (Klein 2020). It is more likely that some larger firms in some sectors will seize the opportunity to slash fixed costs by shedding prestige office space in pricy areas and establish smart hubs in more affordable suburban locations. Where workers telecommute from is not their concern, but in adopting such a workstyle reform, the costs of work-space are shifted onto workers who must adapt their living environment to work requirements.

Teleworking disparities

Japan's sharp digital divide carries enormous implications. According to McKinsey, 'COVID-19 accelerated three groups of consumer and business trends that are likely to persist: remote work and virtual interactions, e-commerce and digital transactions, and deployment of automation and AI. Our research suggests that the disruptions to work sparked by COVID-19 will be larger than we had estimated in our pre-pandemic research, especially for the lowest paid, least educated, and most vulnerable workers' (McKinsey

2021a). McKinsey forecasts significant job losses and need for retraining by 2030 affecting about 11 per cent of workers in Japan compared to 28 per cent in the US and 21 per cent in Germany. While the burden of adjustment may be smaller, that means more than 6 million workers in Japan's precariat are facing a rough reckoning.

The pandemic has exacerbated the digital divide in Japan and increased existing disparities by gender, occupation, income, and firm size. Keio University economist Okubo Toshiro concludes, '[H]igh-income workers and large corporations actively use telework and digital tools, which will increase their productivity in the future, lower-income strata and small and medium-sized enterprises are not riding the wave of digitalization. As a result, economic disparities are becoming more conspicuous due to the existence of digital disparities' (Okubo 2020b). He argues that the middle-class and unskilled workers were already facing declining fortunes, and the pandemic had accelerated this trend, while the adverse impact on workers in large firms has been limited. The spread of telework increases with income and firm size, and there was little growth in lower income brackets or in SMEs indicating that 'the income gap and the digitalization gap are linked' (Okubo 2020b). It appears likely that the benefits of further digitalization will disproportionately benefit larger firms and their employees. Overall, large firms are better positioned to introduce videoconferencing, data sharing software, attendance management tools, ICT tools for office procedures, accounting, human resources, and sales operations, and are ahead of SMEs in adopting robotic process automation (RPA) systems and virtual offices. This uneven advance of the digital revolution is intensifying disparities and casts a cloud over the prospects of SMEs that are falling behind. The digital revolution will also disrupt labour markets as some jobs will cease to exist and others will change dramatically with the potential for significant social problems and greater disparities.

Employers' reluctance to allow non-regular workers to telecommute is a significant obstacle to expanding teleworking and sharing the fruits of flexibility (*Asahi* 2020a). We speculate that the sharp divide between the core workforce of regular workers and non-regular workers in terms of employment conditions extends to teleworking due to issues of trust and loyalty. Non-regular workers operate on the corporate periphery and are not treated as insiders and extended the trust this implies. They are more vulnerable to layoffs and downsizing and not treated as part of the corporate family. Managers are reluctant to forgo supervising non-regular workers because their commitment to the firm is considered weaker, mirroring the firm's limited commitment to them.

Yamaguchi and Osawa (2021) found women are more likely to work as non-regular workers, are more likely to work in smaller firms, and more likely to work in the industries where teleworking is not suitable such as restaurants, hotels, and retail industries. The practice of many firms barring, discouraging, or not supporting telecommuting by non-regular workers impacts women more than men. Temp agencies that provide non-regular workers to corporate clients helped enforce the teleworking exclusion (*Asahi* 2020a). For many working mothers, non-regular jobs provide a degree of flexibility essential to juggling multiple roles as mothers, homemakers, wives, and caregivers for elderly relatives.

In 2020, pandemic countermeasures pushed many women out of the workforce as they assumed most of the burdens of childcaring and the commensurate increase of household duties. PM Abe abruptly declared, with only 72 hours' advance notice, that schools would be closed from the beginning of March 2020, leaving parents scrambling to cobble together childcare arrangements. Having the family at home also meant an increase in housework and this too fell more heavily on women as 37.5 per cent of women with toddlers reported an increase in household chores due to the emergency declaration, while only 19.8 per cent of men did so (Cabinet Office 2020a). Teleworking thus not only excluded women, but also burdened them with increased unpaid housework due to the presence of their teleworking spouses.

Moreover, the pandemic-induced plunge in economic activity disproportionately hit the precariat as firms reduced staff to cope with shrinking revenues. These staff reductions were more pronounced in the service sector—hospitality (hotels, restaurants, and bars), retail, and transportation—due to the plunge in tourism, travel, and consumption. Firms in the service sector tend to have a higher proportion of non-regular workers and often rely on the physical presence of staff to provide services for customers, also reducing the option of telecommuting. In April 2021 the Cabinet Office (2021) released a report that highlighted how women disproportionately suffered from job losses, a lack of employment opportunities, domestic violence, and suicide during the pandemic. Researchers concluded that the pandemic reinforced existing gender disparities, and larger job losses for women due to their concentration in more vulnerable sectors (Okabayashi 2021; Nikkei 2020).

From April 2020 to April 2021 the number of female non-regular workers dropped by 500,000 compared to a decline of 260,000 among men (Cabinet Office 2021). Single women's unemployment rate increased significantly, while women with elementary school age children who dropped out of the workforce when schools were closed had a hard time returning due to a lack of opportunities. The Cabinet Office report concludes that deep-seated gender inequality and a strong sense that men are household 'breadwinners' contributed to the bleak job outlook for women. Based on this breadwinner ideology, wives are relegated to contributing supplemental income, and there is an assumption among employers that men merit preferential treatment in the labour market. The social security and tax systems reinforce women's marginalization by encouraging them to limit their income or lose benefits if they exceed the threshold of just over JPY 1 million, about US$7,000 in 2022.

The Ministry of Labour, recognizing the uneven impact of the pandemic, in early 2021 expanded coronavirus relief to non-regular workers (*Nippon* 2021). Compared to regular workers, twice as many nonregular workers at large firms received no compensation from employers despite being forced to take leave during the pandemic. The Japan Institute of Labour Policy and Training found in August 2020 that 33.4 per cent of nonregular workers received no compensation compared to 14.8 per cent of regular workers, and that 68.3 per cent and 60.8 per cent respectively had been asked to take leave. The national labour law requires employers to pay at least 60 per cent of salaries to workers regardless of status if the firm orders them to go on leave. The government's initiative aims to rectify this discriminatory treatment. Many firms eligible for government subsidies to maintain employment did not apply, apparently due to excessive red tape, and claim they are not responsible for compensating employees who had to take leave due to the pandemic. In June 2020 the government set up a compensation programme targeting workers at SMEs, enabling them to directly apply for state assistance to cover lost earnings, but nonregular workers at large firms were not eligible, based on the assumption that the employer would cover this. The February 2021 measure allows such workers to receive 80 per cent of the wages earned pre-pandemic, capped at JPY 11,000 a day, but they need to apply directly.

Pathologies of telework

Teleworking tires people out and is linked with various ailments, physical and mental (Tsuji 2020). Working long hours on PCs and more sedentary lifestyles generate fatigue, physical ailments, stress, and sleeping disorders (Tsutsui 2020). Zoom burnout is a common lament that reduces job satisfaction, increases anxieties, affects relationships, and can undermine work performance.

During the pandemic there was a 50 per cent increase in the number of domestic violence (DV) consultations and a 20 per cent increase in consultations for sexual crimes and sexual violence, attesting to the grim toll of the pandemic on women (Okabayashi 2021). In Japan, the toll of the pandemic is also evident in the spike in suicides as job losses and financial distress drove some 21,000 people to take their lives in 2020, the first rise in eleven years. Of that total, nearly 7,000 were women, up 15 per cent from 2019. This rise is attributed to the concentration of women in more vulnerable nonregular jobs, but also may be linked to isolation and an increase in DV (Ando 2020). Teleworking and staying at home directives are forcing couples to spend far more time together, cut off from friends and relatives, while some households experience heightened financial troubles due to lower income, developments that are boosting the misery index.

The surge of DV in Japan during 2020 seems linked to telecommuting. This shadow pandemic is surely underreported but even so, the statistics are dire. Social isolation reinforces the sense of helplessness that victims often feel. Covid-19 counter measures encourage people to stay home as a way to contain transmissions but puts many people at greater risk by confining them with abusive partners (Ando 2020). The option of walking away from abusive situations is diminished, and many victims suffer their traumas in isolation without recourse to counselling or shelter. In addition, more time together and no breaks makes it difficult for couples to manage any existing relationship problems, while adjusting to telework presents various new challenges that may boost stress for telecommuters and their partners. The time away from each other during work gives partners important space, and losing that interval generates frictions. In addition, lower income households where one or both partners are working in more vulnerable occupations are at greater risk of financial dislocation due to the pandemic and typically live in less spacious housing.

Hidden overtime is another risk of remote working. The flexible work-from-home system is opening up new opportunities for side-jobs and extra income as firms offer part-time remote gigs to employees of other companies to supplement in-house staff and expertise, especially in IT (Horigomi 2021). On the downside, having multiple jobs makes it more difficult to monitor and curb excessive working hours. Japanese workers log some of the highest number of hours per annum, but these understate the actual situation due to many hours of unrecorded free overtime (*sabisuzangyo*) that is embedded in Japan's business culture. There is justifiable concern that teleworkers and temporary gig workers are vulnerable to unreasonable work expectations and, because there no longer is a clear border between work and home, unreported overtime is a significant risk. Indeed, a 2020 survey reported that two-thirds of workers did unpaid overtime while teleworking (Rengo 2020). Death from overwork (*karoshi*) is a health risk as employees are pressured to work beyond their limits for prolonged periods of time, causing some to die from related health problems or commit suicide.

Freelancers have had a tough time during the pandemic due to job insecurity, less work, lower and unreliable income, and the absence of government social welfare programmes targeting them (Uno and Oday 2020). The mantra of deregulation in twenty-first century Japan has been *jiko sekinen* (personal responsibility), meaning that freelancers and other nonregular workers understand that during a crisis, they are on their own, just as in 2008 following the Lehman Shock and mass layoffs. The threadbare safety net means they have to scramble to cobble together various gigs to make ends meet. Many are millennials (b.1980–1994), lurching from disaster to crisis, including the bursting of the asset bubble in the early 1990s, the 1995 Kobe earthquake, the 1998 and 2008 financial crises, the 2011 tsunami and nuclear disasters, and now the pandemic. This generation has experienced sustained uncertainty and exploitation as many are in the ranks of the working poor precariat. For them telework may be empowering in that many may have the requisite IT skills, but translating those skills into a satisfying and sustainable livelihood remains difficult, and during the pandemic marginalization has been a more common outcome.

Conclusion

Japan has lagged behind other advanced industrialized nations in embracing teleworking, but the pandemic shock forced firms to navigate the pitfalls while realizing some of the untapped potential. The doubling of the overall rate of telework (including hybrid arrangements) from 13.3 per cent of workers in 2016 to 27.3 per cent in 2021 marks a massive shift in the Japanese employment paradigm. In Tokyo alone, teleworking surged from 16.9 per cent of employees in 2016 to 42.1 percent by 2021, but the revolution has been uneven. Clearly, teleworking has gained momentum from the pandemic, but the potential gains in productivity and work–life balance are constrained by limitations in Japan's digital infrastructure, the shortage of IT skills, and more pronounced weaknesses in the capacity, resources, and management practices at SMEs. It does seem that large firms are ramping up plans to expand teleworking and that investments in doing so will bolster the realization of productivity gains. But the digital divide by firm size will magnify existing disparities in pay and performance. Remote working provides new options to some workers and firms, but many workers and firms will not share the fruits of this revolution and digitalization will be disruptive by eliminating jobs. Non-regular workers, nearly 40 per cent of the workforce, have not benefitted because they are concentrated in the sectors hit hardest by the pandemic, such as restaurants, hotels, and transportation, and most are not allowed to telework. Women have been disadvantaged by the pandemic, both because they are disproportionately nonregular workers and because the breadwinner ideology and other patriarchal inclinations favour men; the gender division of housework remains deeply entrenched. It does seem, however, that teleworking might eventually help women better balance the demands of work and home as it becomes a new normal, and management rethinks how it integrates remote working. Japan's stodgy, inflexible business culture is often cited as a significant impediment to the expansion of telework, but this is a misleading generalization that overlooks how some of Japan's leading firms are shedding old ways and embracing telework as a growth and survival strategy. As they do so, they are grappling with various teething problems, especially the flow of knowledge and information that is essential to teamwork and innovation. This is a work in progress, but 'doable' as communication tools improve and employees and employers get better at adjusting to the demands of teleworking. Again, this highlights the brighter future for larger firms and their employees, and the relatively bleak implications for SMEs. For the government, addressing the various digital divides, upgrading the digital infrastructure and ensuring employee protections for remote working is an urgent agenda.

References

Abegglen, James C. (2006) *21st-Century Japanese Management: New Systems, Lasting Values*. Houndmills, Basingstoke, Hampshire; New York: Palgrave Macmillan.

Ando, R. (2020) 'Domestic violence and Japan's COVID-19 pandemic'. *Asia Pacific Journal Japan Focus*, 18:18:7, 15 September. Available at: https://apjjf.org/2020/18/ando.html/.

Asahi (2020a) 'For nonregular workers, request to "stay home" does not apply'. *Asahi Shimbun*, 27 April. Available at: www.asahi.com/ajw/articles/13331716/.

Asahi (2020b) 'Asahi survey: 20% of major companies scaled back on telework'. *Asahi Shimbun*, 15 December. Available at: http://www.asahi.com/ajw/articles/14021893/.

Cabinet Office (2020a) 'Survey on the impact of Covid-19 pandemic from gender equality perspectives' (男女共同参画の視点からの新型コロナウイルスの感染症拡大の影響等に関する調査). Available at: https://www.gender.go.jp/kaigi/kento/covid-19/siryo/pdf/5-5.pdf/.

Cabinet Office (2020b) 'Survey on general public views on change in lifestyle and behavior under Covid-19 pandemic' (新型コロナウイルス感染症の影響下における生活意識・行動の変化に関する調査). Available at: https://www5.cao.go.jp/keizai2/manzoku/pdf/shiryo2.pdf/.

Cabinet Office (2021) 'Report of Impact of Covid-19 pandemic on women: Toward post-Covid-19 society where everybody is included' (コロナ下の女性への影響と課題に関する研究会報告書 ～誰一人取り残さないポストコロナの社会へ). Available at: https://www.gender.go.jp/kaigi/kento/covid-19/index.html/.

Horigomi, T. (2021) 'Companies lure teleworkers seeking side jobs for extra income'. *Asahi Shimbun*, 21 September. Available at: www.asahi.com/ajw/articles/13747932/.

Horiuchi, J. (2020) 'Japan corporate culture remains obstacle to expansion of telework'. *Kyodo News*, 3 January. Available at: https://english.kyodonews.net/news/2020/01/5422161af5a2-feature-japan-corporate-culture-remains-obstacle-to-expansion-of-telework.html/.

Klein, S. (2020) *Urban Migrants in Rural Japan: Between Agency and Anomie in a Post-Growth Society*. Albany, NY: SUNY Press.

McKinsey (2021a) 'The future of work after COVID-19'. McKinsey Global Institute, 18 February. Available at: https://www.mckinsey.com/featured-insights/future-of-work/the-future-of-work-after-covid-19/.

McKinsey (2021b) 'What employees are saying about the future of remote work'. McKinsey and Associates, April. Available at: https://www.mckinsey.com/business-functions/organization/our-insights/what-employees-are-saying-about-the-future-of-remote-work/.

Mainichi (2021) 'Japan's telework rate still far from 70% target during state of emergency'. *Mainichi*, 26 April. Available at: https://mainichi.jp/english/articles/20210426/p2a/00m/0bu/015000c/.

MLIT (2022) 'テレワーク人口実態調査 -調査結果(概要)' (Survey on telework) Ministry of Land, Infrastructure and Transportation. March. Available at: https://www.mlit.go.jp/toshi/daisei/content/001471975.pdf.

Morikawa, M. (2019) 'Japan's low labor productivity: The gap with the U.S. and complex causes'. RIETI, 13 March. Available at: https://www.rieti.go.jp/en/papers/contribution/morikawa/12.html/.

Morikawa, M. (2020) 'COVID-19, teleworking, and productivity' RIETI, 26 April. Available at: https://www.rieti.go.jp/en/columns/v01_0137.html.

Mukoyama, J. (2021) 'The need to digitalize Japanese society as a whole'. *Japan Times*, 8 January. Available at: https://www.japantimes.co.jp/opinion/2021/01/08/commentary/japan-commentary/api-digital-agency-3/.

Nikkei (2018) 'Hitachi boosts telecommuting to unprecedented 100,000 staffers'. Nikkei, 2 August. Available at: https://asia.nikkei.com/Business/Companies/Hitachi-boosts-telecommuting-to-unprecedented-100-000-staffers/.

Nikkei (2020) 'Women bear brunt of Japan's pandemic job losses'. Nikkei, 7 September. Available at: https://asia.nikkei.com/Spotlight/Datawatch/Women-bear-brunt-of-Japan-s-pandemic-job-losses/.

Nippon (2021) *Japan to expand virus aid to nonregular workers at large firms. Nippon.com.* 5 February. Available at: https://www.nippon.com/en/news/yjj2021020500522/.

OECD (2020) 'Productivity gains from teleworking in the post-Covid-19 era: How can public policies make it happen?' Paris: OECD, 7 September. Available at: https://www.oecd.org/coronavirus/policy-responses/productivity-gains-from-teleworking-in-the-post-COVID-19-era-a5d52e99/.

Okabayashi, S. (2021) 'Pandemic hitting women harder due to lack of gender equality'. Asahi Shimbun, 30 April. Available at: www.asahi.com/ajw/articles/14340607.

Okubo, T. (2020a) 'COVID-19 and teleworking in Japan'. CEPR Policy Research, 25 June. Available at: https://voxeu.org/article/covid-19-and-teleworking-japan/.

Okubo, T. (2020b) 'Expansion of disparities during the COVID-19 pandemic: The income gap and the digitalization gap'. Nippon Institute for Research Advancement, NIRA Opinion Paper, No.53, September. Available at: https://english.nira.or.jp/papers/images/e_opinion53.pdf/.

Ono, H. (2022) 'Japan must reform its inflexible work culture' *East Asia Forum*, 24 November. Available at: https://www.eastasiaforum.org/2022/11/24/japan-must-reform-its-inflexible-work-culture/.

Ozimek, A. (2020) 'The future of remote work'. Upwork, June. Available at: https://content-static.upwork.com/blog/uploads/sites/6/2020/05/26131624/Upwork_EconomistReport_FWR_052020.pdf.

Rengo (Japan Trade Union Confederation) (2020) 'Survey on teleworking' (テレワークに関する調査 2020). Available at: https://www.jtuc-rengo.or.jp/info/chousa/data/20200630.pdf/.

Tsuji, T. (2020) 'Study: Telework taking a toll as workers report more fatigue'. *Asahi Shimbun*, 8 June. Available at: www.asahi.com/ajw/articles/13440457/.

Tsutsui, R. (2020) 'Stress levels soaring with more husbands staying at home'. *Asahi Shimbun*, 3 June. Available at: www.asahi.com/ajw/articles/13426902/.

Uchiyama, O. (2020) 'Fujitsu adopts telework for all staff, cuts 50% of office space'. *Asahi Shimbun*, 7 July. Available at: www.asahi.com/ajw/articles/13523634/.

Ueda, M. (2020) 'Urban exodus in cards as people find freedom in teleworking'. *Asahi Shimbun*, 8 July. Available at: www.asahi.com/ajw/articles/13485555/.

Uno, S. and O'Day, R. (2020) 'Japanese freelance workers struggle during the COVID-19 pandemic: Social media, critique, and political resistance'. *Asia Pacific Journal Japan Focus*, 18:18:8, 15 September. Available at: https://apjjf.org/2020/18/Uno-ODay.html/.

Yamaguchi, K. and Osawa, M. (2021) 'Promoting teleworking and unequal opportunities among men and women under Covid-19' (新型コロナ下における在宅勤務機会の男女の不平等). Research Institute of Economy, Trade and Industry. Available at: https://www.rieti.go.jp/jp/publications/nts/21j002.html/.

Yamamoto, T. (2020) '1 in 4 teleworkers mulling ditching Japan's big cities for rural areas'. *Asahi Shimbun*, 22 June. Available at: www.asahi.com/ajw/articles/13479412/.

Zhou, Y. (2021) 'How women bear the brunt of COVID-19's damages on work'. *Japan Labor Issues*, 5(28), January: 2–8.

4
Organizing around Precarity in China

Jude Howell

Introduction

Worker precarity is a global issue. The increasing use of zero-sum contracts constitutes yet another ruse by employers to push labour costs towards the bottom of the pyramid. Ideologically veiled in tropes of offering worker choice and flexibility, such contracts reflect an acceleration of processes of informalization and casualization. They mark a step backwards, diluting the gains made in past struggles for improved employment conditions and labour protection. Too invested in a labour strategy that revolves around formal labour, many trades unions across the world have proven to be ill-prepared to challenge this form of exploitation and slow to mobilize informal workers. It might be expected that a socialist country with a history of worker security, an ideological commitment to the working class, and a long record of trade unionism such as China might fare better than capitalist countries in resolving the issue of precarity. As will be seen, this is far from the case.

This chapter focuses on China, a country ruled by the Chinese Communist Party (CCP) for over 70 years, with a historical and ideological commitment to the working class. We examine whether its armoury of labour protection in the form of legislation, ideology, and the largest trade union in the world has been resilient to the new wave of capitalist exploitation. We begin by examining how worker security was developed during the Maoist decades, only to be gradually dismantled during the reform period with the introduction of labour contracts. We explore measures the government and the official All-China Federation of Trades Unions (ACFTU) have taken to protect labour in the workplace and the frequent piecemeal implementation. Given the gap between rhetoric and reality, we trace the emergence of non-governmental alternatives to securing workers' rights through the development of labour NGOs from the late 1990s onwards to their subsequent demise during the Xi Jinping era.

We first clarify how we use the term 'precarity' in this chapter. Precarity is defined here as living in a state of instability and uncertainty. In relation to worklife, precarious work refers to unstable employment that is not formalized through a contract or agreement, fails to provide employment protection that guarantees decent employment conditions, health and safety, and minimum wages, including the right to establish a trade union. It is often referred to also as casual or informal employment. The instability of employment and thus the uncertainty of a regular and adequate living wage render precarious other parts of life such as having affordable, permanent housing, maintaining a family, and achieving food security.[1] From an employer's perspective precarious labour offers flexibility, that is, the ability to hire and fire labour according to fluctuating market conditions and so maintain profits. It absolves employers of responsibility to provide a healthy and safe workplace, unemployment benefit, injury compensation, pensions, and other benefits that commonly accrue to permanent employees. The neo-liberal ideological discourse of flexibility and individual choice for the worker masks the reality of working life for the informal and casually employed, which is typically characterized by long hours, poor working conditions, and minimal, if any, welfare benefits. What is flexibility for the employer heralds precarity for the worker.

Organizing around precarity is particularly difficult in any context. Informal labour can be employed in the same workplace for long periods but without any contract or agreement to govern employment terms. It can also be highly mobile, with day-to-day employment in different workplaces as might occur through agency work or street labour markets. It is typically invisible, in that companies do not keep records of their employment of their casual and informal workers, which in turn makes it difficult for workers to organize and make claims against employers. Multiple layers of sub-contracting render claim-making by aggrieved workers particularly challenging as it is unclear who the ultimate employer is. In the gig economy informal workers are atomized through digitalized and algorithmically determined processes of production control that ultimately weaken potential bonds of solidarity and resistance (Wu et al. 2019).

Compared with formal employment where the physical concentration of workers can facilitate organizing and solidarity, and legal contracts guarantee some modicum of rights that can be appealed to, precarious labour often lacks a common, permanent site of collective employment that can serve as a nodal point of resistance. As Swider (2015: 43) poignantly illustrates in her research on construction workers in China, there is considerable variation in the 'employment configurations' of informal workers, whereby labour markets and employment relations intertwine. She identifies at least three types of configuration in the construction industry, namely, mediated, embedded, and individualized, which in different ways present barriers to collective action (Swider 2015: 46–53). Though she does not probe the implications of these for labour organizing, it might be conjectured that individualized configurations such as in street labour markets provide the least opportunity for organized action, whilst mediated configurations involving contracting agencies could provide a focal point of action. However, the complexity of and variation in employment configurations renders collective action challenging.

In liberal democratic contexts, independent trades unions, workers' centres, civil society organizations, labour lawyers, and journalists can bring issues of precarity to the attention of the public and politicians. Moreover, the right to form a trade union is usually enshrined in legislation. In authoritarian contexts such as China where civil society is highly constrained, political and civil rights are constricted, an independent judiciary and media barely exist, and the right to form independent trades unions is prohibited, organizing around labour issues is subject to surveillance, harassment, and repression (Brooker 2000; Friedrich and Brzezinski 1956; Wintrobe 1998). Given these structural differences, what then are the possibilities in authoritarian contexts for organizing around informal and casualized labour?

In this chapter on China we explore how different actors organize around precarity to protect workers in China. In particular, we look at the role of labour legislation, the official ACFTU, labour NGOs, and workers in organizing around precarity in the reform period. We examine three key periods: from 1978, the period of the 'iron rice bowl' to the late 1990s when employment contracting and precarity are seeded, fertilized, and legitimized in law; the second phase from the late 1990s to 2011, when contracting deepens, protective legislation is enacted to drive industrial conflict into individual rather than collective action, the ACFTU innovates with democratic elections and community trades unions, and labour NGOs emerge; and the phase from 2012 onwards which marks the decline of labour NGOs, the stalling of trade union reform and deepening of digital forms of labour precarity.[2] In the conclusion we reflect on our findings and consider the prospects for challenging precarity through organized resistance.

From security to precarity: 1978–1990

The precarious nature of work experienced by gig workers such as street vendors, drivers, cleaners, and housemaids has not always characterized employment practices in China. During the era of socialist planning from

1949 up until late 1978 the work unit was both a site of production and reproduction, where workers and leaders were bound together through relations of organized dependence that ensured stability in the workplace (Walder 1986). It provided a 'cradle to grave' existence for its employees, guaranteeing employment and various welfare benefits such as housing, pension, schooling, and health provision (Tang and Parish 2000: 34–41). In this socialist social contract, workers enjoyed an 'iron rice bowl', protected from the risks of unemployment, homelessness, and precarity. Still, there were differences in the quality and accessibility of welfare between workers in large state-owned enterprises and smaller ones, and between state-owned enterprises and urban collective enterprises, though such variation was not stark.

In rural areas, agricultural production was collectively organized through the commune system, that similarly provided some degree of welfare protection, albeit of lesser quality and extent than in urban areas. Labour was allocated through the planning system, so that moving between work units or rural communes was highly constrained. Furthermore, the household registration system, that is '*hukou*', blocked mobility from rural to urban areas (Naughton 2007: 124–126). The *hukou* system, introduced in the 1950s, divided China's population into urban and rural, not only limiting mobility between urban and rural areas but also excluding rural migrants from the numerous welfare benefits accruing to urban citizens (Swider 2015: 20–29). When labour shortages appeared in urban areas, temporary and seasonal labour was hired to fill gaps without, however, changing the residency status of the rural worker and the prospects of an improved package of welfare. The planning system offered a high degree of livelihood security, except during the years of the Great Leap Forward and subsequent famine between 1958 and 1960. Rather than market-induced unemployment, there was planning-induced underemployment. Apart from some temporary and seasonal labour, there was guaranteed employment in lieu of precarity.

In this context the role of the ACFTU departed significantly from trades unions in capitalist countries (Clarke and Pringle 2011). Given that the interests of the state and the working class were deemed to be one, there could be no serious conflict of interests as would be found in a class-divided capitalist economy. This is not to say that workers did not have grievances; indeed, there were strikes in the 1950s, 1960s, and mid-1970s around demands for improved working conditions and the right to establish trades unions (Perry 1994; Wilson 1990). Grievances in general were handled informally in a context of 'organized dependence' (Walder 1986). Moreover, such 'non-antagonistic' grievances were not akin to any class-based antagonism as the concept of 'class' in a 'workers' state' was deemed to be no longer relevant. The

ACFTU was a pillar of the CCP and served as a 'transmission belt' between the Party and workers, relaying workers' concerns upwards and party policies downwards (Harper 1969; Howell 1997b; Taylor et al. 2003). The ACFTU played the role of organizing entertainment, attending to the needs of poor workers, distributing ration cards, and resolving grievances (Harper 1969; Howell 1997b; Lee 1986).

This was all to change with the onset of market reforms from 1978 onwards. Mao had died in 1976, leading to the downfall of the Gang of Four and the concomitant rise of the reformers. Under the leadership of Deng Xiaoping, China's reformers embarked upon a new path to development that hinged on the introduction of market forces. Central to this strategy was the opening up of China to the global capitalist economy through the creation of four Special Economic Zones (SEZs) in the south of China (Howell 1993). Labour contracts were first experimented with in the SEZs, heralding the end of stable employment in China (Howell 1993). At a time of continuing factional struggles within the Chinese Communist Party (CCP), this was a highly contentious move. Ideologically, it symbolized a step towards capitalism as it introduced a differentiation between 'employer' and 'employee' that did not technically exist under socialist planning. This differentiation embodied a class relationship that could lead to 'antagonistic contradictions'. For several decades the CCP, ACFTU, and indeed many social science scholars in China astutely avoided the notion of class, for admitting its existence was to acknowledge that China had taken the 'capitalist path'. Apart from contracts, other reforms such as bonuses and piece-rate payment that rewarded workers according to how much they produced, wage reforms that allowed for greater differentiation amongst workers and between workers and managers (Takahara 1987), and the creation of labour markets in place of state allocation contributed to new hierarchies in the workplace, competition, and performance-related employment (O'Leary 1998).

As labour markets gradually spread across China, the structure of the working class underwent a seismic change. In the early days of the SEZs, state enterprise workers were loath to work in the zones, as they would have had to give up their 'iron rice bowl' for the uncertainty of a labour contract. In order to provide a supply of workers and address the issue of surplus labour in rural areas, the CCP loosened the strictures on rural–urban migration. Enticed by the opportunities and related status of factory work, rural migrants headed in their millions to coastal areas of China (Chang 2008; Pun 2005a, 2005b; Swider 2015). By the early 1990s rural migrants constituted the mainstay of manufacturing and construction but lacked the employment protection and welfare benefits of urban workers.

The nature of the working class now changed from state, collective, and temporary/seasonal workers to migrant workers employed on a contractual basis, laid-off state enterprise workers, unemployed workers, dispatch workers hired out to factories by employment agencies, and student interns (Chan and Pun 2009). In practice, many migrant workers either did not have contracts or were unaware that a collective contract had been agreed at enterprise level. Furthermore, even if they were aware of a contract, it was difficult to ensure its implementation, not least because many factories did not have trade union representation, and even where they did, the trade union representatives were often the owner or relatives of the owner (Chan 2005; Pun 2005a, 2005b). The introduction of piece-rate work, where wages varied according to output, was a forerunner to the digitalized and algorithmically determined 'gig work' that emerged over three decades later, both globally and in China. By the early 1990s grievances around excessive working hours, delayed wages, unsafe working conditions, and inadequate housing were coming to a head.

It might be expected that in a socialist state the trade union would step in and defend aggrieved workers. However, though the ACFTU had made many adaptations in the first decade of reform, such as creating new legal divisions to address disputes, it proved structurally hampered in defending workers and even in establishing unions in private enterprises (Pringle 2013). As a pillar of the CCP, the ACFTU faced a dilemma as to whether it should defend workers or national interests (Harper 1969). Too often than not, union leaders prioritized national interests over workers' well-being. Added to this, workers could not set up alternative trades unions, hence the ACFTU enjoyed a monopoly of representation. Unable to rely on the ACFTU to defend their interests, most workers voted with their feet and moved to workplaces with better conditions. However, from the late 1980s onwards, workers increasingly turned to spontaneous action such as striking, demonstrating, sitting-in, and lobbying labour department officials to press for improved conditions of work (Chan and Pun 2010; Chen and Tang 2013).

With the rise of the Democracy Movement in 1988, workers, too, organized to campaign for the right to free trade unions (Leung 1988; Lu 1990). Some ACFTU leaders sympathetic to the demands of protestors and eager to gain greater autonomy from the CCP to better defend workers' interests also joined in. Indeed, at a national conference in 1988 some ACFTU officials sparked debates around increasing the autonomy of the union from the Party with the goal of better protecting workers and prioritizing their interests over national production (Howell 1997b; Pringle 2013). However, the tragic events of June 1989 brought an abrupt end to the incipient workers' movement and key leaders either fled China or languished in prison.

Smashing the iron rice bowl: 1990–2002

The clampdown on the 1989 student- and worker-led Democracy Movement brought a halt to most autonomous civic organizing. The Chinese government faced international sanctions for its brutal handling of protestors in Tiananmen Square on 4 June 1989. Concerned about rapid inflation, corruption, and public dissatisfaction, senior conservative leaders put a brake on further economic reform. With growth stagnating, Deng Xiaoping travelled to the south of China in 1992 to galvanize support for faster economic reform. This marked a turning point, leading to the further advances in China's opening up to foreign trade and foreign investment.

Alert to the impact on stability of unaddressed workers' grievances, central Party leaders ushered in a raft of new labour legislation to protect labour and rein in the excesses of unfettered capitalism. These included the 1991 Law on the Protection of Women Workers' Rights, the 1992 Trade Union Law, and the 1994 (effective 1995) Labour Law, which amended and updated the previous 1950 law (Gallagher et al. 2011). The laws were framed in a way that channelled workers' grievances towards legal resolution on an individual basis rather than through collective action that might grow eventually into a class-based, labour movement. In the mid-1990s the ACFTU finally recognized the need to bring migrant workers into the scope of the union's work. Though the ACFTU had played a key role in drafting these laws, it had neither the capacity nor sufficient autonomy to effectively implement these laws and tackle workers' grievances. Many private enterprises were without any union representation, not least because owners prevented local trades unionists from entering the premises (Friedman and Lee 2010). Moreover, local government officials, keen to attract foreign investment and improve their promotion prospects by increasing economic development, colluded with domestic entrepreneurs and foreign businesses to curb industrial unrest. As a bureaucratic appendage to the Party, ACFTU cadres lacked skills of bargaining and union activism and failed to properly implement the new labour laws. With the ACFTU unable to effectively address the lamentable conditions of employment, workers continued to spontaneously mount strikes, protests, and sit-ins (Pringle 2013; Taylor et al. 2003). The new architecture of labour laws provided a legal framework which workers could appeal to and safely claim their legally given rights. The raft of new labour laws spawned the emergence of a cortège of labour rights' lawyers, some of whom were former workers and self-taught, who took up the cases of migrant workers (Gallagher 2017).

The 1994 Labour Law was significant, not only in setting boundaries around exploitative workplace practices but also because it cemented the shift towards the labour contracts and the concomitant smashing of the iron rice bowl. It paved the way for a deepening and acceleration of state-owned enterprise reforms in 1996, leading to massive strikes in the north-east rustbelt of China (Lee 2007). China's working class became even more fragmented and differentiated, with state workers protesting in the north-east against layoffs and migrant workers protesting against wage arrears and unsafe working conditions. As unemployment was masked as underemployment in the Maoist decades, the concept of workers losing their jobs as occurred in capitalist countries was also discursively veiled in the language of 'workers stepping down from their positions' or *xiagang*. This reflected the reluctance of Party leaders to acknowledge openly that China was treading the capitalist path and that workers constituted a class, albeit increasingly fragmented and differentiated.

Aware of the limitations of the ACFTU, workers made several attempts throughout the 1990s to establish free trades unions. For example, in 1992 the Preparatory Committee of the Free Labour Union of China distributed leaflets in Beijing calling for free trades unions, while in 1998 Zhang Shanguang was detained for trying to establish the Shu Pu Association for the Protection of the Rights of Laid-Off Workers (Howell 2003). In all cases such attempts to create independent trades unions were immediately clamped down upon and the protagonists swiftly detained. For the CCP, the prospect of independent trades unions was intolerable, hence the repeated efforts by senior Party leaders to push the ACFTU to reform and become more proactive in addressing workers' grievances.

The sweatshop employment conditions of many migrant workers gained significant domestic and international media attention when 53 workers lost their lives in the Zhili Handicraft factory blaze in 1993. This spurred labour activists, students, researchers, and journalists in Hong Kong to raise funds for emergency support to victims and to reflect strategically on ways of supporting migrant workers in China. With China hosting the Fourth World Summit on Women in Beijing in 1995, a raft of new autonomous women's organizations emerged, including a few concerned with female migrant workers such as the Beijing Migrant Women's Club (Franceschini 2014; Howell 1997a; Kaufman 2012). This provided an opening for the Hong Kong supporters of the emergency campaign for victims of the Zhili factory fire to forge closer connections with women workers in nearby Shenzhen. Female activists from Hong Kong set up the Chinese Working Women's Network in 1996, with an outpost in Shenzhen, to empower women migrant workers in China (Pun and Chan 2004). This was one of the first labour NGOs to be formed in China.

Furthermore, in 1994 Han Dongfang, a key leader in the 1989 autonomous workers' movement, who had eventually fled to Hong Kong, established the *China Labour Bulletin* with the goal of keeping international trade unions abreast of the situation of workers in China and providing information to workers in China about the role of trades unions and labour events. As will be seen in the next section, from the late 1990s onwards, labour NGOs began to grow, often with the support of Hong Kong groups, blossoming during the more politically open administration of Hu Jintao and Wen Jiabao (Hu-Wen).

New ways of labour organizing in China: The Hu-Wen period (2002–2012)

In 2002 China entered the World Trade Organization and Chinese enterprises were encouraged to 'go global'. This economic openness not only deepened China's engagement with the global capitalist economy but also fostered opportunities for civic groups in China to make international links. The Hu-Wen administration was a more open period of governance. It set the stage for closer international ties and alliances between Chinese and international workers' organizations, including trades unions, labour NGOs, and labour researchers. It also paved the way for further legislation aimed at curbing violations of labour laws, bolder efforts by progressive trades unionists to experiment with reform, and a deepening of labour movement organizing reflected in the 2010 Honda strikes. It was also during this period that civil society in general and labour NGOs in particular began to proliferate.

During the first decade of the millennium, workers were becoming more adept at organizing protest, appropriating the language of law to legitimize their claims, taking their cases to mediation committees and the courts, and accumulating skills, tactics, and experience (Chen and Tang 2013; Elfstrom 2019). As observed by many scholars, there was considerable variation in the scale, sources of grievances, forms of collective action, and worker–state relations across industries and regions (Elfstrom 2019: 249; Lee 2007). There were continuing efforts to set up alternative trades unions, though as before these were quickly suppressed.

On the legislative front two pieces of legislation were introduced during the Hu-Wen period: the 2008 Contract Law and the 2011 Social Insurance Law. The Contract Law sought to temper the excesses of contracting practice, such as keeping workers on short one-year contracts for many years and denying them the benefits accruing to permanent employees. It also sought to address the precarious situation of dispatch workers and student interns, whose companies used to deal with fluctuations in market demand. It required employers to sign a contract with workers within thirty days, if not, it could be assumed there was a contract (Leung and So 2013). Workers who had more than two terms of service or ten years of employment were to be given an open-ended contract. It allowed greater room for the trade union to engage in collective negotiation with employers. The draft law met with considerable opposition from the US and European chambers of commerce. However, employers soon found ways to circumvent the law by pushing workers with many years of employment to resign and be reappointed as new employees (Leung and So 2013: 148–149). The 2011 Social Insurance Law was also significant in that it attempted to make provision for informal workers to access welfare by contributing to social insurance schemes, and enabled workers to transfer their social insurance entitlements from province to province. Both laws provided a legitimate vehicle through which to make their claims to individual (but not collective) rights. After the 2008 Contract Law, for example, there was a sharp increase in the number of cases taken to the mediation committees and courts (Leung and So 2013: 150).

The ACFTU, too, was under pressure from the central government to reform. To this end it experimented with collective bargaining in state enterprises (Chan and Hui 2014; Zhou and Yan 2020) and democratically elected enterprise-based trades unions (Howell 2008). The ACFTU played a key role in drafting legislation for the 2008 Contract Law and coordinating the wide public consultation process that was held with employers, lawyers, experts, and some labour NGOs. It went on to establish over 800 legal aid centres to ensure implementation of the law, though at enterprise level, where unions tended to be subordinate to management, enforcement remained problematic (Chen 2009; Leung and So 2013: 150). It set up community trades unions, regional trades unions, and regional trades unions based on industry as a way to better protect informal workers (Liu 2011). It should be noted that the ACFTU was not a wholly monolithic organization. At the local level there were enthusiastic and committed trade union cadres who pushed the boundaries in the more open Hu-Wen period around issues such as democratically elected trades unions and collective bargaining.

Parallel to this, ex-workers, labour activist lawyers, and academics began to set up labour NGOs, often with the support of Hong Kong labour groups (Elfstrom 2019). A labour NGO focuses its goals and activities on addressing workers' interests, rights, and needs. It is different from a trade union in that it is not a representative organization. Labour NGOs differ in their origins, goals, size, activities, their relations with local governments, and sources of financing. Some were established by ex-workers, others by journalists or rights lawyers or academics. Their goals can vary from building a labour movement through rights' awareness and leadership training to providing cultural activities for workers (Chan 2012). Some focus on particular workers such as injured workers or female workers, while others provide legal counselling and rights training. Most are unregistered, small, grass-roots' organizations, with a small number of staff, usually no more than five, and a cortege of volunteers, often students. They carry out a range of activities, such as providing services such as legal advice, second-hand clothes sales, and libraries; organizing cultural activities such as choirs, theatre groups, walks, or after-school activities for their children; rights' awareness training and leadership training; corporate social responsibility work such as monitoring; and organizing international events that bring Chinese and international labour activists together. Some labour NGOs have managed to grow in scale, particularly those carrying out monitoring work in factories for international companies engaged in CSR work or carrying out research for international agencies.

Most were located in Guangdong province, where export-oriented manufacturing dominated, but over the decade they sprouted in other major industrial centres across China (Chan 2012; Froissart 2011; Xu 2013). As many labour NGOs were not registered with the authorities, it was impossible to know precisely how many existed. Various researchers estimate that there were between 40 and 100 labour NGOs across China by the end of the decade (Franceschini 2014; Froissart 2011; Howell 2015). As Gallagher et al. (2011: 13–14) observed, labour NGOs, in the context of poorly implemented labour laws and an ineffective official trades union, provided a potential avenue for protecting workers from processes of informalization and casualization.

The bulk of labour NGOs' funding came from international sources such as project funding from Hong Kong groups that had in turn applied for grants from international foundations and trades unions. Some labour NGOs received money directly from embassies, international foundations, and NGOs. Labour NGOs that cultivated good relations with local government officials or local trades unions might receive small amounts of government funding to run training events or organize cultural activities. Companies also provided some funding to labour NGOs for organizing cultural activities or carrying out CSR tasks such as monitoring of factory codes. In addition, labour NGOs could charge fees for legal advice or raise money through sales of goods such as second-hand clothes. However, NGOs could not rely on a steady source of income. Some were adept at attracting sufficient funds from various international donors to sustain themselves for several years or develop in scale; most relied on short-term project money, unable to guarantee organizational development or retain staff.

As Lee and Shen observe (2011), labour NGOs face the dual risks of co-optation by government and commercialization through market demands. As with all types of NGOs, labour NGOs that cooperate with government in services provision can become subject to mission drift (Froehlich 1999) and loss of autonomy (Bennett and Savani 2011), adopting the goals of their funders rather than pursuing the interests and needs of the people for whom they claim to work. New funding opportunities through government or company contracts can push NGOs towards focussing on the survival and development of the organization over and above the needs of workers, a trend from which labour NGOs are not exempt. As will be seen in the Xi period, pressures of co-optation increased with the extension of nationwide, formal contracting.

As labour issues are deemed sensitive in China, labour NGO relations with local government officials can be fraught, with many facing persistent harassment, eviction, and on occasions the brute force of gangs hired by companies or local government officials. NGOs forced to move offices or close down have resisted by relocating elsewhere and/or changing their names. However, some gained the confidence of local government officials and local trades unions. From the perspective of local governments, labour NGOs could fill valuable gaps in services for migrant workers such as cultural activities, legal counselling and support, and education. They were invited to assist them with organizing events, receiving in return a small amount of funding, a venue for activities, and legitimacy from government approval (Cheng et al. 2010). Some labour NGOs preferred to keep local officials at bay and pursue their goals without interference. In general, labour NGOs avoided directly mobilizing workers to take action against poor working conditions in factories, focussing more on behind-the-scene rights' awareness, putting pressure on government to revise labour laws, and developing migrant workers' bargaining and negotiation skills (Froissart 2011).

However, there were a small number of labour NGOs which supported workers in collective bargaining processes and strikes. In 2010, workers at a Honda factory in Guangdong province went on strike for higher wages. The forward-thinking head of Guangdong provincial TU supported the idea of electing workers to negotiate with employers through a collective-bargaining process. The central government had been promoting the idea of collective bargaining for several years, primarily in state enterprises, but the model of collective bargaining promoted did not include worker representation (Chan and Hui 2014). A few labour NGOs, along with labour scholars, played a role in providing legal advice to Honda workers around negotiating for worker representation. The success of the Honda workers in achieving higher wages led to a wave of strikes across the province and boosted the confidence of workers in other sectors to put forward demands. This in turn encouraged some labour NGOs, particularly those with relations to Hong Kong labour NGOs, to focus increasingly on developing leadership and collective-bargaining skills amongst workers, with the ultimate aim of building a labour movement across China. Similarly, in 2014, when workers in the Yu Yuan shoe factory in Dongguan, Guangdong province, struck to demonstrate their dissatisfaction with the poor implementation of the 2011 Social Insurance Law, a labour NGO from nearby Shenzhen provided crucial legal advice to the workers (Jakimow 2021: 3).

Though labour NGOs played a variety of roles in supporting migrant workers, they also faced criticism from some labour studies scholars. Lee and Shen (2011), for example, wrote a provocative piece describing labour NGO as 'anti-solidarity machines'. The argument ran that labour NGOs providing legal counselling channelled workers into finding individual solutions to their predicaments through the law, rather than collective solutions calling for solidarity. Franceschini (2014) similarly queries the assumption that labour NGOs are a positive force of political change, highlighting their tenuous relationship with workers and their lack of social capital. Such critiques in turn reflect the expectations that different actors had of labour NGOs. As Franceschini points out, there was an expectation within the international labour movement that labour NGOs were nascent independent trades unions, though there is little evidence to support such an assumption.

Labour NGOs can also be criticized in terms of their willingness on occasions to perpetuate stereotypic depictions of migrants. For example, some NGOs that received government funding to assist in integrating migrant workers into the cities were complicit in perpetuating images of migrants' 'low quality' (*suzhi di*) and the need for them to conform to an acceptable notion of being modern and urban (Jakimow 2021: 218–219). However, as Jakimow's detailed study of migrant worker NGOs revealed, there were also a good number of migrant worker NGOs that used this funding to raise awareness about the structural discrimination against migrant workers and in particular the exclusionary hukou system. The precarity of the workplace was thus closely aligned to the existential precarity of migrants in the cities and their exclusion from citizenship (ibid.).

As Gallagher et al. (2011: 12–13) noted, labour NGOs, in the absence of an effective trades union and laws, offered a way forward in addressing the issues of informalization and casualization that migrant workers experienced. Initially, most labour NGOs' attention focussed on the manufacturing and construction sectors. However, their work also shifted as new issues, such as student interns and the use of dispatch workers as a reserve army of labour, emerged (Friedman and Lee 2010). As China from 2010 onwards embarked on upgrading its industrial strategy and moving away from overreliance on export-oriented processing and assembly production, the services sector became increasingly prominent as a key source of employment. The application of digital technology and algorithms to the organization of work in the services sector marked a deepening of processes of casualization and informalization. As elsewhere in the world, this type of work was often, and misleadingly, conceptualized as self-employed as a way of reducing production costs, transferring risks, and minimizing any duties of care.

Digital platforms using algorithms to determine the intensity of work, distribution of orders, and assessment of workers' performance reflected new technology-based ways of controlling labour in the gig economy. Food delivery workers, warehouse workers employed in packing goods purchased online, couriers, and taxi drivers represented a growing body of casual workers, who were paid according to assignment, resulting in unstable incomes. However, so-called gig workers were beyond the scope of the official ACFTU and unprotected by existing labour legislation. Due to the casual and atomized nature of their work, they were particularly hard to organize. With the demise of labour NGOs, an increasingly harsh political environment, and the structural limitations of the ACFTU to address formal, let alone informal sector workers' needs, the challenges for organizing gig workers were profound.

As the Hu-Wen period drew to a close, new opportunities and risks arose for labour NGOs in the form of government funding for welfare services contracting. Though experiments with contracting out welfare services to social organizations had taken off from 2007 onwards in cities such as Shenzhen, Beijing, and Guangzhou, these mainly focussed on basic services such as care of the elderly or youth services (Chan 2018; Leung and Xu 2015). Signs of a turn in the government's approach came in 2011 when the Ministry of Civil Affairs announced plans to ease the registration process to facilitate NGOs in applying for government contracts to deliver services. In Guangdong province, the trade union organized a special conference for NGOs interested in delivering services for the trade union, such as legal counselling or organizing cultural events for workers (Franceschini 2014). Labour NGOs invited to this event reacted with surprise and scepticism at this overture, given local government's persistent harassment and suspicion of labour NGOs. However, some saw it as an opportunity to access government funding and foster better relations with local officials. As will be seen in the next section, the new Xi Jiping administration was to roll out the policy of welfare services' contracting across the country, whilst also clamping down on groups it deemed troublesome.

Organizing around precarity under Xi Jinping

Under the Xi administration (2012–) the situation for labour NGOs, rights lawyers, and labour activists worsened. The nationwide extension of welfare services contracting to NGOs signalled in the 2013 Guiding Opinions built upon the previous experimentation in services contracting to NGOs under the Hu-Wen regime. As the policy unfolded, it became increasingly clear that contracting was part of a broader strategy to strengthen services-focussed NGOs that were instrumentally useful to the government, while simultaneously reducing the space for rights-based NGOs, including labour NGOs, to operate and survive (Howell 2015, 2021).

Labour NGOs reacted in different ways to the invitation to collaborate with government in services provision. Some refused because they did not expect to be granted a contract as they were too small in scale, lacked qualified social workers, or did not have close relations with government which they perceived as necessary to obtain a contract. Others refused on the grounds that working with government could compromise their autonomy and restrict the type of work they could do. As the leader of a labour NGO that sought to organize workers through music commented, 'We are in the government's eye ... they would not welcome us. We wouldn't be able to do the things they wanted ... We would need to change our style, the content of what we do ... and the songs we sing would not be what they wanted.'[3]

However, some labour NGOs took the opportunity of applying for government funds. Those that had already worked with government before were well positioned to obtain contracts, not just through competitive application but also through entrustment. For example, a well-established NGO working with migrants in Beijing had already conducted numerous projects for the city government and was approached to serve as a third-party agency tasked with capacity-building of NGOs.[4] Not all labour NGOs with past records of working with government could secure contracts. For example, a labour NGO in Beijing that had done considerable work on dispute mediation and enjoyed good relations with local officials found this work dried up after contracting. Unwilling to forgo rights work, the NGO leader was reluctant to engage in services contracting. In his words, 'In Shenzhen it is not possible to do rights work. It is all about services, legal services . . . We've learned that there is no way to do government contract work because the government decides what you do and there is no way you can do rights work.'[5] Some NGOs found ways of pursuing their goals of advocacy and rights work while also obtaining government contracts. This might be by securing other sources of funding and running advocacy and rights work through these channels. For example, the aforementioned labour NGO that specialized in mediation work planned to establish a social enterprise as a way to continue with their rights work.[6] In other instances it might be by altering the name of their organization to obscure some of their activities or establishing a separate organization to do rights work.

While the Party-state was on the one-hand incorporating services-oriented NGOs through the technique of contracting, it was also clamping down on organizations and individuals it deemed sensitive and threatening to stability. Since their emergence in the late 1990s, labour NGOs had always faced harassment, surveillance, and on occasions state violence. Some had had to move offices several times as local government officials, keen to preserve the interests of employers, pressured them to halt their work. Under the Xi administration, the Party/state unleashed an enduring wave of repression against rights lawyers, feminists, labour NGO leaders, and labour activists in 2015,[7] affecting too the ACFTU's appetite for any further reforms.

The situation was compounded by the passing of the Overseas NGOs Law in 2016 (effective 2017). A first step towards this law took place in Yunnan province in 2010 when the provincial government signalled its intention to register overseas NGOs, triggering alarm amongst domestic and international NGOs that it portended a tightening up of foreign NGO activity (Teets 2015). According to the 2016 Law, overseas NGOs were required to register with the Ministry of Public Security, in contrast to domestic NGOs that registered with the Ministry of Civil Affairs. This suggested the degree of sensitivity within the Party/state about overseas NGOs' activities and funding in China, and particularly the risk that foreign agencies might have a political agenda of undermining the regime, as had purportedly occurred in the Colour Revolutions in Kyrgyzstan, Georgia, and Ukraine. The law had a chilling effect on international NGOs, which now faced much tighter scrutiny and control of their activities and limitations on their funding scope. For labour

NGOs, the 2016 Law signalled the shrivelling up of external funding, which had been crucial for NGOs working on the margins of society that could not readily raise funds locally due to government suspicion and social discrimination. Though some labour NGOs were still able to access some funds from the UN and foreign embassies, most were left floundering. Some began to consider alternative sources of funding such as setting up social enterprises or approaching companies for cultural activity projects. With the option of foreign funding severely reduced, the state became the dominant provider of funding to the emerging service-focussed NGO sector.

The repression intensified further following the strike of workers at a JASICS factory in Huizhou, Guangdong province, in the summer of 2018. The workers planned to form an independent trade union to organize around low wages and poor working conditions. The firing of the striking employees led to further demonstrations in Shenzhen and an upsurge of support in social media and amongst students. A group of neo-Maoist students travelled south to organize in solidarity with the workers. However, a potential alliance of workers and students triggered alarm bells for the CCP leaders, who perceived this as a threat to social and regime stability. Added to this, the JASIC strike was attracting considerable international attention. Security forces swiftly swept down on the apartment where the students were based, arresting several activists and weakening the alliance between workers and students.

Repression has continued to date, with numerous labour NGOs closed down or cowed into self-censorship and inactivity. As the director of a Hong Kong labour NGO recounted, 'There were once 80 labour NGOs across the country. Now there are only about 10 to 20 left.'[8] Similarly, another Hong Kong labour NGO commented, 'It is more difficult now for us to position ourselves in China as a Hong Kong NGO. It is a death or life point. Before we had ten groups we worked with. After the JASIC incident in Pingshan, which involved new Maoists, only 10–20% of labour groups are left in the South. Even before JASIC, only a few groups were left after the 2015 wave of suppression.'[9] In the wake of widespread protests against the National Security Law in Hong Kong, the Hong Kong government, under pressure from the CCP, has arrested rights lawyers, democratic activists, local democratic representatives, and numerous protest leaders. This in turn has affected the possibilities for Hong Kong labour NGOs to form alliances with mainland labour NGOs.

This has put further pressure on labour NGOs to focus on services that correspond to government priorities and move away from rights work to more politically innocuous activities such as after-school clubs for migrant workers' children and cultural activities. For example, a labour NGO in Shenzhen that had focused on women workers and labour rights switched to running activities for the children of migrant workers and women workers.[10] Following the crackdown on public interest lawyers, labour activists and feminists in 2015, a legal advice NGO transformed itself into a social work organization to access government contracts for working with youth and children of migrant workers, and integrating migrant workers into the community. However, they continued to do their legal work through other sources of funding and connections advice work.[11]

The final nail on the head came with the March 2021 Notice 'Eliminating the Breeding Ground for Illegal Organizations' which sought to constrict the spaces where independent civic organizing could develop. Several lists of illegal organizations were drawn up, including both national and provincial level organizations. The Notice heralded a crackdown on those grey, limbo areas where NGOs were unregistered yet tolerated. The future of labour NGOs was now under considerable threat. Even if they agreed to compete for government services contracts, such funding was still precarious, administratively burdensome, and limited to service activities rather than rights or advocacy work. The future development of labour NGOs looked bleak. However, the activities, new approaches to mobilizing workers, strategies, connections, and personal bonds of labour NGOs and activists that had been built up over 20 years formed a legacy of activism that could still be revived in the future.

As well as repressing groups and individuals perceived as socially destabilizing, the Party-state also intensified its grip over society by requiring all non-state institutions, including registered labour NGOs to establish Party cells. In September 2015 the central government issued Notice 51 'Opinion on Strengthening Party-building in Social Organizations'. Though some labour NGOs perceived that as a formality that would have minimal impact on their activities, subsequent legislation suggested a much more intrusive Party presence. For example, the following year Shenzhen government issued a notice requiring social organizations to include Party work in their constitutions and provide room for the Party to express its views on internal policies such as activities, external events, and donations.[12] In some localities forming a Party cell became a condition for receiving a government contract.

Given the crushing and co-optation of labour NGOs, the weakness of the ACFTU, and the increasingly harsh political climate, organizing around informal workers has become harder. There is some evidence that despite the digitalized control of gig workers, some forms of resistance can and are emerging. Current work on gig workers in China suggests that gig workers' grievances as in the manufacturing sector and construction sectors tend to pivot around wages, health and safety, and the intensity of work. Piece rates have formed a key point of contention amongst gig workers in China, informing both public and more hidden collective action. Globally, gig economy workers have found it difficult to organize. While there are some independent trades unions such as the Independent Trade Union in the UK, the atomized nature of work with individuals employed on highly variable terms makes collective action difficult. In an authoritarian regime that curtails independent collective action, the possibilities for action are highly constricted and the stakes of resistance are much higher. Despite tight censorship of digital media in China, social media has still been able to provide a vehicle not only for venting grievances but also for mobilizing resistance to exploitative labour practices.

In their study of the food delivery company, Ele.me, Liu and Friedmann (2021) recount how platform delivery workers employed through a system of sub-contracting developed forms of resistance to their immediate employers. The system of sub-stations where workers were given their delivery orders were paid and assessed on their performance also provided them with some bargaining power. The platform technology also exerted control over the managers of sub-stations, whose performance would be assessed according to the numbers of orders they received and customer feedback. Liu and Friedmann (2021) describe how workers in a sub-station coordinated their actions online through WeChat to interrupt the delivery flow, effectively mounting a strike. By refusing to sign on for delivery orders, workers reduced the supply of delivery workers, causing customer dissatisfaction and eventually affecting the performance of the sub-station and the rewards to the manager. Unlike the Honda strikes of 2010, these work stoppages were short-lived, defensive, and hidden, as they took place online rather than on the streets (Liu and Friedmann 2021: 79). Being hidden, they attracted little media attention and were less politically risky compared to factory sit-ins, petitioning outside government departments, or demonstrating in the streets. Unlike the large-scale Honda strikes the ACFTU at the central or local level played no role in mediating or resolving these collective acts of resistance. This contrasted with the role of traditional unions in some Western countries such as the UK in organizing food-delivery workers such as at Deliveroo.

In 2020, the China Labour Bulletin's (CLB) Strike Map documented 27 protests by couriers in 2019, increasing to 25 up to September 2020, the main grievances being around wage arrears. In October 2020, the Beijing municipal trade union finalized a collective agreement on health and safety of workers with the Industry Federation of Express Delivery. This covered issues such as the legally required payment of work-related injury insurance contributions for workers. According to the CLB, the ACFTU had reportedly prioritized delivery workers as a major sector to focus on, but this has had little impact on their situation, and gig workers continued to find their own ways of resisting. Though the Xi administration has either co-opted or crushed labour NGOs, it has not been able to halt worker protest or address the fundamental structural problems underlying informalization.

Conclusion

In this chapter we traced the shift from employment and livelihood security during the Maoist decades to labour precarity in the post-Mao era. This was a gradual process that had its roots in the introduction of labour markets through contracts in the Special Economic Zones. The 1994 Labour Law legitimized the use of contracts across all forms of ownership, smashing the 'iron rice bowl' of state enterprise workers once and for all. In practice many workers were employed without any form of agreements. Informalization and casualization were increasingly becoming the norm. The 2008 Contract Law sought to rein in some of the excesses of informalization enabling, in theory at least, contract workers employed for 10 years to become permanent. By this time the gig economy brought in digital ways of controlling informal labour, involving digital platforms, algorithms, and highly atomized service workers in a range of industries. This posed new challenges to worker organizing and opened up forms of resistance through disrupting the digital flow of production.

We considered the roles of workers, unions, and labour NGOs in improving labour conditions of migrant informal workers. Whilst the more open political climate of the Hu-Wen period allowed for some advances in trade union reform, albeit limited, and for the blossoming of labour NGOs, the subsequent Xi period led to the demise of labour NGOs and the stalling of any further trade union reform. Though Xi Jinping had urged trades unions to be more proactive and effective in dealing with workers' grievances, the closed and constrained political environment dampened enthusiasm and inhibited the initiative of trade union cadres.

Given the multiple employment configurations of informal workers, the possibilities for collective action are varied. Mobilizing gig workers employed in service industries is challenging, given the highly atomized nature of the work. Nevertheless, as recent studies have shown, social media and deliberate disruption of digitally controlled production can provide an avenue for expressing grievances and mounting some resistance. In an authoritarian context such as China, the absence of multiple free trades unions, a constrained civil society, internet censorship, and an incorporated, official trades union present significant obstacles to worker mobilization, whether factory-based or app-led. Informal workers will continue to use classic modes of resistance such as voting with their feet, sabotage, slow-downs, and using personal connections to express grievances. Social media, despite high levels of state censorship, still provides a way of contesting oppressive working conditions and forging worker solidarity. Looking ahead, the new approaches, achievements, experiences, skills, tactics, and worker leadership-building worker that emerged during the Hu-Wen era provide a legacy of activism that can still inspire in the future.

Notes

1. See Mallet (2020: 273–274) for a useful, instructive discussion of narrower and broader understandings of precarity that focus respectively on labour insecurity and precarity as a condition of broader life.
2. There are other ways of periodizing labour organizing. For example, Gallagher et al. (2011) map out three phases of 1978 to 1995, 1995–2007, and 2007 onwards. While these pivot around key labour legislation, our periodization contextualizes the changes within different leaderships. This is crucial for understanding how the more open politics during the Hu-Wen era facilitated the flourishing of labour NGOs, some innovative reform steps in the ACFTU, and worker-led struggles for representative collective bargaining.
3. Leader of labour NGO in southern city, December 2018.
4. Interview 40, director of labour NGO, December Beijing, 2018.
5. Interview 46, labour NGO leader, December 2018.
6. Interview 46, labour NGO leader, December 2018.
7. Franceschini and Nessosi (2018).
8. Interview 71, Director, Hong Kong Labour NGO, April 2019.
9. Interview 70, Director, Hong Kong Labour NGO, April 2019.
10. Interview, 34, NGO Director, C, November 2018.
11. Interview 33, B, Director, November 2018.
12. See Shenzhen City Social Organizations Committee and Shenzhen City Social Organizations Management Bureau Notice regarding promoting social organizations to put Party work into their constitution (Shenzhen City Social organizations Management Bureau 2017).

References

Bennett, R. and Savani, S. (2011) 'Surviving mission drift: How charities can turn dependence on government contracting to their own advantage'. *Nonprofit Management and Leadership*, 22(2): 217–231.

Brooker, P. (2000) *Non-Democratic Regimes: Theory, Government and Politics*. Basingstoke: Macmillan.

Chan, A. (2005) 'Recent trends in China labour issues—Signs of change'. *China Perspectives*, 57, January–February: 23–31.

Chan, C. K. (2012) 'Community-based organisations for migrant workers' rights: The emergence of labour NGOs in China'. *Journal of Community Development*, 48(1): 6–22.

Chan, C. K. (2018) 'Introduction: Contracting out social services in China'. In J. Lei, and K. Chan (eds.), *China's Social Welfare Revolution: Contracting Out Social Services*. Abingdon: Routledge, pp. 1–11.

Chan, C. K. and Hui, E. S. (2014) 'The development of collective bargaining in China: From "collective bargaining by riot" to "Party State-led wage bargaining"'. *The China Quarterly*, 217: 221–242.

Chan, C. K. and Pun, N. (2009) 'The making of a new working class? A study of collective actions of migrant workers in South China'. *China Quarterly*, 198: 287–304.

Chan, J. and Pun, N. (2010) 'Suicide as protest for the new generation of Chinese migrant workers: Foxconn, global capital and the state'. *The Asia-Pacific Journal*, 37(2): 1–50.

Chang, L. T. (2008) *Factory Girls: Voices from the Heart of Modern China*. London: Picador.

Chen, F. (2009) 'Union power in China: Source, operation and constraints'. *Modern China*, 35: 662–689.

Chen, F. and Tang, M. (2013) 'Labour conflicts in China: Typologies and their implications'. *Asian Survey*, 53(3): 559–583.

Cheng, J., Ngok, K., and Zhuang, W. (2010) 'The survival and development space for China's labour NGOs: Informal politics and its uncertainty'. *Asian Survey*, 50(6): 1082–1106.

Clarke, S. and Pringle, T. (2011) *The Challenge of Transition: Trade Unions in Russia, China and Vietnam*. Palgrave, Macmillan.

Crane, G. (2000) *The Political Economy of China's SEZs*. New York: M.E.Sharpe.

Elfstrom, M. (2019) 'A tale of two Deltas: Labour politics in Jiangsu and Guangdong'. *British Journal of Industrial Relations*, 57(2), June: 247–274.

Franceschini, I. (2014) 'Labour NGOs in China: A real force for political change'. *The China Quarterly*, 281, June: 474–492.

Franceschini, I. and Nessosi, E. (2018) 'State repression of Chinese labour NGOs: A chilling effect?' *China Journal*, 80: 111–129.

Friedman, E. and Lee, C. K. (2010) 'Remaking the world of Chinese labour: A 30-year retrospective'. *British Journal of Industrial Relations*, 48: 507–533.

Friedrich, C. and Brzezinski, Z. K. (1956) *Totalitarian Dictatorship and Autocracy*. Cambridge, MA: Harvard University Press.

Froehlich, K. A. (1999) 'Diversification of revenue structure: Evolving resource dependency'. *Non-Profit and Voluntary Sector Quarterly*, 28(3): 246–268.

Froissart, C. (2011) 'NGOs' defending migrant workers' rights: Semi-union organisations contribute to the regime's dynamic stability'. *China Perspectives*, 2: 18–25.

Gallagher, M. (2017) *Authoritarian Legality in China: Law, Workers and the State*. Cambridge: Cambridge University Press.

Gallagher, M. E., Lee, C. K., and Kuruvilla, S. (2011) 'Introduction and argument'. In S. Kuruvilla et al. (eds.), *From Iron Rice Bowl to Informalisation: Markets, Workers and the State in a Changing China*. Ithaca, NY: Cornell University Press.

Harper, P. (1969) 'The Party and the Unions in Communist China'. *The China Quarterly*, 37, January–March: 84–119.

Howell, J. (1993) *China Opens Its Doors: The Politics of Economic Transition*. Boulder, Colorado: Lynne Rienner Publishers.

Howell, J. (1997a) 'Post-Beijing reflections: Creating ripples, but not waves in China'. *Women's Studies International Forum*, 20(2): 235–252.

Howell, J. (1997b) 'Looking beyond incorporation: Chinese trade unions in the reform period'. *Mondes En Developpement*, 25: 73–90.

Howell, J. (2003) 'Trade unionism in China: Sinking or swimming?' *Journal of Communist Studies and Transition Politics*, 19(1), March: 102–122.

Howell, J. (2008) 'All-China Federation of Trades Unions beyond reform? The slow march of direct elections'. *The China Quarterly*, 196: 845–863.

Howell, J. (2015) 'Shall we dance? Welfarist incorporation and the politics of state-labour NGO relations'. *The China Quarterly*, 223, September: 702–723.

Howell, J. (2021) 'From green shoots to crushed petals: Labour NGOs in China', *Made in China*, 6(1): Jan–Apr. 102–107.

Jakimów, M. (2021) *China's Citizenship Challenge: Labour NGOs and the Struggle for Migrant Workers' Rights*. Manchester University Press.

Kaufman, J. (2012) 'The global women's movement and Chinese women's rights'. *Journal of Contemporary China*, 21(76): 585–602.

Lee, C. K. (2007) *Against the Law: Labour Protests in China's Rustbelt and Sunbelt*. University of California Press, Berkeley, CA.

Lee, C. K. and Shen, Y. (2011) 'The Anti-Solidarity Machine? Labor Nongovernmental Organizations in China'. In S. Kuruvilla et al. (eds.), *From Iron Rice Bowl to Informalisation: Markets, Workers and the State in a Changing China*. Ithaca, NY: Cornell University Press, pp. 173–187.

Lee, L. T. (1986) *Trade Unions in China: 1949 to the Present*. Singapore: University of Singapore.

Leung, J. C. B. and Xu, Y. B. (2015) *China's Social Welfare*. London: Polity Press.

Leung, P. and So, A. Y. (2013) 'The new labour contract law in 2008: China's legal absorption of labour unrest'. *Journal of Studies in Social Sciences*, 4(1): 131–160.

Leung, W. (1988) *Smashing the Iron Rice Pot: Workers and Unions in China's Market Socialism*. Hong Kong: Asia Labour Monitor Centre.

Liu, C. and Friedman, E. (2021) 'Resistance under the radar: Organization of work and collective action in China's food delivery industry'. *The China Journal*, no. 86 (July 2021) (Published online by The Australian National University).

Liu, M. (2011) '"Where there are workers, there should be trade unions": Union organising in the era of growing informal employment'. In S. Kuruvilla et al. (eds.), *From Iron Rice Bowl to Informalisation: Markets, Workers and the State in a Changing China*. Ithaca, NY: Cornell University Press, pp. 157–172.

Lu, P. (1990) *China. A Moment of Truth: Workers' Participation in China's 1989 Democracy Movement and the Emergence of Independent Union*. Hong Kong: Asia Monitor Resource Centre Ltd.

Mallet, R. W. (2020) 'Seeing the "changing nature of work" through the precarity lens'. *Global Labour Journal*, 11(3): 271–290.

Naughton, B. (2007) *The Chinese Economy: Transitions and Growth*. Cambridge: MIT Press.

O'Leary, G. (1998) 'The making of the Chinese working class'. In G. O'Leary (ed.), *Adjusting to Capitalism: Chinese Workers and the State*. New York: M.E.Sharpe, Inc., pp. 48–74.

Perry, E. (1994) 'Shanghai's strike wave of 1957'. *The China Quarterly*, 137: 1–27.

Pringle, T. (2013) *Trade Unions in China. The Challenge of Labour Unrest*. London: Routledge.

Pun, N. (2005a) 'Global production, company codes of conduct and labour conditions in China: A case study of two factories'. *The China Journal*, 54, July: 101–113.

Pun, N. (2005b) *Made in China: Women Factory Workers in a Global Workplace*. Durham and London: Duke University Press.

Pun, N. and Chan, W. (2004) 'Community based labour organising'. *International Union Rights*, 11(4): 10–11.

Swider, S. (2015) 'Building China: Precarious employment amongst migrant construction workers'. *Work, Employment and Society*, 29(1): 41–59.

Takahara, A. (1987) 'The politics of wage reform in post-revolutionary China', PhD thesis, IDS, University of Sussex.

Tang, W. and Parish, W. L. (2000) *Chinese Urban Life under Reform: The Changing Social Contract*. Cambridge: Cambridge University Press.

Taylor, B., Chang, K., and Li, Q. (2003) *Industrial Relations in China*. Cheltenham: Edward Elgar.

Teets, J. C. (2015) 'The evolution of civil society in Yunnan province: Contending models of civil society management in China'. *Journal of Contemporary China*, 24(91): 158–175.

Walder, A. (1986) *Communist Neo-Traditionalism: Work and Authority in Chinese Industry*. Berkeley: California University Press.

Wilson, J. L. (1990) '"The Polish lesson": China and Poland 1980-1990'. *Studies in Comparative Communism*, 23(3–4): 259–279.

Wintrobe, R. (1998) *The Political Economy of Dictatorship*. Cambridge: Cambridge University Press.

Wu, Q., Zhang, H., Li, Z., and Liu, K. (2019) 'Labour control in the gig economy: Evidence from Uber in China'. *Journal of Industrial Relations*, 61(4): 574–596.

Xu, Y. (2013) 'Labour non-governmental organisations in China: Mobilising rural migrant workers'. *Journal of Industrial Relations*, 55(2): 243–259.

Zhou, M. and Yan, G. (2020) 'Advocating workers' collective rights: The prospects and constraints facing "collective bargaining" NGOs in the Pearl River Delta, 2011–2015'. *Development and Change*, 51(4): 1044–1066.

5
Precarious Work and Challenges Facing Japanese Unionism

Arjan Keizer

Introduction

The strong rise in non-regular and often precarious employment has posed a major challenge for labour unions. Initial opposition because of a perceived threat to regular jobs and conditions of employment often motivated a strategy of exclusion (Keune 2013) and has informed criticism that unions protect 'insiders' in permanent and full-time jobs while allowing greater flexibilization for 'outsiders' in non-regular employment (Rueda 2005; Standing 2011). The recruitment and organization of non-regular workers has nowadays become a priority for many unions. However, progress has been difficult because of the character of employment (e.g. short duration of contracts, fear among workers to risk future employment opportunities) and the prevalence of precarious employment in relatively under-organized industries (Grimshaw et al. 2016). It explains why unionization rates tend to remain low and improvements to working conditions limited.

These observations also hold for Japanese unions which have often limited organization to regular workers in accordance with the strong dualism in the labour market and dominant gender perceptions that stressed the role of men as breadwinner (Gottfried and Hayashi-Kato 1998; Keizer 2008). The strong rise in the share of non-regular employment to more than one-third of workers has therefore contributed to the decline in the unionization rate to 17.1 per cent in 2020 (Survey on Trade Unions' Structure). Several Japanese unions have responded by increased attempts to organize non-regular workers, and this chapter compares the strategies developed by the two main confederations, Rengo and Zenroren, and their affiliated industrial and enterprise unions. They represented around 70 and 7 per cent of all union members respectively in 2020 (Survey on Trade Unions' Structure). The chapter will show that Japanese unionism has indeed become much more

Arjan Keizer, *Precarious Work and Challenges Facing Japanese Unionism*. In: *Temporary and Gig Economy Workers in China and Japan*. Edited by Huiyan Fu, Oxford University Press. © Oxford University Press (2023). DOI: 10.1093/oso/9780192849694.003.0006 inclusive to non-regular workers. However, three forms of dualism—in the labour market, in industrial relations, and in union identities—fragment the union movement and have hindered its ability to contest the rise in precarious employment.

The analysis draws on semi-structured interviews with over 20 representatives of departments in Rengo and Zenroren with a direct responsibility for non-regular workers and various affiliated unions. The unions affiliated to Rengo included the industrial federation for the retail industry UA Zensen, its predecessor UI Zensen, and affiliated enterprise unions at three major supermarkets.[1] The unions affiliated to Zenroren are the industrial federations Jichiroren (prefectural and municipal workers), JMITU (metal manufacturing, information, and telecommunication workers), and Seikyororen (Seikyo cooperatives' workers).[2] Union and firm documents provided additional data.

The chapter uses 'non-regular' employment as arguably the most neutral term but will refer to 'precarious' and 'contingent' employment when more appropriate. It sets out with a brief description of the structure of Japanese unionism before discussing the organization of non-regular workers by Rengo and Zenroren together with their affiliated unions. The analysis shows how important ideological differences have shaped their respective strategies. At the same time, the structures in the labour market and industrial relations can be considered dominant in explaining the successes and limitations of unionization. The chapter ends with some observations on the role of unions but also the need for more concerted social action to address precariousness.

Structure of Japanese unionism

Both Rengo and Zenroren were formally established in 1989 when the dominant national centres—Sohyo and Domei—merged to form Rengo but some critical Sohyo unions decided to form Zenroren and Zenryoku as alternative confederations. It confirms how the confederations offer *'ideological foci'* (Mouer and Kawanishi 2005: 208) which can be related back to post-war decades when employers motivated moderate employees to establish alternative and less radical enterprise unions to compete with the affiliates of powerful left-wing industrial unions (Jeong and Aguilera 2008). The national confederations, together with their affiliated industrial unions, play a coordinating role, but enterprise unions are dominant as they keep the major share of union dues, provide most officials in industry and national federations, and hold the main decision-making powers (Jeong and Aguilera 2008). Two important aspects define many enterprise unions. First, the prevalence of closed-shop or union-shop agreements means that for most workers it is 'a fairly automatic and natural action' to join the union if present (Tachibanaki and Noda 2000: 27). Secondly, most unions, particularly those affiliated with Rengo, show strong cooperation with management. There is a mutual understanding between management and the enterprise union that they 'are in the same boat' and that 'survival or prosperity is the ultimate goal' (Suzuki 2004: 15).

The dominance of enterprise unions limits the access to unions for workers in two fundamental ways. First, less than 10 per cent of all firms have an enterprise union, with unions much more prevalent among large firms (JILPT 2013). Workers at smaller firms, therefore, have limited access to unionization (Mouer and Kawanishi 2005). Secondly, membership has long been limited to the regular workforce as the sole members of the firm 'community' (Inagami and Whittaker 2005; Jeong and Aguilera 2008; Urano and Stewart 2009; Weathers 2010). Non-regular workers were considered an employment buffer to support the survival of the firm and the employment of regular employees (Chalmers 1990). The unionization rate is indicative: as late as 2000 only 2.6 per cent of 'short-term workers' were union members and they made up a mere 2.3 per cent of total union membership (Survey on Trade Unions' Structure). It shows that Japanese unions have long complemented and confirmed the dualism in the labour market (Yun 2010) and explains why they have been described as 'unable' and 'unwilling' to organize non-regular workers (Broadbent 2008: 168). Urano and Stewart (2009: 28, 35–36) see Rengo and its affiliates as 'unlikely vehicles for alternative strategies' because of their 'exclusionary ideology bound by the perpetuation of the cultural milieu of the secure work force'.

Alternative unions represent workers who are badly served by the enterprise unions. Both Rengo and Zenroren have regional structures with general unions (*gōdō rōso*) which organize workers at small- and medium-sized enterprises and on an individual basis. They particularly engage in assisting members in labour disputes and can be considered to serve as a 'safety net' (Takeuchi-Okuno 2012: 101). Both confederations have strengthened these regional structures and have become more proactive in organizing individuals and smaller firms (Oh 2012). A related development has been the rise in community unions, 'labour unions organized at the regional level with their membership drawn from workers employed by different firms' (Suzuki 2008: 499). Well-known examples include the Edogawa union from 1994, the Tokyo Managers Union from 1993, and the Women's Union Tokyo from 1995

(Oh 2012; Royle and Urano 2012). The lack of enterprise unions and the rise in non-regular employment provide these alternative structures and unions with a large pool of potential members. However, they face important challenges, including small membership, a weak financial base, and a shortage of professional staff (Suzuki 2008; Weathers 2010). Union shop agreements and majority rights also limit their ability to organize employees in unionized workplaces. Consequently, they account for less than 1 per cent of total union membership and have failed to substantially raise the unionization rate among non-regular workers.

The inclusion of precarious workers

The strong rise in non-regular employment means that many workplaces have become highly dependent on these workers. This quantitative importance often has qualitative implications. For example, many part-timers in retail work long hours, sometimes more than 35 hours a week, and are considered part of the core workforce. It has inspired qualifications such as 'quasi part-timers' (Passet 2003), 'core part-time workers', and 'fulltime part-time workers' (Tsuchida 2004). At the same time, working conditions remain secondary to those of regular employees (Keizer 2019). These developments have informed initiatives to organize non-regular workers, albeit with contrasting interpretations as to whether unions are driven by the plight of non-regular workers or the ambition to maintain cooperative industrial relations. The remainder of this section discusses the initiatives by Rengo and Zenroren, including their affiliated unions. It draws on a framework developed by Hyman (1997: 515) which considers three fundamental questions that unions need to answer: 'whose interests they represent, which issues they embrace as relevant . . . and what methods and procedures they adopt in undertaking this task'. Hyman also speaks about the *who* (types of employees), *what* (objectives), and *how* (strategies) of representation.

Rengo

Representatives acknowledged that Rengo 'is sometimes regarded as the union only for the members of the big companies and male workers'. However, it has developed several initiatives to strengthen the organization of non-regular workers, including the establishment of the 'Part-timers Joint Struggle Council' (*Pāto Kyoto Kaigi*) in 2006 and the Department of Non-Regular Employment (*Hiseiki Rōdō Sentā*) in 2007. The latter initially aimed to collaborate with NGOs to respond to social problems such as the rise in working poor, but since 2010 has focused on the organization of part-time workers under the slogan 'Let's start from the workplace' (*'shokunōba kara hajimeyō'*). The industrial federation UA Zensen has been particularly successful in this respect, accounting for more than 80 per cent of all non-regular union members in Japan (Keizer 2019).

The decision to organize non-regular workers was informed by their rising share but also by changes in the character of employment (longer hours, greater responsibilities) and the employees concerned (i.e. non-regular 'breadwinners'). The rising number meant that organization was not only crucial to guarantee a 'future for the union' but also to show that Rengo was 'the sole labour organization to represent Japanese workers'. Greater responsibilities of non-regular employees meant that the differences with regular workers in wages and working conditions were not only considered unfair but also endangered overall working conditions. Full-time contract workers and part-timers with longer hours have been the priority as illustrated by the three enterprise unions affiliated with UA Zensen organizing workers employed for more than 20 hours per week. It shows that the *who* of organization remained largely limited to those who can be relatively easily integrated within the 'firm community'. This was also illustrated by the relatively poor progress in organizing agency workers (Keizer 2019).

The *how* of organization confirmed the dominance of enterprise unions. Almost all Rengo members belong to industrial federations (Table 5.1) which almost exclusively organize members through enterprise unions where they can draw on the established relations with management:

> In such workplaces there is a collective bargaining relation, so it is possible . . . to improve the working conditions of the non-regular workers. If we could succeed in improving the working conditions of non-regular workers in such organized workplaces, it could have a good influence on the working conditions of others and increase the working conditions of all non-regular workers.

Representatives of UA Zensen ascribed their organizing success to the character of the former UI Zensen as more centralized than other industrial federations and thus with stronger leadership over its enterprise unions. Two further aspects defined the initiatives (Keizer 2019). First, most enterprise unions had a union shop agreement which contributed to very high levels of membership, often more than 90 per cent of all employees who qualified. Secondly, both the establishment of new enterprise unions and the inclusion of

Table 5.1 Union membership data (x 1,000)

	2001	2005	2010	2015	2016	2017	2018	2019	2020
All workers	11,212	10,138	9,988	9,882	9,940	9,981	10,070	10,088	10,115
Non-regular workers	280	389	726	1,025	1,131	1,208	1,296	1,333	1,375
Rengo	7,120	6,672	6,876	6,891	6,880	6,929	6,992	6,991	7,020
- Industry affiliation	7,001	6,543	6,732	6,749	6,753	6,799	6,861	6,864	8,893
- Regional membership	119	129	144	142	127	130	131	127	127
UA Zensen*	-	1,025	1,289	1,536	1,607	1,685	1,767	1,772	1,799
Zenroren	1,012	954	869	805	776	771	764	755	738
- Industry affiliation	780	723	635	569	550	542	536	524	511
- Regional membership	232	231	234	236	226	229	228	231	227
Jichiroren	235	211	174	153	149	146	142	139	134
Seiyororen	71	63	66	64	63	63	64	63	63
JMIU/JMITU*	9.5	8.7	8.5	6.3	6.1	5.9	5.6	5.4	-

Note: *The data until 2010 reflect the combined membership of UI Zensen and JSD.

non-regular workers tended to involve cooperation with management. This can be linked to the prevalence of union shop agreements, as they require agreement with management, but also to the advantages that unionization was considered to offer to both employees and employers.

This approach has informed criticism for being top-down, stressing coordination with management rather than the involvement of workers, and undercutting more independent and critical unions (Weathers 2007). Moreover, the organizing success cannot hide important ongoing challenges. First, important differences existed between enterprise unions in their organizing efforts, and there was an ongoing need to change the mindset of existing regular members in some enterprise unions. Another challenge concerned the organization of non-regular workers outside enterprise unions. Rengo's prefectural centres organize both individual members and small enterprise unions. However, increased focus on these groups has not prevented a decline in individual membership, and representatives acknowledged that for 'workers in non-organized companies, it is very difficult to join'.

Cooperation with management has also characterized the objectives (*what*) of organizing as unionization was seen to offer important advantages to both the union and the firm. It gives the former a position as majority union that can act as defence against more critical voices. Unionization was also considered to give management access to the workers' voices and to support the management of so-called 'human relations' in case of poor relations between managers and their subordinates, sexual or power harassment, and conflicts about requests for paid leave. The potential differences in experience and status between regular and non-regular employees can play a major role in this respect:

> Sometimes the part-time workers have been with the company for a very long time and know the job very well. On the other hand, new regular employees have just graduated from university or high school. Part-time workers can teach these employees their job but when it comes to wages, the new employees earn much more. That can be a cause of conflict.

These aspects confirm how unionization has contributed to the inclusion of non-regular workers within the 'firm community'. Their employment security was strengthened as unions negotiated alternative employment or redundancy payments in case of store closure. Moreover, working conditions were negotiated during the annual *shuntō* and no longer set unilaterally by management. Another major improvement was through new personnel systems for non-regular workers, developed in close cooperation between management and the union, that offer better career opportunities and a potential transfer to regular employment (Keizer 2010, 2019). At the same time, the actual improvements were debatable. Only a limited number of workers were promoted, with a large majority remaining in 'standard' part-time positions. Improvements in terms of remuneration were also constrained by an employee's position as a non-regular worker and few were offered a regular position. The improved career perspectives must also be considered against the wider differentiation in employment, with many large firms having introduced regular positions with more limited working conditions such as 'area-specific' types of employment (Keizer 2010). Recent years have seen a debate on 'limited regular employment' (*gentei seiki koyō*), which has been argued to overcome the strict dualism between regular and non-regular employment but also presents a slippery slope towards nominal regular employment driven by firms' needs to control costs.

A particular issue concerns the position that unions have taken on the differences in conditions between regular and non-regular employees. Representatives of Rengo and UA Zensen acknowledged a debate within the union about whether additional compensation for non-regular workers was needed to achieve greater equality, and some enterprise unions have indeed been able to negotiate wage increases and additional bonus payments for specific groups such as contract workers. However, the same conditions that constitute the dualism in the labour market complicated these discussions as illustrated by the following assessment:

> There are some who say that to achieve equal treatment for the part-time workers, they need to be given higher wage increase. However, it is not that cut and dry. Because in the Japanese tax system, there are some people who don't want to earn more. People with such views are also part of this discussion. So, it is not that simple to say that higher wages are needed, there are many factors in play here.

Neither Rengo nor UA Zensen therefore took an explicit position, and their guidelines largely accepted the existing labour market dualism. It confirms the challenges to implementing the principle of equal pay for equal work in the Japanese context (Keizer 2019).

Zenroren

Zenroren has supported the interests of non-regular workers through its Contingent Labour Bureau which organizes various activities such as meetings with representatives of affiliated unions, campaigns to improve working conditions, and an annual congress. The confederation directly organizes almost 30 per cent of members through individual membership, but most workers are organized by the affiliated unions, both through enterprise unions and general workers' sections (Table 5.1). The three unions discussed in this chapter (Jichiroren, Seikyororen, JMITU) have organized non-regular workers from the very establishment of Zenroren, with some initiatives dating back much further. Two main considerations have informed this strategy:

> The increase in precarious workers, with worse working conditions, directly impact the quality of the services and that is why we need to organize. The second reason is [that] we need to increase the bottom, otherwise we cannot maintain the working conditions.

Non-regular members were estimated to constitute about 10 per cent of total membership for Zenroren, about 15 per cent for Jichiroren, less than 10 per cent for the JMITU, and the majority of members at Seikyororen. The latter represents the workers of the various Seikyo, particularly supermarkets and university shops, which have become highly dependent on non-regular workers.

Zenroren organizes all workers as 'precarious or contingent workers are not a group to be separated'. The *who* of organizing was thus highly inclusive, as illustrated by the strategies of the affiliated unions. For example, Seikyororen also offered membership to part-timers working only eight hours per week and subcontracted workers such as the drivers who supply the stores. Jichiroren organized workers at outsourced quasi-public entities such as public halls, swimming pools, and libraries. At the same time, there was an ongoing need to change the mindsets of members, both among regular and non-regular workers, and the leadership of some unions. The JMITU representative acknowledged how regular employees 'are affected both ideologically and politically because Japanese companies and the general political mood regard temporary workers as a kind of revolving employment'. The inclusion of non-regular workers within the unions therefore remained 'an ongoing process', with important differences linked to the share and role of non-regular employment across industries.

In accordance with this wide inclusion, the strategies (*how*) of organization ascribed an important role to individual membership through general workers' sections of prefectural and industrial unions. At the same time, it was highly challenging to increase membership: '[I]t depends on how many organizers we have, if we have more organizers to be active in the local unions, maybe we could increase this number.' The case of JMITU illustrated these challenges. It had seen a strong rise in membership—between 2,000 and 3,000 workers in the 2009–2010 period after the Lehman Shock—but 'it is also the case that when the cases were settled, they quitted the union', resulting in a very high turnover in membership. The latter was not necessarily the outcome of opportunistic behaviour by individual members as many workers lost their jobs.

Most non-regular workers were therefore organized through enterprise structures, and Zenroren acknowledged the reality of enterprise unionism. At the same time, it considered the exclusive focus on the company as a fundamental weakness that needed to be overcome through the inclusion of both regular and non-regular workers within the union and 'bottom-up' organization:

> We focus on the bottom-up style . . . to organize the struggle . . . We need some core members, we convince them to share or try to approach them by sharing the demands; what is their dissatisfaction in the workplace? By sharing their experience, we try to enlarge this small circle, often secretly. That is the initial way of organizing.

This implies the need to consult members, and many affiliated unions motivated their members to join in collective bargaining (e.g. in Seikyororen about 600 workers sit together in preparation). The unions also tried to 'to create leaders or shop stewards among the contingent worker members', not just to make them responsible for their own working conditions but also because their active involvement increases the support from regular workers. When prompted, one representative provided the following comparison to UA Zensen:

> They first go to the management and their relationship with management is very good. That is why they avoid the struggling model and try to avoid any conflict of interests with management. But at Zenroren that is not the case. We believe that management and workers have different interests and often we need to argue more. That's why management hate Zenroren. That is very different.

The differences with Rengo affiliated unions, in particular the greater secrecy of organization and need to consult members, also meant that union shop agreements were less prevalent. Several affiliated unions such as Jichiroren and Seikyororen had union shop agreements as they can strengthen the position of the union and facilitate recruitment. However, the use was not as systematic and cooperative as among Rengo unions, and the main experience concerned the challenges posed by union shop agreements of Rengo affiliated unions which made it 'almost impossible to create a minority union'.

The objectives (*what*) when representing non-regular workers depended on the form of organization. Seikyororen successfully represented non-regular workers through collective bargaining in accordance with their strong position within the firm, similar to the enterprise unions affiliated with UA Zensen. This had, for example, resulted in an agreed target to transfer more than 30,000 non-regular workers from fixed-term to open-ended contracts, new career trajectories for non-regular employees, and a system that enables transfer to regular employment. However, the very different position of the JMITU shaped its objectives and achievements. It also engaged in collective bargaining in about 180 of the 250 enterprises it had organized, but has become best known for its representation of individuals or small groups of non-regular workers. A famous example concerned their successful struggle against discrimination in wages between permanent and temporary workers at Maruko Horn Company during the 1990s. This even created the momentum to renew the Part-Time Employment Law. Another well-known example concerns the successful demand for agency workers in 'disguised outsourcing' at Koyo Sealing Technology to be offered permanent employment.

The bottom-up character of organizing supported the capacity of non-regular workers to express their concerns, and the new members have changed the objectives of representation. For example, 60 to 70 per cent of part-timers at Seikyororen were wives of male regular workers and more interested in working conditions and excessive workload than higher wages. At the same time, male non-regular workers and single mothers tended to consider higher wages as the most important demand and by 'increasing those numbers in our structure, the demands from the part-timers are also changing'. It informed discussions among non-regular members about the appropriate demands to put forward. Across all Zenroren affiliated unions, there was a strong focus on societal issues and in particular the inequalities in the labour market and their implications. For example, representatives of Seikyororen stressed the difficult position of atypical part-timers (i.e. male workers, single mothers), the gap between rich and poor, the need to change the social security system, and better support for education and housing.

Japanese unions and the position of precarious workers

The previous section has shown how Japanese unions have made important progress in the organization of non-regular workers. The rise in membership to almost 1.4 million in 2020 has been impressive and largely compensated for the declining union density among regular employees. Several unions have successfully included non-regular workers at the enterprise level, while the strengthening of regional structures and the rise of community unions has increased access through individual membership. At the same time, improvements to the position of non-regular workers have been limited. Rengo has organized many non-regular workers through UA Zensen and its affiliated unions, but the initiatives have often been top-down, excluded more precarious employment types, and have not addressed the fundamental inequalities between regular and non-regular employment. Zenroren and its affiliated unions have been more inclusive and have supported more precarious workers in the enforcement of their rights. However, they have failed to organize similar numbers of non-regular workers, and Zenroren has seen a strong decline in membership by over 25 per cent since the turn of the century (Table 5.1).

The outcomes are indicative of important differences between Rengo and Zenroren, with strong overlap in each case between the *who* (workers targeted), *how* (types of membership), and *what* (objectives) of representation. Both confederations accepted all types of non-regular workers in principle, but the realities were different. The success of enterprise unions affiliated with UA Zensen meant that almost all new members (*who*) were contract workers and part-time workers with relatively long hours. This links directly to the other two aspects of organizing as enterprise unions (*how*) remained the dominant form, and the representation of non-regular workers followed the established pattern of collective bargaining (*what*). Rengo and its unions also offer individual membership through regional structures, but the focus is clearly on enterprise unionism. The position of Zenroren and its affiliated unions was almost the opposite. Their strategies have been more inclusive through the greater share of individual membership open to all non-regular workers (*who, what*). They have also shown a stronger awareness of the weaknesses of enterprise unions and a less cooperative attitude towards management (*how*).

The inclusion of non-regular workers thus confirms and illustrates the long-term ideological differences. Rengo largely embraces enterprise unionism and this explains its focus on 'core' non-regular workers. In accordance, the inclusion of non-regular workers has not caused a redefinition of its identity, but membership has been extended. On the other hand, the identity of Zenroren is characterized by the more critical attitude towards enterprise unionism, the greater tendency to organize workers in secret, and the larger share of individual membership. The strategies of Seikyororen provide an excellent illustration. It has implemented similar strategies to the enterprise unions affiliated with UA Zensen, but also stressed the difficult position of atypical part-timers such as single parents and the need for wider changes in society. The larger share of individual members also means that Zenroren affiliated unions are more likely to represent precarious workers during litigation or to raise public awareness of their difficult position.

These outcomes show how neither Rengo nor Zenroren have been able to overcome the dualism between regular and non-regular employment. For Rengo, the historical 'embrace' of enterprise unionism has largely limited recruitment to industries with a high share of non-regular employment and workers with relatively long hours and stable employment. Moreover, the cooperative character of enterprise unionism and the predominance of union shop agreements stresses the relationship with management rather than members. It explains why unions have not taken an explicit position on the inequalities in the labour market despite some improvements and internal debate on the issue. The challenge for Zenroren is different as its unions are more inclusive towards non-regular and individual members. However, they remain constrained by the reality of enterprise unionism and the need to compete for recognition with the more cooperative unions affiliated with Rengo.

We can, therefore, distinguish a threefold dualism that hinders the inclusion of non-regular workers. Most fundamental is the dualism in the labour market between regular and non-regular types of employment (Keizer 2008, 2010). Regular employment tends to be limited to those hired after graduation and able to show a strong commitment to the organization, while others are destined for non-regular employment with secondary working conditions. This constitutes a second dualism in industrial relations between membership at the enterprise level and individual membership, with the former an expression of membership to the 'firm community' and therefore limited to those in regular and potentially other forms of stable employment. The two types of membership are formally integrated within single confederations and federations and can be considered a necessary response to the realities of the labour market. At the same time, they remain competing structures and constrain the development of broad solidarities. Finally, there is the ideological distinction between cooperative or top-down and independent or bottom-up types of unionism that tend to be represented by respectively Rengo and Zenroren with their affiliated unions. This can be considered a third dualism successive to those existing in the labour market and union structures.

This explains why Japanese unionism has failed to develop a unified voice. Figure 5.1 illustrates how the three types of dualism—in the labour market, in industrial relations, and in union identities—pull the union movement in opposing directions and fragment its voice. The inequalities in the labour market affect the other two forms of dualism with greater leverage for enterprise unions and top-down, cooperative strategies. These findings feed back, not only to the literature on insiders and outsiders (e.g. Rueda 2005; Standing 2011), but also to the need to differentiate between intentions and outcomes (Palier and Thelen 2010; Pulignano et al. 2015). Several enterprise unions, especially those affiliated with Rengo and UA Zensen, have successfully organized non-regular workers, but inclusion has been limited to more stable forms of employment, and improvements in working conditions have been limited. Unions affiliated with Zenroren have arguably been more inclusive as individual membership is open to more precarious forms of employment. However, these unions have struggled to translate these inclusive strategies into organizational success. These outcomes suggest that the different union strategies should be considered secondary to the dualism in the labour market and the dominance of enterprise unionism. Japanese unions have not initiated this dualism, nor did they support the strong rise in non-regular employment. But just as they were not able to prevent the rise of enterprise

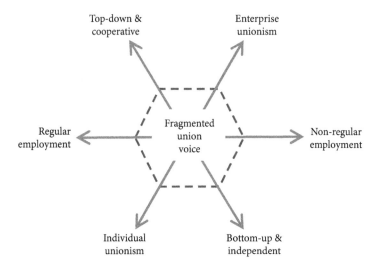

Figure 5.1 Stylized representation of union voice fragmentation

unions during the post-war period (e.g. Gordon 1985; Mouer and Kawanishi 2005), they failed to stop the rise in non-regular employment during recent decades.

The problems it poses for the successful representation of non-regular workers, particularly those in more precarious jobs, are obvious. Enterprise unionism implicitly assumes a continuous employment relationship, and this explains the successful organization of 'core' part-timers by both Seikyororen and the enterprise unions affiliated with UA Zensen. Instead, the inclusion of agency workers and non-regular workers with relatively short hours has proven highly challenging. Moreover, even when organization is successful, representation remains problematic as their cooperative character means that many enterprise unions tend to reinforce the status quo rather than become a strong voice for change. The prevalence of union shop agreements means that the workers in a firm are usually represented by a single enterprise union, and this limits the potential success of the more critical and independent unions affiliated with Zenroren.

Conclusions

The chapter has shown how Rengo and Zenroren with their affiliated unions have made important progress in the organization and representation of non-regular workers. Japanese unionism is more diverse than often given credit for, with regional structures which offer individual membership and organize workers at smaller firms. Unions have also become more inclusive, with a stronger voice for non-regular workers, and this can make a huge difference to the employees concerned. However, the initiatives have not been able to overcome the fundamental dualism in the labour market between regular and non-regular employment. The strong relationship between firms and their regular employees—usually expressed as lifetime employment—continues to ascribe a secondary status to non-regular employment, and any attempt to overcome this dualism also questions the character of regular employment and the wider system of industrial relations and personnel management. This affects both Rengo and Zenroren despite their contrasting identities and strategies with important differences in workers targeted (*who*), types of membership (*how*), and objectives of representation (*what*). It explains why the voice of unions in Japan is fragmented: because of the differences between the different confederations but more fundamentally between regular and non-regular workers and between the different types of representation at the enterprise and individual level. This suggests that ideological differences matter, but that the structures of the labour market and industrial relations are dominant.

These outcomes, when placed in historical perspective, confirm how institutional practices are shaped by dominant cultural values and can contribute to their persistence. The strict distinction between regular and non-regular employment has drawn legitimacy from a range of factors, including prevalent gender perceptions (Gottfried and Hayashi-Kato 1998) and the corporatist re-interpretation of Japan's patriarchal and paternalistic culture (Hazama 1997). Together they have also shaped the structure and identity of Japanese unionism as firms motivated moderate employees to establish cooperative enterprise unions during the post-war period. These unions confirmed the existing dualism in the labour market by almost exclusively representing male, regular workers in accordance with their position as breadwinners. It, for example, informed demands for a living wage based on age and family size to reflect the needs of workers (Gordon 1985). The set of practices thus developed received continued support in subsequent decades as strong economic growth validated the Japanese version of 'welfare corporatism' with lifetime employment as 'a normative model' (Dore 1973). Non-regular, particularly part-time, employment was largely reserved for married women and considered as a complement to the main employment by male breadwinners (Nomura 1998). However, the burst of the economic bubble and the rise of neo-liberalism have increased costs pressures and contributed to the partial transformation of non-regular employment to include more precarious forms, with important implications for workers and society.

The dominance of enterprise unionism has clearly hindered the unions' ability to fight this trend towards precariousness and to represent the workers concerned. It illustrates the constraints posed by path dependence, as enterprise unionism, itself strongly defined by the dualism in the labour market, has become a major limitation in the neo-liberal era; irrespective of its role in the high-growth period. However, it would be short-sighted to simply blame unions for their unwillingness to represent non-regular workers. They remain the dominant and often sole voice in representing non-regular workers, whether through direct representation in collective bargaining, through the presentation of individual members, or through their support for policies that reduce the inequalities in the labour market and wider society. The fact that these initiatives are constrained should not distract from the achievements made. It is without doubt that unions have substantially improved the lives of those workers successfully represented during a labour dispute or profiting from new career opportunities. At the same time, progress remains constrained by the dualism in the labour market. This informs a second observation, equal to the disconcerting but realistic conclusion by Keune (2013: 77) that EU unions are unlikely to 'achieve a substantial decline in precarious employment on their own'. Only a concerted effort across society can confront the dualism in the labour market, and substantial change will require support for greater equality by all social partners, including firms (e.g. because of a shortage of employees) and the state (e.g. because of concerns about gender inequality and the working poor). This leads to a final observation. Without this support, unions will be tempted to defend the existing rights of regular workers where they are able to do so and to represent new workers through the structures that are available to them. Not to do so would merely lower their leverage rather than strengthening the position of 'outsiders' in precarious employment. At the same time, they need to develop strategies to overcome the existing dualisms in industrial relations between cooperative and independent unionism and between individual and enterprise-level representation. The future will show whether any of the current initiatives can contribute to this mission.

Notes

1. UA Zensen was formed in 2013 through a merger between UI Zensen and the JSD.
2. JMITU was formed in 2016 through a merger between the JMIU and Tsushin Sangyo, the Tele-Communications Workers' Union. The initial data collection was limited to the JMIU, but the chapter refers to the JMITU for continuity reasons and as justified by JMIU's dominance in terms of membership.

References

Broadbent, K. (2008) 'Japan: Women workers and autonomous organizing'. In K. Broadbent and M. Ford (eds.), *Women and Labour Organizing in Asia: Diversity, Autonomy and Activism*. London: Routledge, pp. 156–171.

Chalmers, N. J. (1990) *Industrial Relations in Japan: The Peripheral Workforce*. London: Routledge.

Dore, R. (1973) *British Factory, Japanese Factory: The Origins of National Diversity in Industrial Relations*. London: George Allen and Unwin.

Gordon, A. (1985) *The Evolution of Labor Relations in Japan: Heavy Industry 1853–1955*. Cambridge, Massachusetts: Harvard University Press.

Gottfried, H. and Hayashi-Kato, N. (1998) 'Gendering work: Deconstructing the narrative of the Japanese economic miracle'. *Work, Employment and Society*, 12(1): 25–46.

Grimshaw, D., Johnson, M., Rubery, J., and Keizer, A. (2016) 'Reducing precarious work: Protective gaps and the role of social dialogue in Europe'. Available at: http://www.research.mbs.ac.uk/ewerc/Portals/0/Documents/Comparative-Report-Reducing-Precarious-Work-v2.pdf/ (Accessed at: 21 December 2016).

Hazama, H. (1997) *The History of Labour Management in Japan*. London: Macmillan Press.

Hyman, R. (1997) 'Trade unions and interest representation in the context of globalisation'. *Transfer*, 3: 515–533.

Inagami, T. and Whittaker, D. H. (2005) *The New Community Firm: Employment, Governance and Management Reform in Japan*. Cambridge: Cambridge University Press.

Japan Institute for Labour Policy and Training (2013) *Labor Situation in Japan and Its Analysis: Detailed Exposition 2012/2013*. Tokyo.

Jeong, D. Y. and Aguilera, R. V. (2008) 'The evolution of enterprise unionism in Japan: A socio-political perspective'. *British Journal of Industrial Relations*, 46(1): 98–132.

Keizer, A. (2008) 'Non-regular employment in Japan: Continued and renewed dualities'. *Work, Employment and Society*, 22(3): 407–425.

Keizer, A. (2010) *Changes in Japanese Employment Practices: Beyond the Japanese Model*. London: Routledge.

Keizer, A. (2019) 'Inclusion of "outsiders" by Japanese unions? The organizing of non-regular workers in retail'. *Work, Employment and Society*, 33(2): 226–243.

Keune, M. (2013) 'Trade union responses to precarious work in seven European countries'. *International Journal of Labour Research*, 5(1): 59–78.

Mouer, R. and Kawanishi, H. (2005) *A Sociology of Work in Japan*. Cambridge: Cambridge University Press.

Nomura, M. (1998) Koyō Fuan [Employment insecurity]. Tokyo: Iwanami Shinsho.

Oh, H-S. (2012) 'The current status and significance of General Unions: Concerning the resolution of individual labor disputes'. *Japan Labor Review*, 9(1): 63–85.

Palier, B. and Thelen, K. (2010) Institutionalizing dualism: Complementarities and change in France and Germany. *Politics Society*, 38(1) 119–148.

Passet, O. (2003) 'Stability and change: Japan's employment system under pressure'. In P. Auer and S. Cazes (eds.), *Employment Stability in an Age of Flexibility: Evidence from Industrialized Countries*. Geneva: International Labour Office, pp. 159–217.

Pulignano, V., Meardi G., and Doerflinger N. (2015) 'Trade unions and labour market dualisation: A comparison of policies and attitudes towards agency and migrant workers in Germany and Belgium'. *Work, Employment and Society*, 29(5): 808–825.

Royle, T. and Urano, E. (2012) 'A new form of union organizing in Japan? Community unions and the case of the McDonald's 'McUnion'. *Work, Employment and Society*, 26(4): 602–622.

Rueda, D. (2005) 'Insider-outsider politics in industrialized democracies: The challenge to social democratic parties'. *American Political Science Review*, 99(1): 61–74.

Standing, G. (2011) *The Precariat: The New Dangerous Class*. London: Bloomsbury Academic.

Suzuki, A. (2004) *Explaining Japanese Unions' Strategies for Organizing: Examination of the Strategic Choice of Industry-Level Union Federations*. Seoul: IIRA 5th Asian Regional Congress.

Suzuki, A. (2008) 'Community unions in Japan: Similarities and differences of region-based labour movements between Japan and other industrialized countries'. *Economic and Industrial Democracy*, 29(4): 492–520.

Tachibanaki, T. and Noda, T. (2000) *The Economic Effects of Trade Unions in Japan*. London: Macmillan.

Takeuchi-Okuno, H. (2012) 'General unions and community unions, and Japanese Labor Law', *Japan Labor Review*, 9(1): 86–102.

Tsuchida, M. (2004) 'Career formation and balanced treatment of part-time workers: An examination focusing on legal policy'. *Japan Labor Review*, 1(4): 27–47.

Urano, E. I. and Stewart, P. (2009) 'Beyond organised labour in Japan: The case study of the Japanese Community Union Federation'. In J. McBride and I. Greenwood (eds.), *Community Unionism: A Comparative Analysis of Concepts and Contexts*. Basingstoke: Palgrave Macmillan, pp. 121–138.

Weathers, C. (2007) 'Organizing marginalized and non-regular workers: A US-Japan comparison'. Discussion Paper No. 4. Osaka City University: Center for Research on Economic Inequality.

Weathers, C. (2010) 'The rising voice of Japan's community unions'. In H. Vincken, Y. Nishimura, B. L. J. White, and M. Deguchi (eds.), *Civic Engagement in Contemporary Japan: Established and Emerging Repertoires*. New York: Springer, pp. 67–83.

Yun, J. W. (2010) 'Unequal Japan: Conservative corporatism and labour market disparities'. *British Journal of Industrial Relations*, 48(1): 1–25.

6
Organizing Temporary Agency Workers in Japan

Two Types of Inclusive Union Responses

Akira Suzuki

Introduction

How do labour unions respond to non-regular, often precariously employed workers? Unions have two major approaches towards these workers: exclusion or inclusion. These two responses reflect two conflicting roles that labour unions are expected to play: protecting the interests of existing members or representing the broad interests of workers by organizing non-regular workers. Research suggests that the predominant response of labour unions in Japan, Korea, and countries in the West has been to protect the interests of their members by excluding non-regular workers, such as part-time and temporary agency workers (Heery and Abbott 2000; Yun 2010; Song 2012). Only a minority of unions, often social movement oriented, actively engage in organizing non-regular workers (Chun 2009; Kojima 2020).

Japan's 'dualist' labour politics point to cross-class alliances between enterprise unions representing core workers and management at the enterprise and national levels as an institutional factor restraining inclusive union responses towards non-regular workers. Although labour market regulation has been liberalized since the mid-1990s, according to these studies, representatives of enterprise unions and management made a tacit agreement on the partial liberalization of labour markets: labour market liberalization would be applied mainly to non-regular workers such as temporary agency workers and would not threaten the employment security of core workers in large private-sector firms (Yun 2010; Song 2012). In other words, enterprise unions would exclude non-regular workers; they would seek to protect employment for their members, while giving implicit consent to the extensive use of contingent workers.

Akira Suzuki, *Organizing Temporary Agency Workers in Japan*. In: *Temporary and Gig Economy Workers in China and Japan.*
Edited by Huiyan Fu, Oxford University Press. © Oxford University Press (2023). DOI: 10.1093/oso/9780192849694.003.0007

On a closer look, however, we note that despite the general trend of exclusivity, some unions in the mainstream take more inclusive approaches to non-regular workers. Unionized part-time workers jumped from 260,000 in 2000 to 1,333,000 in 2019, more than a five-fold increase. The 2019 figure accounted for more than 13 per cent of all union members (MHLW various years). Enterprise unions in the retail sector (e.g. supermarkets and department stores) have been particularly active in organizing part-time workers, and half of unionized part-timers work in the retail sector. We also note that a minority of leftist unions, acting on a policy of working-class solidarity, have more inclusive responses to non-regular workers, representing the interests of precariously employed workers such as temporary agency workers, who work alongside union members in the same workplace.

This chapter examines inclusive responses of Japanese unions to non-regular workers, especially temporary agency workers (dispatched workers or *haken rodosha*). It presents three cases of union organizing of agency workers and examines how unions with inclusive responses try to represent the interests of these workers. The three cases are the Haken Union (Dispatched Workers' Union, an individually affiliated union),[1] local unions of JMIU (All Japan Metal and Information Machinery Workers' Union, a leftist-oriented union in metal-related industries), and JSGU (Jinzai Sabisu (Human Resources Service) General Union), an affiliate of UA Zensen (formerly UI Zensen), the largest union federation in the private sector. Based on a comparison of inclusive responses, I argue that there are two distinctive types of organizing among non-regular workers: cooperative and arm's length organizing.

This volume's Introduction argues that labour market dualism in Japan is gender-based, a plausible argument because in the second half of the 2010s female workers accounted for about 70 per cent of non-regular workers (e.g. part-time, fixed-term, and agency workers). Gender-based segmentation, however, was less pronounced among agency workers than among part-time workers; it should be noted that the latter constituted by far the largest group of non-regular workers. According to the Labour Force Survey, the number of male agency workers increased from 130,000 (26.0% of all agency workers) in 2003 to 550,000 (39.3%) in 2008. The number dropped to 350,000 (36.5%) in 2010 due to the Great Recession, but increased to 570,000 (40.1%) in 2019 (MIAC, various years). An increase in the number of male agency workers can be explained by the 2004 legalization of dispatching agency workers to manufacturing plants. Among the three cases in this chapter, the target of union organizing by local unions of JMIU and JSGU was agency workers in manufacturing plants. The union organizing I discuss often involves male agency workers (including agency workers disguised as contract workers or *giso ukeoi*).[2]

Studies of union responses to non-regular workers

Studies of Japanese union responses to non-regular workers are roughly divided into two groups. One strand of research consists of critical evaluations of the exclusive responses of enterprise unions in large private-sector firms towards non-regular workers. They criticize the 'self-centered' attitudes of these unions, not only for defending union members' economic interests at the expense of non-regular workers, but also for uncritically accepting social norms of gender discrimination based on 'a corporate-centred, male-breadwinner reproduction bargain' (Gottfried 2014: 465) or 'gender-based vested interests of regular workers' (Watanabe 2015: 525; see also Endo 2011; Kumazawa 2013).

The second strand consists of studies that empirically examine enterprise unions that organize part-time and other non-regular workers. Many of these cases studies depict enterprise unions in the retail sector where part-time workers constitute a majority of the workforce. Some studies in this group examine motivations of enterprise unions to organize non-regular workers, while other studies examine how the interests of non-regular workers are represented once they have been organized.

Concerning the former issue, Keisuke Nakamura argues, based on 10 case studies (four of which were unions in the retail sector), that leaders of enterprise unions are motivated to organize non-regular workers, such as part-time workers and fixed-term workers, not primarily for the sake of these workers but for the sake of regular workers. Nakamura's basic assumption is that enterprise unions representing regular workers have vested interests in maintaining high productivity in the workplace and cooperative labour–management relations (Nakamura 2009). According to him, unless enterprise unions organize non-regular workers and improve their working conditions, productivity suffers because these workers remain undermotivated and are unwilling to cooperate with regular workers in performing tasks. Productivity also suffers due to a high non-regular turnover.[3] He also points out that the failure to organize non-regular workers threatens cooperative union–management relations. If a majority of workers in the workplace are non-regular workers, failure to organize these workers creates an opportunity for a more militant rival union to organize non-regular workers, thus disrupting cooperative labour–management relations (Nakamura 2009; see also Hashimoto 2009 for a similar argument).

Concerning the representation of the interests of non-regular workers by enterprise unions, Iku Kanai, whose work examines eight supermarket worker unions, points out that the participation of part-time workers in decision-making bodies of unions and in negotiations between unions and management is limited. None or few delegates or representatives of part-time workers were elected to union conventions or to higher decision-making committees, and it is rare that part-time workers participate in meetings of labour–management consultation and in collective bargaining (Kanai 2006). Although these unions take inclusive responses to non-regular workers, this union response is what Edmund Heery calls 'subordination', that is, the unions represent the interests of full-time workers primarily, and part-time workers only secondarily (Heery 2009).[4]

Compared to studies of organizing part-time workers by enterprise unions, the number of studies on union organizing of temporary agency workers is limited. This is because union leaders and labour scholars only came to regard agency workers as the target of organizing after the 2004 Worker Dispatch Law (*Haken Ho*) deregulated the use of agency workers in manufacturing and increased their numbers. At the same time, the issue of 'disguised contractors' (*giso ukeoi*) came to the fore (Sekine 2009).

To the author's knowledge, there is only one book-length empirical study of organizing temporary agency workers. Taichi Ito examined how, in 2004, agency workers in an auto parts manufacturing plant (Koyo Sealing Techno in Tokushima Prefecture)[5] formed a union with the assistance of one of the two unions of regular workers in the plant. The agency workers were disguised as employees of contractors (contract workers). Their organizing efforts included struggles for direct employment by the manufacturing company;[6] they won direct employment as fixed-term workers and eventually as regular workers. Almost all members of the union were male workers (Ito 2013; a personal correspondence with Ito, 22 April 2021).

Ito points out three main reasons for the union's successful campaign for direct employment. First, contract workers working at Koyo Sealing Techno were in a 'strategic position'. The company, as a second-tier supplier to Toyota, manufactured piston seals for automatic transmissions, and Toyota could not afford a supply disruption due to labour disputes with the contract workers' union. Second, contract workers assisted each other in the formation and development of their production-related skills and formed a workplace-based group led by the group's senior members. This group became a social base of the union. And third, one of the unions of regular workers at the company, a local union of JMIU, helped form the contract workers' union (a separate union affiliated with the regional organization of JMIU in Tokushima Prefecture) and supported the union throughout its struggle for more secure forms of employment (Ito 2013: 48, 63–64, 74, 87–89). Ito's study indicates that successfully organizing precariously employed workers such as in the case of Koyo Sealing Techno (about 30–40 agency workers were organized into the union) was exceptional in terms of the resources that workers were capable of mobilizing.

Three cases of inclusive responses to temporary agency workers

This section examines three cases of inclusive responses of unions to temporary agency workers, involving the Haken Union, JMIU local unions, and JSGU. Although in the three cases the unions aimed to organize agency workers and/or employees of temporary agency firms, the main targets of organizing were different. The Haken Union organized 'daily' agency workers (*hiyatoi haken*), while local JMIU unions organized agency workers disguised as contract workers. JSGU organized workers whose employment was relatively stable, that is, regular workers of agency firms and 'regular' (*joyogata*) agency workers (those employed by agency firms as fixed-term or regular workers).

Haken Union

The Haken Union[7] (*haken yunion*) is an individually affiliated union organized on the regional level with its membership drawn from workers employed by different firms. Members of these unions (often called 'community unions') include workers who fall outside the coverage of enterprise unions, such as part-time and fixed-term workers, temporary agency workers, workers in small firms, and foreign workers. Individually affiliated unions provide labour-issue counselling, organize workers who seek counselling services into unions, and engage in collective bargaining with employers on behalf of union members with individual grievances, such as dismissals, harassment, arbitrary changes in working conditions, or wage discrimination based on employment status or gender. Thus, the relationship between these unions and employers tends to be tense and conflictual.

The Haken Union, based in Tokyo, has about 300 members (as of 2016). About one-third of its members are temporary agency workers, most of whom are 'registered' (*toroku gata*) agency workers (as opposed to 'regular' or *joyo gata* agency workers).[8] The remaining two-thirds are fixed-term workers and regular workers. Individual affiliation is the main form of joining the union, but the union has about 10 workplace-based locals, usually consisting of four to five members. Although many individually affiliated members quit the union when their labour-related grievances are resolved, some remain union members because they expect that they, as agency and fixed-term workers, may encounter similar labour issues in their next job (Sekine interview).

The Haken Union belongs to the Japan Community Union Federation (JCUF or Zenkoku Yunion), a federation of 11 individually affiliated unions with a total membership of about 2,800. The JCUF is in turn affiliated with Rengo (Japan Trade Union Confederation, Japan's dominant confederation). The union was established in 2005 by leaders of the JCUF as a union specializing in temporary agency workers and regular employees of agency firms. Shuichiro Sekine, General Secretary of the union, had been a full-time activist in the Tokyo Union (another member union of the JCUF) since the mid-1990s. JCUF leaders intended to create a union with the capacity to organize and bargain with agency firms that expanded their operations on a nationwide basis because of deregulation of the temporary agency industry (Sekine interview; JCUF 2005: 8–9).

Agency firms that had rapidly expanded their operations since 2000 included those firms which dispatched 'daily' agency workers (*hiyatoi haken*) to client firms. These agency workers were assigned to the 'light work' of client firms, either on a daily basis or for a short period of time. They worked under precarious employment conditions. The light work to which these workers were assigned included physically demanding loading and unloading work in warehouses and moving companies (Sekine 2009). In 2006–2007, the Haken Union organized daily agency workers at major agency firms such as Fullcast and Goodwill, and demanded the improvement of working conditions, particularly the abolition and restitution of illegally 'skimm(ed) bogus fees from workers' wages' (Kojima 2020: 205; Takai and Sekiguchi 2011). The Fullcast local of the Haken Union, consisting of about 10 workers, engaged in collective bargaining with management and won the abolition and restitution of skimmed fees and improved working conditions. The membership of the Goodwill local grew to be about 150 at one point, but the company refused to reimburse the skimmed fees fully. The union sued the company and won full restitution in an out-of-court settlement in 2009. The labour movement of daily agency workers led by the Haken Union received media attention and created social pressure on other agency firms to abolish the practice of skimming fees and to reimburse agency workers (Sekine 2009; Takai and Sekiguchi 2011).

Local unions of JMIU

JMIU (All Japan Metal and Information Machinery Workers' Union) is affiliated with Zenroren (National Confederation of Trade Unions, the leftist non-mainstream confederation) and represents about 6,000 workers in metal-related industries (as of 2015), many of whom work in small- and medium-sized enterprises (SMEs).[9] JMIU was formed in 1989 by leftist union leaders who opposed the domination of Rengo and its affiliated unions in the labour movement of metalworkers. JMIU adopted a principle of industrial unionism but promoted building a strong union presence in workplaces at the same time. In the 1990s when SMEs in metal industries came under strong market pressure, JMIU and its local unions engaged in struggles against management rationalization policies, such as downsizing, dismissals, the introduction of performance-based wages, and plant closures (Hasegawa 2006).

In the mid-2000s, JMIU adopted a policy to actively organize non-regular workers, including temporary agency workers. The union called upon its local unions to regard non-regular workers working in their workplaces as a potential target of organizing and to start a 'dialogue' with these workers. The first major organizing case was the establishment of the union of disguised contract agency workers at Koyo Sealing Techno in 2004 (Ikuma 2010; Ito 2013). As already discussed, the local union of regular workers assisted in the formation of the contract workers' union. Following this case, other local unions directly organized agency workers (including disguised contract workers) in their workplaces and demanded their direct employment. *Kinzoku Rodo Shinbun* (Metal Labour News), the bulletin of JMIU, reported cases of local unions that had reached out to and/or organized agency workers in their workplaces in the second half of the 2000s. However, the size of these local unions was small because they organized workers of SMEs (often a minority of workers in one plant or firm). According to a JMIU internal document, an average local union in the second half of the 2000s had about 22 members. Thus, the number of newly organized agency workers by each local union was limited. For example, the local union of Himeji Plant of Nippon Thompson (a manufacturer of bearings) organized 13 disguised contract workers in 2009 to protect them from dismissal and demanded direct employment. This seems to be the largest number of agency workers organized by a single local union (*Kinzoku Rodo Shinbun*, 20 February 2009, 5 April 2009).

JMIU also attempted to organize agency workers by establishing new local unions in the workplaces where JMIU had not established its presence previously. One major case was the formation of a new JMIU local union by 19 agency workers at Nichia Corporation in Tokushima Prefecture (a manufacturer of LEDs) in 2006.[10] The workers, many of them in their twenties and disguised contract workers, denounced their employment status and demanded direct employment by the company because they had worked at the company more than one year (the maximum period of accepting agency workers at that time). JMIU and the company reached an agreement that the company would directly employ those contract workers who had worked at Nichia for more than three years as fixed-term workers and would promote qualified workers to regular workers. The company directly employed 31 contract workers out of 251 workers who met the condition but did not employ all union members, thus breaking its agreement with JMIU.[11] JMIU mobilized its members and members of other unions affiliated with Zenroren for mass rallies and demonstrations in support of union members, and these union members (now decreased to six, one female and five male workers) came to be portrayed as a symbol of an increasing number of young workers who suffered from economic injustice due to precarious employment as agency and other types of non-regular workers. JMIU and its local union filed a lawsuit against Nichia Corporation in 2009, demanding direct employment of the six union members. The two sides reached an out-of-court settlement in 2011 in which the union agreed to withdraw the demand for direct employment in exchange for a payment of monetary compensation by the company to the union members.

JSGU

JSGU (Jinzai Sabisu (Human Resources Service) General Union) was established in 2004 with a membership of 17,000 in eight local unions organized at major agency firms, including Pasona and Manpower Japan. JSGU was affiliated with UI Zensen (currently UA Zesen), the largest private-sector union federation affiliated with Rengo. The union first organized regular employees of agency firms, workers who were in charge of dispatching agency workers to client firms and managed agency workers.[12] It then extended its target to organizing *joyo gata* agency workers (those employed by agency firms as fixed-term or regular workers). JSGU also focused on organizing agency firms that specialized in dispatching relatively high-skilled workers such as engineers. In other words, JSGU organized a relatively stable segment of workers in the temporary agency industry. Since males dominated high-skilled agency employment, about 80 per cent of JSGU's membership were male (UI Zensen Shinbun, 25 May 2004, 25 January 2005; Ninomiya interview; Ogata 2014: 18–19).

JSGU also attempted to organize some registered (*toroku gata*) agency workers, including daily agency workers, but only succeeded in organizing a small number of such workers. Thus, there was no competition between JSGU and the Haken Union which organized registered agency workers (Sekine interview).

JSGU grew phenomenally until 2007 when its membership reached 43,000. For example, JSGU organized about 30,000 agency workers in the Crystal Group (the firms specialized in dispatching assembly workers and engineers to manufacturing plants) in 2007 (UI Zensen Shinbun, 15 February 2007; Ninomiya interview). JSGU organized a large number of workers in a short period because of its top-down organizing strategy. The union approached the management of target firms, gained their consent to organizing activities, and then held numerous recruiting meetings. When sufficient workers had been recruited, the union signed union shop and check-off agreements with agency firm management (UI Zensen Shinbun, 15 June 2005; Ninomiya 2012: 161, 165; see also Shukan Toyo Keizai, 7 February 2009). JSGU gained management consent by stressing the union's commitment to cooperative union–management relations and productivity improvement.[13]

However, membership soon declined rapidly. Goodwill, one of the major agency firms where JSGU had organized about 3,000 regular employees, went out of business in 2008 when its senior managers were prosecuted for illegally double dispatching (*niju haken*) agency workers (Fu 2011: 38).[14] The Crystal Group agency firms, where JSGU had organized 30,000 workers, also went out of business in 2010 because of a decline in sales that resulted from a government-ordered suspension of operation in 2006 in the wake of rampant non-compliance with the Worker Dispatch Law. Its noncompliance damaged client trust. Moreover, the global financial crisis of late 2008 and tighter government regulation of illegal practices such as disguised contractors adversely affected the performance of many agency firms. As a result, membership in the JSGU declined to 14,000 in 2009. Its membership has recovered somewhat since then (its 2017 membership is about 19,000) (Ninomiya 2012: 163–164; Ninomiya interview; *Nikkei Shinbun*, 2 June 2010).

JSGU claimed that it organized workers in the temporary agency industry across firms, that is, its organizational form was not a federation of enterprise unions but a unitary body in which firm-based local unions were under the direction of its headquarters. Union dues collected by check-off agreements between the JSGU and agency firms went directly to the headquarters of JSGU, not to local unions. Decision making was not delegated to local unions, occurring only at the headquarters. According to Makoto Ninomiya, first president of JSGU, the headquarters of JSGU, rather than heads of local unions, engaged in collective bargaining with employers during annual rounds of wage negotiations (*shunto*) and signed a framework agreement with the management of agency firms. Firm-level negotiations took place within the framework agreement (Ninomiya, interview; *Tokyo Shinbun*, 3 April 2016).

Rank-and-file members of JSGU, however, did not necessarily have strong union consciousness. Unlike non-regular workers who joined the Haken Union through individual affiliation and those who were organized into local unions of JMIU through workplace-level organizing activities, union members of JSGU were organized either in a top-down way or through union shop agreements. Thus, it is not surprising to learn that regular workers at a major agency firm, where the JSGU local at the firm had signed a union shop agreement with management, were not even aware that they belonged to the union (Sekine 2016).

Comparing the three inclusive response cases

We can distinguish two types of labour–management relations: cooperative and arm's length relations. Cooperative relations, typical of industrial relations in large private-sector firms, are the dominant pattern of labour–management relations in Japan. Enterprise unions form a relationship of mutual trust with management based on shared values of productivity improvement and the economic competitiveness of firms. If unions plan to organize non-regular workers, they seek the consent of management on the grounds of productivity improvement. In contrast, there is social distance between unions and management in arm's length labour–management relations, and the two sides engage in negotiations from their distinctive positions.

Among the three cases, Haken Union and JMIU local union organizing activities took place in the context of arm's length labour–management relations. Since these organizing campaigns originated in workers' grievances, labour–management relations often become adversarial. JSGU, in contrast, gained the consent of agency firm management by emphasizing the union's commitment to productivity improvement. Thus, JSGU's organizing activities took place in the context of cooperative labour–management relations.

Unionization of part-time workers by enterprise unions was relatively successful, especially in the retail sector, where organizing took place in the dominant institutional context of cooperative labour–management relations. A majority of enterprise unions in the retail sector active in organizing part-time workers belonged to two union federations, JSD (Japan Federation of Service and Distribution Workers Union) and UI Zensen.[15] Enterprise unions affiliated with these federations adopted a 'partnership model' of union organizing. The unions gained the consent of management to organizing part-time workers by stressing the merits of organizing matters such as higher worker morale, improved productivity, better workplace communications, and the union contribution to efficient and sound corporate management (Suzuki 2006). JSGU and enterprise unions in the retail sector adopted cooperative inclusive organizing, while the Haken Union and local unions of JMIU adopted an arm's length approach.

The two types of inclusive responses are different in the effectiveness of union organizing and representing workers' interests. The effectiveness of union organizing can be measured in the number of non-regular workers organized into unions. The effectiveness of representation of workers' interests can be assessed by how unions addressed non-regular workers' labour issues, particularly the pressing issues faced by precariously employed workers. Enterprise unions in the retail sector and JSGU, engaging in organizing activities in the context of cooperative labour–management relations, were successful in unionizing many non-regular workers because of top-down organizing based on management consent. In contrast, the Haken Union and local JMIU unions tried to organize temporary agency workers in a bottom-up way and outside the framework of cooperative labour–management relations. Thus, they had difficulty in organizing a large number of non-regular workers.

The effectiveness of union organizing and representation was a trade-off. Enterprise unions in the retail sector organized part-time workers for the sake of regular workers and subordinated the interests of part-time workers to those of regular workers. JSGU's top-down organizing strategy gave priority to representing the relatively stable segment of workers in the temporary agency industry over the unstable segment such as registered agency workers. Moreover, some regular agency firm workers were unaware that JSGU represented them.

Individually affiliated unions such as the Haken Union could effectively address pressing labour issues faced by individual workers such as dismissals.

Table 6.1 Two types of inclusive responses of unions to non-regular workers

	Cooperative type	Arm's length type
Contexts of labour–management relations	Cooperative labour–management relations	Arm's length labour–management relations
Cases	Enterprise unions in the retail sector, JSGU	Haken Union, Local unions of JMIU
The effectiveness of union organizing	high	low
The effectiveness of representation	low	high

The Haken Union also represented the collective interests of daily agency workers, demanding the restitution of skimmed fees to agency firms. Local unions of JMIU organized agency workers disguised as employees of contractors by building workers' unity at the workplace and demanding direct employment. The two distinctive types of inclusive responses of unions to non-regular workers are summarized in Table 6.1.

Conclusion

As the literature of the 'dualist' labour politics in Japan posits, the dominant response of Japanese labour unions to non-regular workers was exclusion, with enterprise unions making a tacit agreement with employers in which the employment security of regular workers in large private-sector firms was protected in exchange for labour market liberalization of non-regular workers. But as the cases presented in this chapter show, individually affiliated unions such as the Haken Union and local unions of the leftist-oriented JMIU organized daily agency workers, registered agency workers, and agency workers disguised as contract workers, and they addressed members' individual and collective labour issues. These unions, small and with limited resources, were still at the margin of the labour movement, dominated by cooperative enterprise unions and their federations. Their conflictual relations with employers made it difficult for these unions to engage in large-scale organizing campaigns of precariously employed workers.

JSGU was the only union among the three cases that succeeded, albeit temporarily, in large-scale organizing of regular agency workers or agency firm employees. It organized a relatively stable segment of workers in the temporary agency industry in the context of cooperative union–management relations but was ineffective in representing the interests of registered agency workers, including daily agency workers. Its cooperative relations became clear when the union sided with advocates of labour market deregulation by opposing Rengo's policy calling for a revision of the Worker Dispatch Law to prohibit registered agency workers (*Shukan Toyo Keizai*, 7 February 2009).

This chapter shows that union organizing of agency workers and workers of agency firms in charge of dispatching these workers involved many male workers, indicating the increasing precariousness of male workers as well as female workers, undermining the 'male-breadwinner reproduction bargain' (Gottfried 2014) that has been the dominant cultural assumption underlying labour market dualism in Japan. The impact of increased male precariousness in the Japanese labour market on the dominant cultural assumption should be a subject of future studies.

What are the implications of this chapter for the labour movement in Japan, especially when the employment crisis due to the spread of Covid-19 has heavily affected non-regular workers, including agency workers? The downsizing and shutdown of business under the Covid-19 crisis since the spring of 2020 has demonstrated the persistence of labour market dualism in the sense that the employment and economic security of regular workers were protected at the expense of dismissals and reduced working hours of non-regular workers. The precarity of agency workers' employment became clear when agency worker jobs decreased drastically due to cancelling employment contracts at the end of June or September (*Asahi Shinbun*, 2 September 2020; *Rengo Tsushin*, 3 August 2020).[16]

In an employment crisis like this, individually affiliated unions such as the Haken Union seemed to respond relatively flexibly in addressing the troubles and complaints of agency and other non-regular workers. For example, JCUF (the federation of individually affiliated unions including the Haken Union) conducted labour-issue telephone counselling and received 106 cases of individual labour disputes by the end of March, many of which were related to discriminatory treatments and employment insecurity under the Covid-19 crisis. JCUF then held a press conference at the Japan National Press Club in May to present problems faced by agency and other non-regular workers, such as non-payment of leave allowances (*kyugyo-teate*) during the suspension of business, the refusal of client companies to allow agency workers to telework (while allowing regular workers to do so), and dismissals of agency workers.[17] Although individually affiliated unions have not been effective on a large scale in organizing agency workers with labour issues under Covid-19, these unions have been effective in raising issues of economic injustice and employment insecurity as social problems, and in making the general public aware of the persistent disparity between regular and non-regular workers.

Notes

1. An individually-affiliated union (*kojin kamei kumiai*) is organized on a regional level, rather than based on a single firm or plant, and recruits its members from different firms in the region. Japanese labor law permits such a union to represent its members in collective bargaining with their employers.
2. Disguised contractors [*giso ukeoi*] means that manufacturing firms, to avoid stipulations of the Worker Dispatch Law ('the payment of health and safety insurance and the obligation to directly employ workers after a certain period'), use de facto agency workers as employees of contractors (contract workers). Contractors are supposed to be in charge of a well-defined segment of the manufacturing process, and contract workers are supposed to work under the supervision of contractors. Agency workers disguised as contract workers work alongside employees of client firms and receive instructions from managers of client firms (see Fu 2011: 37).
3. That non-regular workers perform key, rather than auxiliary, job tasks but receive treatment inferior to regular workers is said to contribute to grievances and lack of motivation (Hashimoto 2009).
4. Edmund Herry identifies subordination is one of the four union responses to contingent workers. He characterized this union response as 'acceptance of contingent workers as both participants in the labor market and part of union constituency, but on a secondary basis' (Heery 2009: 431).
5. Ito used the pseudonym 'Aizumi Tech.'
6. According to the Worker Dispatch Law (as of 2004), the maximum period for accepting agency workers in manufacturing plants was one year, and client companies were required to directly employ agency workers who had worked more than one year (the maximum period was extended to three years in 2007).
7. Information on the Haken Union, JMIU local unions, and the JSGU is based on the author's interviews with Shuichiro Sekine (General Secretary of Haken Union) on 12 December 2016, with Makoto Ninomiya (first President of JSGU) on 30 January 2017, and on bulletins and union documents of JMIU and UI Zensen, and other secondary sources.
8. Registered agency workers are employed by agency firms and work in client firms only when client firms request agency workers be dispatched to their workplaces. Their employment is thus precarious. Regular agency workers, on the other hand, are employed by agency firms as fixed-term workers or even as regular workers, and their employment is relatively secure.
9. JMIU merged with Tsushin Roso (Telecommunication Workers' Union, a minority union in the telecommunication industry) to form JMITU (Japan Metal Manufacturing, Information and Telecommunication Workers' Union) in January 2016. This chapter uses JMIU, the name of the union before the merger.
10. The following description of the case of agency workers at Nichia Corporation is based on articles of *Kinzoku Rodo Shinbun* (*Metal Labor News*), the bulletin of JMIU.

11. When JMIU and Nichia negotiated conditions for direct employment of contract workers, representatives of the company promised that they would not discriminate against union members in the selection of directly employed workers.
12. Employment of regular employees of agency firms is not as secure as that of regular workers in more established firms. Many agency firms were newly established and entrepreneurial and often went out of business (see below).
13. A Zensen Domei (the predecessor of UI Zensen) manual for organizing part-time workers stressed four merits from a management perspective of organizing part-time workers: a better grasp of opinions and complaints of employees, a lower turn-over rate of employees, a higher employee morale, and preventing leftist unions from organizing dissatisfied employees (Zensen Domei 2002). It seemed that JSGU organizers stressed similar points to the management of agency firms.
14. Double dispatching is the practice of agency firms dispatching workers to workplaces of firms other than client firms (often workplaces prohibited by the Worker Dispatch Law, such as stevedoring). The practice of double dispatching is prohibited by Employment Security Law.
15. Since UI Zensen and JSD covered retail and other service industries and organized part-time workers based on a similar organizing philosophy, the two federations merged in 2012 to form UA Zensen with a membership of 1.5 million.
16. According to the Labor Force Survey, the number of agency workers in July, August, and October 2020 declined by 160,000, 130,000, and 100,000, respectively, compared to the number in the same months in 2019 (MIAC, monthly figures).
17. See Press Conference of JCUF (https://www.youtube.com/watch?v=Zrs-PY4O3og), accessed on 29 April, 2021.

References

Asahi Shinbun (2020) 'Kyujin Bairitsu 7kagetsu Renzoku Akka, "6 gatsu Kiki" Haken Rodo 16mannin Gen' (The ratio of job offers to job applicants declined 7 months in a row, agency workers declined by 160,000 due to 'the June crisis'), 2 September.

Chun, J. J. (2009) *Organizing at the margins: The symbolic politics of labor in South Korea and the United States*. Ithaca: Cornell University Press.

Endo, K. (2011) 'Hiseiki Rodosha no Soshikika' (Organizing non-regular workers) *Keiei Ronshu*, 58(3): 1–16.

Fu, H. (2011) *An Emerging Non-Regular Labour Force in Japan: The Dignity of Dispatched Workers* London: Routledge.

Gottfried, H. (2014) 'Precarious work in Japan: Old forms, new risks?' *Journal of Contemporary Asia*, 44(3): 464–478.

Hasegawa, Y. (2006) 'Chusho Kigyo Rodosha o Taishotoshita Soshiki Kakudai'. (Union organizing targeting workers in SMEs). In Akira Suzuki and Seiichiro Hayakawa (eds.), *Rodo Kumiai no Soshiki Kakudai Senryaku*. Tokyo: Ochanomizu Shobo, 183–208.

Hashimoto, S. (2009) 'Kigyobetsu Kumiai ni okeru Hiseiki Jugyoin no Soshikika Jirei no Shimesu koto' (What cases of organizing non-regular employees by enterprise unions show). *Niho Rodo Kenkyu Zasshi*, 591: 41–50.

Heery, E. (2009) 'Trade unions and contingent labour: Scale and method'. *Cambridge Journal of Regions, Economy and Society*, 2: 429–442.

Heery, E. and Abbott, B. (2000) 'Trade unions and the insecure workforce'. In Edmund Heery and John Salmon (eds.), *The Insecure Workforce*. London: Routledge, 155–180.

Ikuma, S. (2010) 'Hiseiki Rodosha no Soshikika Katsudo kara Miete Kitamono' (What we have learned through organizing non-regular workers) *Rodo Soken Quarterly*, 76(77): 69–77.

Ito, T. (2013) *Hiseiki Koyo to Rodo Undo* (Non-regular employment and the labour movement). Kyoto: Horitsu Bunkasha.

JCUF (the Japan Community Union Federation) (2005) *Zenkoku Yunion Dai Yonkai Teiki Taikai* (The fourth convention of the JCUF). Tokyo: JCUF.

Kanai, I. (2006) 'Kigyobetsu Kumiai ni okeru Pato Kumiaiin to Ishiketteikatei heno Kanyo' (The position of part-time workers within enterprise unions and the extent of their involvement in the decision-making process of the unions). *Ohara Shakaimondai Kenkyujo Zasshi*, 568: 39–55.

Kojima, S. (2020) 'Social movement unionism in contemporary Japan: Coalitions within and across political boundaries'. *Economic and Industrial Democracy*, 41(1): 189–211.

Kumazawa, M. (2013) *Rodo Undo toha Nanika* (What is the labour movement?). Tokyo: Iwanami Shoten.

MHLW (Ministry of Health, Labour and Welfare) (various years) *Rodo Kumiai Kiso Chosa* (Basic Survey of Labour Unions).

MIAC (Ministry of Internal Affairs and Communications) *Rodoryoku Chosa* (Labour Force Survey).

Nakamura, K. (2009) *Kabe o Kowasu* (Breaking the wall). Tokyo: Daiichi Shorin.

Nikkei Shinbun (2010) 'Gyomu Ukeoi no Kyu Kurisutaru Tokubetsu Seisan no Kaishi Kettei, Konpura Fubi Shinrai Ushinau' (The former Crystal will be liquidated. It has lost credibility due to its lack of compliance), 2 June.

Ninomiya, M. (2012) *Ninomya Makoto Oraru Hisutori* (Oral History of Makoto Ninomiya). Tokyo: Kyodosha.

Ogata, Y. (2014) 'Haken Rodosha no Hogo, Koyono Antei to Hakenkiseino Nozomashii Arikata' (Protection of agency workers, stability of their employment, and how agency work should be regulated), *Rodo Chosa* (January 2014): 18–21.

Rengo Tsushin (2020) 'Haken Rodosha no Koyoiji wo Yosei' (Requesting the maintenance of employment of agency workers). *Rengo Tsushin*, 3 August.

Sekine, S. (2009) *Haken no Gyakushu* (Counterattack by agency workers). Tokyo: Asahishinbun Shuppan.

Sekine, S. (2016) 'Yuki Rodo no Kisei ga Hitsuyo' (Regulation of fixed-term workers is necessary). *Gekkan Rodo Kumiai*, 629: 11–14.

Shukan Toyo Keizai (7 February 2009) 'Honto ni Rodoshano Mikataka Rodo Kumiaino Shonenba'. (Are labour unions really friends of workers? The crucial moments for labour unions). *Shukan Toyo Keizai* 6186: 72–75.

Song, J. (2012) 'Economic distress, labor market reforms, and dualism in Japan and Korea'. *Governance*, 25(3): 415–438.

Suzuki, A. (2006) 'Sanbetsu Soshiki no Soshiki Kakudai Senryaku' (Organizing strategies of industry federations). In Akira Suzuki and Seiichiro Hayakawa (eds.), *Rodo Kumiai no Soshiki Kakudai Senryaku*. Tokyo: Ochanomizu Shobo, pp. 285–309.

Takai, A. and Sekiguchi, T. (2011) *Tatakau Yunion* (Militant Unions). Tokyo: Junposha, 285–309.

Tokyo Shinbun (2016) 'Watashino Shunto JSGU Kaicho Umeda Hiroshi san'. (My shunto, Mr. Hiroshi Umeda, president of JSGU), 3 April.

Watanabe, H. R. (2015) 'The struggle for revitalisation by Japanese labour unions: Worker organising after labour-market deregulation'. *Journal of Contemporary Asia*, 45(3): 510–530.

Yun, J. (2010) 'Unequal Japan: Conservative corporatism and labour market disparities'. *British Journal of Industrial Relations*, 48(1): 1–25.

Zensen Domei (2002) *Pato Taimu Rodosha no Soshikika ni Mukete* (Toward organizing part-time workers).

Bulletins of Labour Unions

Kinzoku Rodo Shinbun (Metal Labour News), JMIU.
UI Zensen Shinbun (UI Zensen News), UI Zensen.

Interviews

Shuichiro Sekine (general secretary of Haken Union), 12 December 2016.
Makoto Ninomiya (first president of JSGU), 30 January 2017.

7
Negotiating Gender, Citizenship, and Precarity

Migrant Women in Contemporary China

Nana Zhang

Introduction

Receiving much attention from scholars across different disciplines, the concept of 'precarity' has become a buzz word in recent years (Barchiesi 2011; Neilson and Rossiter 2005, 2008; Schierup et al. 2015; Suliman and Weber 2019; Tsianos and Papadopoulos 2006a and b). While much of the earlier literature examines the problems of precarious employment (Neilson and Rossiter 2005; Tsianos and Papadopoulos 2006a, 2006b), increasingly, more attention is given to exploring the wider meanings of precarity and its very intricate relations with modernization and globalization (Schierup et al. 2015, Suliman and Weber 2019) as well as its commonplace nature (Neilson and Rossiter 2008). As Tsianos and Papadopoulos (2006b) suggested, 'Precarity is where immaterial production meets the crisis of the social systems which were based on the national social compromise of normal employment.... Precarity means exploiting the continuum of everyday life, not simply the workforce.' In this context, precarity is best exemplified by the lived experience of rural migrant women in contemporary China.

Since the market-oriented reforms of 1979, China has undergone rapid industrialization and urbanization. Accompanying these dramatic social and economic transformations is one of the world's largest internal migrations, with an estimated 286 million people from rural areas migrated to China's urban centres searching for waged employment by 2020, and among them, around 35 per cent are women (NBSC 2021).

Despite their relatively new encounter with capitalism, Chinese rural women have been engaged in negotiating and contesting different subject positions in the migration process, like their counterparts in other parts of

Asia and South America (Mills 1997; Moore 1994; Silvey 2003; Tiano 1994). They are, indeed, exposed to the 'vicissitudes of every day symbolic struggle' (Bourdieu 1997: 242). Taking employment in low-paid, gender-specific jobs, mainly in the textile and manufacturing industries and the service sector (Davin 1996; Fan 2003; Gaetano and Jacka 2004; Lee 1998; Pun 1999; Solinger 1999, 1995; Zhang 2006), rural women migrants are said to 'occupy a liminal position in space and time' (Gaetano 2008: 629). Some researchers suggest that rural migrant women are 'the most oppressed' (Au and Nan 2007) and the 'victims of exploitation' under a triple oppression of 'global capitalism, state socialism, and familial patriarchy . . . along lines of class, gender and rural-urban disparity' (Pun 2005: 4). Precarity is thus engraved in the everyday lived experience of rural migrant women.

Drawn from a qualitative study of 33 rural migrant women in two popular destination cities in China—Beijing and Shantou, and two sending provinces, Hebei and Henan, this chapter seeks to investigate how Chinese rural migrant women negotiate gender, citizenship, and precarity in their migration process and how they construct and perform identities during the negotiation. It also explores the situatedness of their identity negotiation, construction, and performance, and how they draw on different resources to establish a sense of selfhood and belonging.

'Suzhi', 'hukou', 'dagongmei', and rural migrant women's identity negotiation in contemporary China

Seen as a 'new Chinese working class' in the making, rural migrant workers have been at the forefront of encounter with global capital and the new international division of labour (Pun 2005: 4). The politics of their identity negotiation is intrinsically linked to China's fast economic reform and development, modernization, and urbanization, and the dichotomy between rural and urban space, as well as to the disparity between regions and genders (Davin 1999; Jacka 2006; Lee 1998; Pun 1999, 2005; Solinger 1995).

Rural migrant workers are said to be China's most valuable economic asset (Harney 2008); however, their labour is devalued by the new conceptualization of value and a 'new logic of value coding' within the new context of rapid transformations in China (Anagnost 2004). The devaluation is attained through the use of 'suzhi'[1] as a measurement, where rural people are believed to have low quality and hence, rural migrant labour is also devalued as having 'low quality' (Anagnost 2004: 190). Their labour, therefore, can be purchased at a lower price, which allows for the extraction of surplus value that enables capital accumulation (Anagnost 2004). Not only is the extraction of surplus value from rural migrant labour justified, but the new regimes of social differentiation and governmentality are also legitimized, through the value coding of 'suzhi' quality of the population, which has a direct impact on the identity negotiation of rural migrants—being a rural migrant itself implies having 'low quality' and less human capital (Anagnost 2004).

Furthermore, the Chinese government also deploys different strategies and migratory apparatus to differentiate rural migrants from urban residents and keep rural migrants afloat. In so doing, it manages to keep migrant labour cheap and flexible, and hence remain competitive within the global market. The hukou system (household registration system) is but one of the many institutions that label and maintain these divides and differentiation.

Being a peasant in China is not an occupation which one can easily change, but an identity or status that one is destined to carry and pass on to one's descendants. Under the hukou system, rural migrants are denied permanent settlement in the cities due to their 'agricultural' hukou status, which they inherit from birth. Rural migrant workers in China are thus referred to as 'nongmin gong' (peasant workers). Classified as peasants in the city, rural migrant workers are not only valued as having 'low quality' (*di suzhi*), but are also denied equal access to social welfare, such as state-subsidized medical care, education, and social benefits in the city that are guaranteed for people with urban hukou, even if have migrated to the city and worked there for a number of years. Although the hukou system has undergone a series of reforms, the conversion from 'agricultural' to 'non-agricultural' status remains problematic, and the distinction between 'agricultural' and 'non-agricultural' hukou and related social welfare distribution, which privileges urban hukou holders, remains intact. With the hukou system in place, rural migrants' 'low quality' ('*di suzhi*') is clearly labelled, their transient and secondary status is legitimized, and the source of cheap, flexible labour is secured.

In addition to the 'official naming' of rural migrant women by the state using terms such as 'blind migrant', 'floating population', and 'peasant workers', the rhetoric of 'maiden workers', 'dagongmei',[2] and 'disposable labour' also appears in recent research in the area (Gaetano and Jacka 2004; Pun 2005; Wright 2006; Yan 2008). In documenting rural women's lived experience of new forms of control generated by the combination of state power and global capital, these discourses, conversely, not only engender 'hegemonic effects' that 'limit what individuals perceive as the subject positions available to them' (Mills 1997: 38) but also institute an almost homogeneous representation of rural migrant women, caught up in binary identity categories such as rural/urban and traditional/modern.

For instance, recent research on Chinese rural migrant women's identity and subjectivity has preferred to centre on the 'dagongmei' subject and the power of the state, institutions, and media in shaping rural women migrants' identity (Au and Nan 2007; Beynon 2004; Fan 2002; Gaetano 2008; Jacka 2006; Lee 1998; Pun 1999, 2005; Sun 2004; Yan 2008; Zhang 2001; Zheng 2009).

Lee's study on rural migrant women working on the production lines in Shenzhen establishes an early picture of 'dagongmei', or in her words, 'maiden workers', as a contested identity for Chinese rural migrant women. She argues that while the factory management conceives maidens as docile, short-term, ignorant, but quiescent labourers, for rural migrant women, 'dagongmei' has a somewhat positive connotation—'a relatively independent, modern, and romantic lifestyle in anticipation of marriage and adulthood' (Lee 1998: 135, 136). Based on her study of female rural migrant workers in a factory in Shenzhen, Pun argues that although 'dagongmei' signifies 'an inferior working identity inscribed with capitalist labour relations and sexual relations', it is not necessarily a negative term for the young rural migrant women in her study; rather, the term provides new identities and new senses of the self that rural women can acquire once they work inside a global factory (Pun 2005: 111). As a contested identity for rural migrant women, 'dagongmei' has also been undergoing various interpretations. Recent studies on rural migrant women for example, have extended its coverage to refer to rural migrant women in general (Beynon 2004; Gaetano 2008; Jacka 2006; Sun 2004; Yan 2008; Zheng 2009). Yan, on the other hand, argues that dagongmei are liminal subjects caught up 'between the city and the countryside, between disposable and necessary, between possibilities of absence and those of presence, and between disarticulation and articulation' (Yan 2008: 248).

In *Gender Trouble*, Butler convincingly argues that gender identity is performatively constituted and is always a doing (Butler 1990). The very process of rural migrant women's identity negotiation is key to our understanding of their everyday lived struggles and resistance as both women and migrants in the city. Whilst the aforementioned studies have challenged different aspects of rural migrant women's identity shaping and their lived experiences as migrant labour, to date, the situated, fluid nature of rural women's identity construction has not been sufficiently explored.

As a symbiosis of performed story and the social relations, identity and experience are materially embedded: sex, class, race, ethnicity, sexuality, geography, religion, and so on (Langellier 1999: 129). It is not an already accomplished fact, but a 'production' that is always in process and always constituted within representation (Hall 1990). Despite facing multiple constraints in negotiating their identity, rural women migrants are by no means passive recipients in the process. Rather, they 'accept, resist, choose, specify, invent, redefine, reject, actively defend...' their identities (Cornell and Hartmann 1998: 77). For migrant women, identity is not so much a static label but a threshold, a transition, which always produces itself through 'the combined processes of being and becoming' (Fortier 2000: 2). Their agency lies in the very act of their identity construction and deconstruction, albeit the subversion itself is conditioned and constrained by discourse (Butler 1990).

To understand more fully the reactions and resistance of rural women as new entrants of the global capitalist system in transforming China, it is necessary to consider rural migrant women's 'alternative interpretations' in their everyday lives and in their daily negation of the 'hegemonic definitions' of their identity in ever changing material circumstances during their migration process (Ong 1991).

Performing identities and searching for belonging—Chinese rural women in the internal migration circuit

Migration involves more than a shift in physical location (Mills 1997). It influences all stages of the life course of rural women regardless of whether they are migrants, migrant returnees, or non-migrants (Murphy 2002). On the one hand, rural migrant women may experience a series of transformations when they change from being invisible labourers in rural households to being urban wage earners. Conversely, by taking on this 'modernity project', rural women also have to face new modes of control and power relations. Rural migrant women are far from being a homogenous group. Indeed, their transformations and struggles, which intersect with gender and class, amongst other factors, are shaped by every aspect of women's identity negotiation, construction, and performance. As was noted by a young migrant women in this study, '(After all these years of migration[3]) there is one thing I understand most clearly: when your circumstances change, your views also change. My experience of migration forced me to change greatly.'[4] In the following section I will explore the shifting identities negotiated and performed by rural migrant women at different stages in the migration cycle in order to illustrate the fluidity and plurality of their identity construction and performance.

Discarding peasant identity?

Based on her study of rural migrant women in Beijing, Gaetano (2008) concludes that upon migration, rural women reject rural identity and all that it signifies, preferring instead to embrace 'a more sexualized, urban femininity' through a discourse of 'eating spring rice' (*chi qingchunfan*)[5] (Gaetano 2008: 641–642). Whilst it is undeniable that the impact of their experience of the 'modern, outside world' upon rural migrant women is not only immediate but also profound, and that many rural women are at the forefront in performing such impacts and changes, it is worth pointing out that embracing an 'urban lifestyle' or having a desire to be modern does not necessarily mean that migrant women can easily discard their peasant identity or the low quality (*di suzhi*) that is linked to it. Their rural hukou registration, their temporary and secondary status in the urban labour market and their gender-specific waged work, along with the disparity between rural and urban space, invariably differentiate migrant women from an 'urban, modern identity' that is connected to high quality (*gao suzhi*). Such alienation and other institutional barriers that rural migrant women have to face in the city force them to rely heavily on their family and kinship *guanxi* networks for support, which may further push women to reconcile themselves to peasant identity.

By interpreting migration as a 'troubled process of subject formation' particularly for rural young women, Yan concludes that in the post-Maoist discourse of modernity, the countryside is produced as 'a wasteland' both materially and ideologically (Yan 2008: 37). Yet subject formation is not only a troubled process for rural youth, but in fact, for all rural people. Despite the government's effort to reduce the rural–urban disparity, the income gap between rural and urban areas continues to widen, and agricultural work is still considered to be 'unprofitable, unattractive and even redundant economic activity' by both rural and urban people (Croll and Huang 1997: 129). Given that they endure a living standard that is far below that of the urban sector, are labelled as an underclass having low quality (*di suzhi*), and linked with feudal backwardness and the possession of a limited outlook, rural people do not readily accept such a peasant identity without complaint. Many, indeed, find ways to counter the negative discourses of a peasant label. One such strategy is to disassociate themselves from land and farming altogether. Many migrant women's parents interviewed in this study took pride in the fact that their children never worked in the fields and had no knowledge of agricultural work. Rural migrant women also told me proudly that they did not have arable land at home, and that they were not involved in any work in the field, like 'other' peasants. Such a strong denunciation of farming and the peasant label seems to occur well before rural women embark on their migration journey.

Once in the process of migration, rural women became active performers of 'modernity' from many points of view. Their fellow villagers can readily list the 'big changes' in women after their migration: 'The way they talk is different from people in the village. They speak in a civilized way. They also eat and dress differently.'[6] Through their 'urbanized' appearance and lifestyle, migrant women send out a clear message that they are different from their fellow villagers, and have renounced their relationship with land, agricultural work, and peasantry. However, women's performances of such changes are not always well received by their families or fellow villagers. Migrant women themselves are also sensitive in observing boundaries, which exactly reflects their careful preservation of aspects of peasant identity.

Ping, who is 23, migrated to work in Beijing in 1999 at the age of 19. In talking about her fashionable outfits, she admitted that she had to make compromises with her parents back in her home village. Even though her parents had loosened their control over her as she grew older, and she had had a longer migration experience, Ping still carefully observed the boundary, making every effort to have a 'proper' appearance when visiting home: '. . . If I was young, in my 18, 19, or 20, they would definitely not allow me to wear what I liked. They would forbid me to wear this or that. But now they don't say anything about it as long I don't wear something too fashionable.'

Fully aware of their own changes, rural migrant women generally identify themselves as different from their fellow villagers. Some also try to distance themselves from their fellow villagers. Although Ping was not able to wear her fashionable heels in her home village, she was happy that unlike most of the girls at her age in her home village who had already got married and had children, she was still in migration. For Ping, they were from 'disparate worlds'—'I feel that those of my playmates who grew up with me . . . we are from totally different worlds. They cannot accept me, while I can't accept them, either. . . They feel I look strange (*kanbuguan*) and I feel they are very conservative and very feudal-minded (*fengjian*).'

Such changes do not only happen among young, single women migrants. Married women migrants also experience the transformation and feel they can no longer fit into the 'old' circle of friends and fellow villagers in their home villages. They also identify themselves as different from their 'left-behind' fellow villagers. Fen had been selling eggs in a local market in Beijing for nearly ten years when I met her. Talking about her fellow villagers, she commented: 'They stay in the villages and talk about the things that happen in the village, about which I have no idea at all. We do not have anything in common to talk about, and I am not interested in that kind of talk anymore.' Fen also managed to stay away from her fellow villagers by making fewer visits to her home village.

Rural women may, in fact, be able to give up their peasant identity more readily than rural men as they are less attached to the villages due to their 'temporary' status in the family as daughters and their role of an 'outsider and stranger' as wives when they move into their husbands' villages upon marriage. However, it might be too soon to conclude that rural migrant women actually discard their peasant identity. Due to women's transient status as rural migrants in the city, they have limited *guanxi* networks in the urban area. By drawing boundaries against their fellow villagers in the countryside, rural women migrants thus further confine their *guanxi* networks to only family members, relatives, and a handful of home fellows. Paradoxically, this strengthens their village-based family and kinship networks. Deeply embedded in their village kinship networks[7] throughout the migration circle, rural migrant women are required to strike a balance between their desire to be modern and non-rural and villagers' conventional moral codes for peasant women, even though urban waged work may provide them with the ability to resist to some extent the dominant patriarchal control over their lives.

Embracing urban modernity?

Just as they carefully preserve some aspects of peasant identity, rural migrant women do not 'embrace urban modernity' and pursue an urban identity blindly, either. Instead, they consciously evaluate different circumstances and make choices. Whether embracing urban modernity or not, migration opens up the arena for rural migrant women to contemplate and to perform the identities that are appropriate for them.

Rural migrant women, especially young women, may make an effort to look 'urban' by wearing fashionable clothes and using make-up, yet they are fully aware of the inequality between urban and rural areas and the superior status of the urban locals. In consequence, they generally identify themselves as different from urbanites, especially in terms of their hukou status, job security, pension, welfare, and education. Rural migrant women might be able to achieve with ease a modern, urban look, yet to feel modern and urban is not easily achievable for many.

Zheng was among the very few informants who had managed to enter the urbanites' world in her migration—with the help of her parents' network, she had secured a job as a bookkeeper in a local trade union office at the Beijing

Railway Bureau at the age of 21, where she could sit in the office along with local Beijingers and enjoy a stable salary and fixed working hours. However, just before she turned 25 years old, she resigned and returned home to Hebei province. Working along with local Beijingers day in and day out for nearly four years did not draw her closer to Beijing; rather, it pushed her further away from the city. As Zheng recounted:

> I am not saying that all of them (Beijing locals) are bad. I mean that everyone has his own living circle and his own friends and acquaintances. I don't fit into their circle at all. . . . People are sophisticated in Beijing . . . The people from the countryside are different. . . . They will not make up something about me to report to the boss behind my back.

Zheng's narrative shows a rather complicated picture of the boundaries and connections she built up through contact with those that surrounded her. She identifies herself as different from local Beijingers—'they' (Beijingers) grow up in a different environment and she does not fit in 'their' circle. She also draws a boundary between local Beijingers and people from the countryside—Beijingers are sophisticated, whereas rural people are different. However, she does not consider herself as one of 'them'—rural people are described as 'they' and there is a clear boundary between her and rural people in her narrative.

The majority of the rural women migrants interviewed held similar attitudes towards urban locals and people from the villages. Rural migrant women's transiency and status as both an underclass and a stranger and outsider in the city alienate them from urban local residents. This alienation, nonetheless, pushes rural women to re-evaluate 'those villagers' they once wanted to be distant from. This engenders a sense of belonging to their home villages and a way of reconnecting to their fellow villagers from whom they once tried to disassociate themselves. However, this reconnection is not sufficient for rural migrant women to reposition themselves back among their fellow villagers due to the profound impact of their exposure to the urban world, at least not in a short period of time. Even for those women migrant returnees who do muck in with farm work eventually, the return to the home village is seen as a temporary interruption to their migration project, rather than a long-term settlement. They manage to reconstruct an imagined identity as 'a migrant in the city' by differentiating themselves from their 'fellow peasants', reiterating memories about their life in the city and planning migration for the future.[8]

Becoming dagongmei?

'Dagongmei', as a contested identity for rural migrant women, has been undergoing various interpretations in recent years. However, contrary to the findings of the aforementioned studies, this study shows that 'dagongmei' is not in the vocabulary that rural migrant women would normally use to express their subjectivities. Neither does 'dagongmei' appear to offer a positive subject position that rural migrant women can relate to. None of the interviewed migrant women in this study referred to themselves as 'dagongmei'. In fact, 'dagongmei' never appeared in our conversations, and even 'dagong' was seldom used by rural migrant women when talking about their own work. Rather, 'dagongmei' as a label differentiates rural migrant women from both urban locals and rural migrant men. The implied low quality (*di suzhi*) that is connected to this label put migrant women off making any links with 'dagongmei'. Instead, rural migrant women actively drew different boundaries to exclude some rural migrants or to differentiate themselves from other migrants, and in so doing, constructing a positive Self in contrast to the negative Other.

Little solidarity has been demonstrated by rural migrant women who work on the assembly line in this study. A range of factors such as gendered hierarchical structures in the management and production systems in different factories, strong presence of home fellow based guanxi networks and temporalities of the relations between rural migrant women workers as well as women's age, education, marital status, and so on, all work together to differentiate rural migrant women in the workplace, which has a great impact on their identity negotiation and construction. For example, factory workers can be differentiated into various categories such as handyman/woman, temporary workers, probationary workers, general workers, skilled workers, etc., with different working time, work intensity, and wages. For those who can get into the managerial system, they can work as reserve cadres (*chugan*),[9] line leaders, monitors, heads of workshop, department managers, and so on. Indeed, as argued by Ong (1991), 'Rather than a homogeneous spread of Fordist production and "despotic" labor regimes, we find local milieu constituted by the unexpected conjunctures of labor relations and cultural systems, high-tech operations and indigenous values' (Ong 1991: 280). However, rural migrant women are by no means passive in these complicated power relations. They are creative performers, taking on various strategies in resisting different forms of control. Nevertheless, their acts and performances at times work towards further differentiation among women.

Dong, who is 20, migrated with her sister from a village in Guangdong province to work in Shenzhen in 2001 and together they were recruited by an electronics factory as 'reserve cadres'. However, Dong and her sister had very different job prospects later on—as Dong' had a diploma from a vocational college, she was assigned to help with recording stock, while her sister was assigned to the assembly line. Working in the same factory as her sister, Dong saw her own work as different from her sister's—'Mine (work) was actually much better. Pu gong's work (those who work at the assembly line) was the hardest. It really was.' Different types of work led to very different life journeys for the two sisters. While Dong gained the opportunity to become a technical worker later on, her sister became a real dagongmei. 'She worked (*dagong*) in the factory for a few years and then changed to another factory and several others... and couldn't make much money and has now gone back home and got married.'

Young, single migrant women also found it hard to identify with women who were older, married, and had children, even if they all worked on the same assembly line. Age and marital status are salient factors in undermining gender solidarity among rural migrant women. Xia, who is 22, migrated from Jiangxi to Shantou when she was only 15 years old. Working as a seamstress in a garment factory, she differentiated herself from most other workers in the factory, especially the temporary workers who worked as handywomen. Xia told me,

'You see those nannies (handywoman) outside? They are married and have a lot of children. They need money and they just want to work here temporarily. They are very lazy. They don't think about the future and they don't want to make any progress any more. I am so young. Of course I want to do something (make achievements).'

For Xia, age, marital status, having children, being lazy, having no plan for the future and money driven are linked directly to the hegemonic discourse of poor rural migrants with low quality, which she wished to dissociate from. Although working in the same factory together day in and day out, Xia did not realize that the handywomen she referred to also had to work 19 hours a day, with meagre wages. They had to leave their children behind in the villages to take on the hardest work in the factory. Although their mind and body had been stretched to an extreme, they, too, had a solid future plan—supporting their family.

Migrant women keep changing, constructing, and reconstructing their identity boundaries in accordance with their migration experiences and different circumstances. Many do not have just one boundary; instead, they create several boundaries to exclude/include other migrants. Shu (26 years old) migrated from a village in Hebei in 2000 because her father needed a helping hand for his rented counter in a local shop, where he sold construction workwear. Living in a migrant compound for more than four years, she could not identify with any of the rural migrant neighbours who were also working as shop assistants or bookkeepers in the neighbourhood. As she stated, 'The migrant girls here have a very hard life. I can't bear it at all.' Shu clearly identified herself as different from young rural migrant girls with less migration experience because they looked rural, endured hardship, had poor wages, and were easily contented with their life in the city. However, at the same time, Shu also drew up a clear boundary against those who had become 'too modern' when they had transgressed the patriarchal moral code set for women. Shu continued to relate:

> There was once a girl who migrated from a village in Hebei and she also lived in this compound. She was very nice and moderate then. And she looked like a girl from the countryside. . . . She has changed a lot. Her hair has been dyed yellow and she also wears that kind of very short skirt. She sleeps with whoever has money. . . . Those migrant girls don't care about anything at all, as long as they can get money! I try my best to stay away from them.

By trying to stay away from these two types of 'rural migrant girls', Shu is in fact attempting to refuse two dominant discourses pertaining to the identity of 'dagongmei'—one which depicts rural women as rustic, naïve but who could 'eat bitterness' (*chi ku*), working in harsh conditions; and the other which describes rural women migrants as the source of crime and immorality in the city. By setting boundaries against other rural migrants and by disassociating themselves from the dominant public discourses on 'dagongmei' identity, rural migrant women attempt to reject the identity labels pinned onto them, and the low quality that is implied.

Furthermore, rural migrant women's transient status, diverse geographical origins and the temporalities of relations among rural migrant women workers also restrict them from identifying with each other, as related by one of the young women:

> Although there were a lot of girls, they were not all from this part (of the country). . . . It was impossible to make real friends with them. They might be your friends when you lived and worked in the same yard but they might not recognize you once you stepped out of the gate. That is the reality.

Apathy and lack of trust towards fellow women migrant workers no doubt undermines the solidarity among rural migrant women, which reinforces women's sense of transiency and rootlessness in the city.

Self-employed women migrants who worked as street vendors or rented counters in local stores or markets differentiated themselves from other waged rural migrants, often with an emphasis on their freedom and profit, although most of them have to work as long and hard as other waged rural migrants. Jia, who is 24, migrated to Beijing from a village in Hebei. Renting a counter selling hardware with her husband in a department store, she was tied to the shop counter all day long. However, she was content with her life as compared to other migrant workers. As she emphasized, 'It is our own business and the time is ours . . . Those migrant workers definitely have no free time.'

Few rural migrant women identify themselves with rural migrant men. For rural migrant women, the 'peasant worker' identity, while appearing gender neutral, is used to refer to male rather than female rural migrants. Ning, who is 48, migrated to Beijing from a village in Hebei in 2001. Through the help of her son-in-law's uncle, who was a contractor of a building project in Beijing, she ran a canteen for rural migrant workers on the construction site. When I asked her in the interview whether she had ever had a chat with the rural construction workers she had been working with, she almost jumped up from her chair with disbelief that I had asked such a question and exploded in an outcry,

> Those people! Who were they?! They were all peasant workers. How could I have something to talk to them about! They were all strangers and spoke in very, very strong dialects, and it was impossible to talk to them at all.

Despite the fact that Ning was a rural migrant and had been working on the construction site along with other rural construction workers, she clearly refused to retain a peasant worker identity. In our interview, Ning continued to draw lines between herself and the rural construction workers on the same building site, and kept referring to them as 'those peasant workers', 'those labourers', and 'those strangers'. The boundaries were drawn on the basis of geographical origin (her home village was near Beijing), dialect (her dialect was closer to Mandarin), and social networks (her son-in-law's uncle was one of the contractors), as well as types of work (other workers did hard, manual work while her work, although equally hard, fell into the service sector). These boundaries invariably point to the implied low quality (*di suzhi*) that is connected to rural migrants and low value that is associated with them.

In emphasizing their differences in having more free time, more income, a more stable job, higher moral standard and less hardship compared to 'those peasant workers', rural migrant women try to construct and perform a different kind of self in the urban world. In so doing, they attempt to disassociate themselves with the hegemonic discourse on rural migrants and rural migrant women, and the low value associated with these labels. Conversely, such differentiation further reinforces their secondary status in the city. Their identity construction does not challenge the traditional patriarchal moral code set for women. Differentiating 'self' from other rural migrant women also undermines the solidarity among women migrant workers.

In search of a sense of belonging?

Writing about women workers in Asia, Ong (1991) convincingly argues that the remaking of working women's identities is closely linked to their awareness of how their status as daughter/woman is linked to the domination by family, industry, and society, and they are capable of constructing a sense of selfhood and belonging while manipulating, contesting, or rejecting different claims (Ong 1991).

Waged work transforms rural women from an invisible labourer in the household to a visible cash earner in the city, enables them to be financially independent from their families, and gives women an opportunity to recognize their own value and ability and gain confidence in themselves. This may serve to assist rural women in increasing their bargaining position within the household. Working in the cities, rural migrant women are believed to have more experience and more information about the cities and the labour market, and their opinions are valued more by their family members, which allows them to have greater involvement in decision-making on various matters in the family. Nan had been working as a shop assistant in Beijing since 1998. Reflecting on her achievements in migration, she observed:

> It may be because I have been in migration for such a long time—I now feel I am more mature than before in every aspect. In my family, when my parents have some problems, they all turn to me and ask for my opinion.

However, the new 'Self' women construct also has a clear gender imprint—it is closely linked to their being a better performer of the gender stereotypes of a devoted mother, a dutiful wife, and a filial daughter. Xia's account of the happiest moment in her migration as a garment factory worker in Shantou represents every woman in this study:

> Especially when I see my parents buying something with the money I earned and when I buy something for them with my own money, I feel really good. I have a sense of achievement. And I feel like I earned a lot of face (*hen you mianzi*).

Rural migrant women's sense of selfhood and achievement is always accompanied by an equally strong sense of temporariness. In her research on women factory workers, Pun concludes that 'Transience is the dominant characteristic of the lives of Chinese dagongmei. . . . This transient working life is not the choice of the women migrant workers, but rather, is a consequence of the legacy of socialist control and the residue of the Chinese patriarchal family' (Pun 2005: 5). Further to Pun's conclusion, I would argue that transience not only characterizes the lives of Chinese dagongmei, but those of all rural migrant workers in China, and this transience was felt and clearly articulated by rural women migrants themselves regardless of their age, marital status, or migration experience. Many rural women share the feeling of being a stranger in the city, rootless, isolated, and inferior. Their departure from the peasant identity does not erase their rural origin, just as their attempt to embrace modernity does not grant them legitimate urban membership. This feeling was well illustrated by Fen, who migrated from a village in Hebei and had been selling eggs in a local food market in Beijing for nearly ten years:

> When we are here, we always feel that what we are doing now is only temporary. We just work for today and we are not sure what is going to happen tomorrow. It is hard to say, isn't it? What if we cannot stay here any longer in the future? We still have to go back home. We live by day.

Fen's expression of 'live by the day' appeared repeatedly in rural women migrants' accounts of their life in the city in this study, especially when they talked about their plans for the future, which resonate with the transitory feeling of young migrant women in Beynon's (2004) study. However, women deal with such transience in various ways. While some women may endure more hardship during migration so as to maximize the migration return, some women, especially young, single women many translate their feeling of transitoriness into increased consumption,[10] as related by 22-year-old Nan who worked as a shop assistant in Beijing,

> We don't know what we are going to do yet. Sometimes . . . I just want to live for this very day. I spend all the money I have today and I will let tomorrow take care of it itself. I do it this way. Sometimes I feel life is not interesting at all. It is boring (*meijin*), indeed very boring (*zhenmeijin*).

Rural women's 'temporary status', both as a rural migrant and a woman, and their sense of 'rootlessness' further strengthen women's sense of precarity, just as Solinger put it, '[T]hey are unrooted noncitizens, wanderers; they are the elements of the 'floating population' (Solinger 1999).

Conclusion

In its search for 'nimble fingers' and 'disposable labour' (Elson and Pearson 1981; Wright 2006), global capital has created a new international division of labour, which has transformed China into a 'world factory' (Pun 2005). Not only this, but it has made the sexual and class exploitation of women and the working population more mobile, more extensive, and more complex (Ong 1991). Yet global capital has also opened up the possibility of new forms of power and politics, as well as new sites of resistance and action (Sassen 2007). As argued by Silver, '[T]here is no reason to expect that just because capital finds it profitable to treat all workers as interchangeable equivalents, workers would themselves find it in their interest to accept this' (Silver 2003: 177). As individuals who encounter global capital, Chinese rural women migrants, like their counterparts in other parts of Asia and South America, have to face 'evolving forms of insecurity, vulnerability, contingency and exploitation' (Strauss 2018: 626). They actively negotiate gender, citizenship, and precarity in the migration process and are true producers and performers of their identities.

However, their negotiation is not without its restrictions. Rather, it is shaped by 'the intersection of state agencies, the local workings of capital, and already configured local power/culture realms' (Ong 1991: 305). Rural migrant women's identity negotiation is directly influenced by the hegemonic discourse on 'suzhi' (quality), which devalues rural migrant women's labour, and 'hukou', which labels and differentiates rural (*di suzhi*, low quality) and urban (*gao suzhi*, high quality) and legitimizes the devaluation.

To distance themselves from the low quality and hence the low value that is connected to peasant identity, rural migrant women attempt to depart from their 'peasant' identity. Many rural women, especially young women, disassociate themselves from agricultural work even before they migrate to the city. Once in migration, rural migrant women identify themselves as being different from their fellow villagers. However, their desire to leave behind their peasant identity does not automatically grant women membership of urban space. A range of institutional barriers, as well as their lesser status in the city, force women to rely on their family and kinship networks in the city, which paradoxically strengthen their link to their homeland, and to their 'peasant' identity.

In contrast to Lee (1998) and Pun's (2005) conclusion that 'dagongmei' provides rural migrant women with a new, positive identity, this study shows that for rural migrant women, the identity of 'dagongmei', like 'nongmingong', represents a specific modality of the wretched victims of China's urbanization and a lower class in the city, characterized by insecurity. More importantly, it implies low quality hence low value of rural migrant women's labour. It is an identity label that rural migrant women reject. There can be many potential boundaries that women draw against other migrants, such as gender, age, marital status, types of work they do, their geographical origin, dialect they speak, their social networks in the city, and so on. In doing so, they attempt to live outside the identity of 'dagongmei' as defined by dominant discourses, to negotiate and perform a series of alternative identities in different contexts, and to create different meanings of 'Self' and 'Other' in their gendered migration process. However, such attempts undermine the solidarity among migrant women, even when they work on the same assembly line. Paradoxically, it also confirms and reinforces the differentiation between rural and urban and the low value that is assigned to rural women migrants' labour which is legitimized by the state through different institutions that label and maintain these divides and differentiation, (i.e. *hukou*).

Women migrants are fully aware of their status as transient and as an underclass in the city. Their efforts to negotiate new identities do not necessarily make women feel that they belong to the city. Few women identify themselves with urban locals. Many migrant women, indeed, share the feeling of being transient in the city, rootless, isolated, and inferior. Such alienating feelings reinforce women's attachment to their home in the villages. Through the flow and exchange of remittances, gifts, and information, rural women's sense of belonging to their home in the countryside thus comes to be renewed, and their ties with the home are strengthened.

Rural migrant women keep constructing/reconstructing their gendered identities and drawing boundaries in accordance with their migration experiences throughout their migration project. The boundaries they draw are, however, not static, but are fluid and ever changing in different circumstances and contexts. Many women do not have just one boundary, but create several boundaries to exclude or include others, creating different layers of 'Self' and 'Other'. However, the processes of their identity negotiation are inevitably constrained because of their gender. In negotiating their identities, rural migrant women continue to uphold the patriarchal moral code set for women. These identities and boundaries have a clear gender imprint— they are always linked to women's role as a devoted mother, a dutiful wife, and a filial daughter.

Rural women's everyday struggle as women peasant workers in contemporary China is reflected in this seemingly contradictory, negotiated passage of identity and belonging, characterized by fluidity—a dynamic, a 'reception place for differences at play' (Preis 1997: 98). It is through this process of denunciating, recognizing, and drawing on the boundaries of Self and Other that rural migrant women start to redefine the meaning of being a rural migrant woman. The processes of the construction and deconstruction of identities form the very scenes of agency. Although the process is conditioned by structural forces, they cannot determine it (Tiano 1994: 212). Rather, the process is itself a significant force. As argued by Cornell and Hartmann, although identities are shaped by circumstances, they are also capable of reorganizing actions in ways that can transform the circumstances (Cornell and Hartmann 1998).

Acknowledgement

The chapter is adapted from N. Zhang (2014), 'Performing identities: Women in rural–urban migration in contemporary China'. *Geoforum* (54): 17–27.

Notes

1. 'suzhi' (roughly means 'quality' in English), first appeared during the early 1980s in the state documents on population quality (*renkou suzhi*). As Anagnost convincingly argued, the term encompasses the changing relationship between value and bodies. In popular discourses, the low quality (*di suzhi*) of the population, especially rural population, became the impediments to China's modernization (Anagnost 2004: 190). For more discussion on suzhi, please also see Anagnost 2004; Yan 2008.
2. 'Dagongmei' is a Cantonese word and is commonly translated as 'working sisters' in recent research literature. According to Pun, 'Dagong means "working for the boss", or "selling labour", connoting commodification and a capitalist exchange of labour for wages. Mei means younger sister. It denotes not merely gender, but also marital status—"mei" is single, unmarried and younger (and thus of a lower status)' (Pun 1999: 3).
3. Words in brackets were added by the author.
4. Interview with 25-year-old Shan, who migrated from Henan in 1996.
5. A popular saying during the 1990s which implies young women live off their youth and youthful beauty. The 'rice of the youth' does not last for ever, just as one's youth that fades.
6. Villager from Hebei.
7. For a more detailed discussion, please see Zhang 2006, 2011.
8. Please see Zhang 2013 for a more detailed discussion on rural women migrant returnees in China.

9. 'Chunagan' is a shortened term for Chubei ganbu in Chinese. It refers to enlisted personnel who, after training, will fill managerial roles. However, in reality, those who are recruited as 'chugan' work like handymen/women.
10. See Yu and Pun (2008).

References

Anagnost, A. (2004) 'The corporeal politics of quality (suzhi)'. *Public Culture*, 16(2): 189–208.
Au, L. and Nan, S. (2007) 'Chinese women migrants and the social apartheid'. *Development*, 50(3): 76–82.
Barchiesi, F. (2011) *Precarious Liberation: Workers, the State and Contested Social Citizenship in Postapartheid South Africa*. New York: SUNY Press and the University of KwaZulu-Natal Press.
Beynon, L. (2004) 'Dilemmas of the heart'. In A. Gaetano and T. Jacka (eds.), *On the Move: Rural-to-Urban Migration in Contemporary China*. New York: Columbia University Press, pp. 131–150.
Bourdieu, P. (1997) *Language and Symbolic Power*. Cambridge: Polity Press.
Butler, J. (1990) *Gender Trouble: Feminism and the Subversion of Identity*. London: Routledge.
Cornell, S. and Hartmann, D. (1998). *Ethnicity and Race: Making Identities in a Changing World*. Thousand Oaks: Pine Forge Press.
Croll, E. and Huang, P. (1997) 'Migration for and against agriculture in eight Chinese villages'. *The China Quarterly*, 149: 128–146.
Davin, D. (1996) 'Gender and rural-urban migration in China'. *Gender and Development*, 4(1): 24–30.
Davin, D. (1999) *Internal Migration in Contemporary China*. London: Macmilla
Elson, D. and Pearson, R. (1981) 'Nimble fingers make cheap workers': An analysis of women's employment in third world export manufacturing'. *Feminist Review*, 7: 87–107.
Fan, C. (2002) 'The elite, the natives, and the outsiders: Migration and labor market segmentation in urban China'. *Annals of the Association of American Geographers*, 92(1): 103–124.
Fan, C. (2003) 'Rural-urban migration and gender division of labor in China'. *International Journal of Urban and Regional Research*, 27(1): 24–47.
Fortier, A. (2000) *Migrant Belongings: Memory, Space, Identity*. Oxford: Berg.
Gaetano, A. (2008) 'Sexuality in diasporic space: Rural-to-urban migrant women negotiating gender and marriage in contemporary China'. *Gender, Place & Culture*, 15(6): 629–645.

Gaetano, A. and Jacka, T. (eds.) (2004) *On the Move – Women in Rural-to-Urban Migration in Contemporary China*. New York: Columbia University Press.

Hall, S. (1990) 'Cultural identity and diaspora'. In J. Rutherford (ed.), *Identity: Community, Culture, Difference*. London: Lawrence and Wishart, pp. 557–568.

Harney, A. (2008) *The China Price*. New York: The Penguin Press.

Jacka, T. (2006) *Rural Women in Urban China: Gender, Migration and Social Change*. London: ME Sharpe.

Langellier, K. (1999) 'Personal narrative, performance, performativity: Two or three things I know for sure'. *Text and Performance Quarterly*, 19(2): 125–144.

Lee, C. K. (1998) *Gender and the South China Miracle: Two Worlds of Factory Women*. Berkeley: University of California Press.

Mills, M. B. (1997) 'Contesting the margins of modernity: Women, migration, and consumption in Thailand'. *American Ethnologist*, 24: 37–61.

Moore, H. (1994) *A Passion for Difference: Essays in Anthropology and Gender*. Cambridge: Polity Press.

Murphy, R. (2002) *How Migrant Labour is Changing Rural China*. New York: Cambridge University Press.

NBSC (2021) Report on national survey of rural migrant workers 2020. Available from http://www.stats.gov.cn/tjsj/zxfb/202104/t20210430_1816933.html/ (Accessed at 1 June 2021).

Neilson, B. and Rossiter, N. (2005) 'From precarity to precariousness and back again: Labour, life and unstable networks'. *Fibreculture Journal*, 5. Available at http://journal.fibreculture.org/issue5/neilsonrossiter.html/ (Accessed at 1 June 2021).

Neilson, B. and Rossiter, N. (2008) 'Precarity as a political concept, or, fordism as exception. Theory'. *Culture & Society*, 25(7–8): 51–72. doi:10.1177/0263276408097796 (Accessed at 1 June 2021).

Ong, A. (1991) 'The gender and labor politics of postmodernity'. *Annual Review of Anthropology*, 20: 279–309.

Preis, A. S. (1997) 'Seeking place: Capsized identities and contracted belonging among Sri Lankan Tamil refugees'. In K. F. Olwig and K. Hastrup (eds.), *Siting Culture: The Shifting Anthropological Project*. New York: Routledge, pp. 87–102.

Pun, N. (1999) 'Becoming dagongmei (working girls): The politics of identity and difference in reform China'. *The China Journal*, 42: 1–19.

Pun, N. (2005) *Made in China: Women Factory Workers in a Global Workplace*. Durham: Duke University Press.

Sassen, S. (2007) 'The global city'. In D. Nugent and J. Vincent (eds.), *A Companion to the Anthropology of Politics*. Oxford: Blackwell Publishing Ltd, pp. 168–178.

Schierup, C. U., Munck, R., Likic-Brboric, B., and Neergaard, A. (eds.) (2015) *Migration, Precarity, and Global Governance: Challenges and Opportunities for Labour*. Oxford: Oxford University Press.

Silver, B. (2003) *Forces of Labor: Workers: Movements and Globalization since 1870.* New York: Cambridge University Press.

Silvey, R. and Elmhirst, R. (2003) 'Engendering Social Capital: Women Workers and Rural-Urban Networks in Indonesia's Crisis'. *World Development*, 31(5): 865–881.

Solinger, D. (1995) 'China's Urban Transients in the Transition from Socialism and the Collapse of the Communist "Urban Public Goods Regime"'. *Comparative Politics*, 27(2): 127–146.

Solinger, D. (1999) *Contesting Citizenship in Urban China: Peasant Migrants, the State, and the Logic of the Market.* California: University of California Press.

Strauss, Kendra. (2018) 'Labour geography 1: Towards a geography of precarity?'. *Progress in Human Geography*, 42: 622–630. 10.1177/0309132517717786 (Accessed at 6 June 2021).

Suliman, S. and Weber, H. (2019) 'Global development and precarity: A critical political analysis'. *Globalizations*, 16: 4,525–4,540. doi: 10.1080/14747731.2018.1463739 (Accessed at 6 June 2021).

Sun, W. (2004) 'Indoctrination, fetishization, and compassion: Media constructions of the migrant women'. In A. Gaetano and T. Jacka (eds.), *On the Move: Rural-to-Urban Migration in Contemporary China.* New York: Columbia University Press.

Tiano, S. (1994) *Patriarchy on the Line: Gender, Labor, and Ideology in the Mexican Maquila Industry.* Philadelphia: Temple University Press.

Tsianos, V. and Papadopoulos, D. (2006a) 'Precarity: A savage journey to the heart of embodied capitalism'. Available at: https://transversal.at/transversal/1106/tsianos-papadopoulos/en/ (Accessed at 6 June 2021).

Tsianos, V. and Papadopoulos, D. (2006b) 'Who's afraid of immaterial workers? Embodied capitalism, precarity, imperceptibility'. Available at: http://www.preclab.net/text/06-TsianosPapado-Precarity.pdf/ (Accessed at 6 June 2021).

Wright, M. (2006) *Disposable Women and Other Myths of Global Capitalism.* New York: Routledge.

Yan, H. (2008) *New Masters New Servants: Migration, Development and Women Workers in China.* Durham: Duke University Press.

Yu, X. and Pun, N. (2008) 'Xiaofei shehui yu "xinshengdai dagongmei" zhutizaizao' (Consumer society and the subject reconstruction of new generation dagongmei). *Shehuixue yanjiu* 3: 143–171.

Zhang, L. (2001) *Strangers in the City: Reconfigurations of Space, Power, and Social Networks Within China's Floating Population.* Stanford: Stanford University Press.

Zhang, N. (2006) 'Social networks and women's rural-urban migration in contemporary China'. *Capital and Society*, 39(2): 104–125.

Zheng, T. (2009) *Red Lights: The Lives of Sex Workers in Postsocialist China.* Minneapolis: University of Minnesota Press.

8
Hierarchies, Shadows, and Precarity
Cultural Production on Online Literature Platforms in China

Elaine Jing Zhao

Introduction

Informality in the labour market has been a long-standing feature of the Chinese economy. Since the reform and opening up, the ideological shift towards economic developmentalism has seen the accelerated rise of informal labour. This parallels the rise of informal and often precarious labour underwritten by neoliberalism and its variants in different parts of the world (Kalleberg and Hewison 2013). While existing literature has built knowledge about precarious positions of informal workers in China (Chang 2009; Qiu 2017; Swider 2016), the shifted gears in the economic development path demand attention to non-regular labour in emerging industries. The turn to creative industries and internet industries is particularly noteworthy. The policy discourse of creative industries since the late 1990s in the UK has quickly attracted attention from policymakers in China (Keane 2007, 2013; Wang 2004). Contrary to the approach to cultural sectors as receivers of state subsidies, the creative industries discourse stresses the potential for market growth and job creation. The prospect of job creation is clearly manifested in China's promotion of creative industries in the policy discourse, defined as 'those industries that rely upon creative ideas, skill and advanced technology as core elements, increase value in production and consumption, create wealth and provide extensive jobs for the society through a series of activities' (Li 2008: 3). As internet penetration gathers pace, the convergence between creative industries and digital technologies is considered as holding transformative potential to drive economic development. In China's Thirteenth Five Year Plan (2016–2020), digital creative industries became recognized as one of the five strategic emerging industries.

Indeed, amateur creativity and informal labour have been key sources of economic and cultural value in China's digital transformation (Zhao 2019). In analysing the social and economic impact of creative industries in China, leading industrial economist and policy adviser Li Wuwei (2008) points out that creative industries are not only creating new employment opportunities for Chinese society but also changing the traditional employment structure of China, with conspicuous growth of unregistered labour. The growing penetration of digital platforms further accelerates such development. According to the forecast of AliResearch (cited in Sohu 2017), up to 400 million people in China will be self-employed in the gig economy by 2036, constituting 50 per cent of the total labour force in China. Among this growing population are professionalizing amateurs engaged in creative and cultural production on digital platforms. While much has been written about amateur creators such as guild labour in online gaming (Zhang and Fung 2013) and volunteering subtitlers (Davis and Yeh 2017), increasingly professionalizing creators harvesting both economic returns and cultural reputation warrant further studies.

Existing research on creative labour features both championship and critique. Celebratory accounts tend to focus on elite creative workers and emphasize flexibility, mobility, and autonomy as their defining characteristics (Florida 2002; Howkins 2001). As Lobato and Thomas (2015) insightfully point out, informality in such discourses 'takes on a positive character, associated with freedom, autonomy and liberation from Fordist routinization' (p. 72). Such boosterism about creative labour has triggered noticeable critique. This body of literature reveals that creative professionals tend to be subject to precarious conditions and self-exploitation (Deuze 2007; McRobbie 2002; Ross 2009). Creative and cultural workers are not immune to existential, financial, and social insecurity (Gill and Pratt 2008). As digital platforms open up opportunities for 'ordinary' users to create content and seek audience, a growing body of literature in internet and digital media studies has focused on entrepreneurial creators and their experiences in navigating various platforms (Banet-Weiser 2012; Burgess and Green 2009; Duffy 2016; Poell, Nieborg, and Duffy 2021; Nieborg and Poell 2018). The debate so far has been productive in revealing mixed realities of creative labour and their development in the platform economy.

This chapter examines aspiring creative labour on digital platforms with reference to online literature writers in China. The online literature field is a significant case here, not only for its size and scale in China's digital creative industries, but also for the insights it affords into the platfomization of cultural production in China. The analysis draws on in-depth interviews with aspiring online literature writers and publicly available resources. Specifically, 26 interviews were conducted between 2014 and 2016 with online literature writers publishing on a range of platforms including qidian.com, 17k.com, zongheng.com, jinjiang.com, and hongxiu.com. The interviewees are carefully selected to include writers across the spectrum of experience and status. Face-to-face interviews were supplemented with conversations with writers in industry gatherings and online forums as well as secondary sources such as industry literature and news reports to capture the nature of their experiences.

The rest of this chapter begins with a brief overview of the evolution of the online literature market in China, outlining how digital platforms have carved out an alternative space of cultural production for aspiring creators. Then I reveal how hierarchies and shadows emerge from the creative labour market and unpack how aspiring writers experience multiple realities of precarity. I explain how these writers experience precarity and at the same time exhibit an entrepreneurial ethos as they navigate four aspects of platform politics, namely, those in relation to (1) access, (2) temporality, (3) visibility, and (4) copyright protection. The focus on creative labour adds to the current research on the informal labour in China, which has predominantly focused on migrant workers and laid-off state-owned enterprise workers as a result of economic deregulation and restructuring (Hong 2011; Sun 2014), or conventional labour-intensive sectors (Swider 2016; Wu et al. 2019). Drawing on creative labour studies, platform studies, and informal media economics, this chapter contributes to the wider debate on relationships between creativity and commerce, capital and labour in the age of platforms.

The platformization of the online literature market in China

Before the emergence and adoption of online media, literature in China is largely an elite undertaking, the privilege of a minority of people (Ouyang 2011). The high entry barrier to literary production in the country is closely connected to the formal literary production system, which is strictly controlled by the state through book numbers issued to state-run publishing houses (Latham 2005). Private publishing houses can only obtain book numbers through collaborations with state-owned publishers. Elitism and state control in the literary production system is also evidenced in the institutional mechanism of China Writers' Association (CWA, *zhongguo zuojia xiehui*). It has been unique worldwide since the disintegration of the Soviet Union as a nominal association of writers actually operated by a national government. The government provides financial support to the CWA, which gives writers an 'iron rice bowl' to produce the 'major melody' works in the centrally planned cultural production system (Martinsen 2006). Such financial support from the state has waned since the 1980s, giving rise to a market-driven literary field under state control.

As the internet opens up creative space for amateurs and enthusiasts, literary production has re-established its popular orientation (Ouyang 2011). As well as a lower entry barrier, the internet provides relatively more creative freedom as the sheer volume of works creates a loophole in the censorship mechanism. Readers find an alternative site for literary consumption on the internet, which addresses popular taste, rather than producing literary works for the imagined readership of the cultural bureaucracies. As such, the online literature space fills the market gap left by the state-controlled literary production market.

While the ethos of internet literature writing resided in non-monetary motives, equality, and truthfulness at an early stage (Ouyang 2002), this alternative creative space has witnessed the rise of digital platforms with the establishment of a successful freemium business model. A crucial platform here is Qidian, launched in 2003 by Chinese Magic Fantasy Union, a group of amateur writers of fantasy novels. The platform hosts online literature works published in serial form, and derives revenue mainly from user subscription to premium content, at 0.02 to 0.05 yuan per thousand Chinese characters in most cases. Moreover, the 'tipping' (*dashang*) feature allows authors opportunities to receive rewards from readers in the form of a platform-specific virtual currency. Such tips can be converted into real currency based on a certain ratio and split between the platform and the author on a revenue-sharing basis. The freemium model, with the capacity to allow both readers and platforms to share the risks inherent in creative production, has been a key factor in Qidian's success (Xiang and Montgomery 2012). Other online literature platforms such as Hongxiu, Jinjiang, Xiaoxiang, and Zongheng soon followed suit. The successful commercialization strategy has driven the rapid growth of the online literature market, with its market size reaching over 9 billion RMB and catering to over 333 million users by the end of 2016 (*People's Daily* 2017).

Over the past two decades, the market has consolidated through multiple rounds of mergers and acquisitions. Previously mentioned sites have become a part of the internet literature divisions of China's leading internet platforms, such as the interactive entertainment media company Shanda Interactive Entertainment Ltd. (Nasdaq: SNDA), China's leading search engine Baidu (NASDAQ: BIDU), the social media giant Tencent (OTCMKTS: TCEHY), and the leading online game developer and operator Perfect World (formerly NASDAQ:PWRD, privatized in 2015). The merger of Tencent Literature and Shanda Literature (later known as Cloudary) in 2015 further consolidated the market. The resulting China Literature (also known as Yuewen Group) owns multiple online literature platforms and has since established market dominance.

As the market matures, it has witnessed the diversification of revenue streams propelled by copyright transactions. In addition to user subscription, downstream licensing has become a noticeable revenue source, where platforms sell adaptation rights to filmmakers, TV producers, or game developers (Zhao 2011, 2017). The rapidly growing online video industry has also increasingly sought to obtain the rights to adapt online literature, as streaming platforms start to develop original screen content (Zhao and Keane 2013). Through these deals, online literature platforms not only receive licensing fees but also gain a share of the advertising revenue associated with the screen products. Consumption data such as clicks, subscriptions, favourites, comments, and tips inform various kinds of metrics, serving as indicators of readers' ephemeral tastes. These assist platform owners in the attempt to identify promising writers and further commercialization opportunities. Therefore, readers as produsers/prosumers are an important part in capital accumulation (Andrejevic 2009). In this context, what was previously a space for hobbyists writing online with little commercial aspiration has transformed into a market-driven, platform-dominated, and copyright-centred industry.

Concomitant with the commercialization logic of digital platforms in the online literature field is the rise of genre fiction. From time travel fantasies and warrior legends to romance and science fiction, these genres transport readers to an imaginary space where they can fulfil their desires for fame, fortune, power, love, and sex, which are often hard to attain in real life. As such, Chinese online genre fiction is also widely known as 'YY fiction', where YY stand for yiyin, or 'lust of the mind' (Hockx 2015). By creating such a mind space, commercially viable works are able to capture an expanding readership in contemporary China.

The rapidly scaling industry has witnessed an increasing number of registered writers at various publishing platforms. By the end of 2016, market leader China Literature claimed close to 5.3 million writers on its platforms (China Literature 2016). Another sign of rapid commercialization is a rich list dedicated to online literature writers in China, published annually since 2012. In 2016, Zhang Wei, who publishes on Qidian under the name of Tangjia Sanshao, became the first Chinese author to earn more than 100 million yuan (about US$14.5 million) a year. He topped the Chinese Online Writers Rich

List for the fourth consecutive year with royalties of 110 million yuan (around US$16 million) (*China Daily* 2016). However, while top-earning writers feature prominently in the media spotlight, many more are struggling at the bottom of the pyramid.

Traversing platform politics of access: Hierarchies and shadows

While aspiring writers become more commercially motivated, the market is in fact characterized by politics of access, with hierarchies and shadows. First, the tiered contracting system and the freemium business model constitute platform hierarchies for writers to navigate. The initial target for aspiring writers to aim for is to become contracted writers to platforms. Indeed, while anyone can self-publish on online literature platforms, not everyone can secure a contract. As writers keep uploading new instalments of their works, online editors review these work-in-progress and offer contracts to commercially viable ones. Editors' decisions are informed by data as well as their professional experience. Once contracted, writers may see their works promoted on digital platforms, which often means a more prominent position or more exposure on platforms. Most writers agree that platform promotion is crucial in elevating visibility and driving readership. For contracted writers to receive remunerations from user subscription, further performance targets need to be met before part of their books are moved behind the pay wall.

In addition, the contracting system takes various forms, with different approaches to and tiers of remuneration. Some contracts offer remuneration based on a fixed price per thousand words regardless of subscription figures. Other contracts offer revenue-sharing deals based on user subscription, where revenue is usually split 50:50 between platforms and authors. In either case, the unit prices vary from case to case. On China Literature's platforms, authors are categorized into four classes, where 'platinum authors' receive the best terms. Such variances as well as different commercial prospects of downstream licensing mean that authors' income could vary significantly. As one writer shared his experience,

> I didn't get a cent for the first three months until I received a contract. I get paid 20 yuan per thousand words and that's it. I don't get to share any revenue. Now I usually upload 6000 words a day and receive only 3600 yuan a month. It's much less than a common white-collar's salary.

As the tiered contracting system offers different levels of remuneration and prestige, precarity is framed into the structure of hope. For some writers, a shimmer of hope is what keeps them on platforms despite their precarious status. As one writer said, 'If I keep writing, there's always some hope; if I quit, then all my previous efforts become futile.' Another shared his thoughts thus, 'Some people say I should be more realistic. I think there are always some pathways for the so-called unrealistic. Plus I'm doing what I love.' Such emphasis on hope and passion reveals how the design of the platform labour regime cultivates entrepreneurialism associated with neoliberal subjectivities. While some persist with their creative pursuits, many more tend to give up. In fact, many works are left unfinished once hope and passion becomes unsustainable.

Moreover, hierarchies in the contracting system extend beyond remuneration for creative works. Informality in the platform-mediated labour relations means those without other formal employment face many barriers in life. Most notably, this means the majority of online literature writers are excluded from social security benefits, such as basic endowment insurance, basic medical insurance, work injury insurance, unemployment insurance, and maternity insurance, as well as the public housing fund. Essentially these online writers face the risk of being marginalized in society. In mid-2013, the eleventh anniversary of Qidian, it announced a medical insurance plan for the writers. While this is a step towards improving the protection framework for writers, it was only offered to selected VIP authors, long-term contracted authors, and platinum authors. Therefore, the number of writers who have actually received such support is microscopic compared to the total pool of registered writers.

Furthermore, apart from the visible online literature writers situated at different levels of the hierarchy, many others are invisible. The challenge of securing contracts has given rise to ghost writing as an informal labour practice. For contracted authors, surrogate writing provides a way of buffering against the risk when they run out of inspiration, time, or energy to keep up. For a large number of new entrants who are yet to secure contracts, they can receive a fixed amount of money based on work-for-hire rates. Thus, surrogate writing offers both contracted writers and their non-contracted peers an approach to self-managing risks, which is characteristic of contemporary society (Bauman 2001; Beck 1992).

Based on the atomization of the creative process with a clear division of labour into tradable units and temporal orchestration, surrogate writing is often well planned and organized (Zhao 2017). Hiring advertisements are distributed in online communities where online literature writers gather. Would-be surrogate writers can contact advertisement publishers, who will then send over a plot scenario or chapter synopsis and ask for some sample work. Those who pass such writing tests will be hired. They will then begin the creative process based on the guidelines supplied by the hirers. Usually the deal is based on an oral or informally written agreement, which puts surrogate writers in precarious positions. As one surrogate writer described himself, 'I'm one of many invisible figures in the market. That puts me at the bottom of the pyramid.' Furthermore, the deal indicates a shifted relationship between the writer and the finished creative product. As writers subcontract the work to others, they informally release part of their creative responsibilities yet still claim ownership of the work. In this sense, surrogate writing is a case of the formal sector acquiring skills or services from the informal zone, under informal conditions. This reflects the broader dynamics between the formal and informal, where outsourcing is a mechanism of value capture (Lobato and Thomas 2015; Zhao 2019). As creative works generated from the shadow market essentially accrue to the interest of the platform, the accumulation process occurs at the expense of those in the shadows.

Despite the invisible status, some writers treat surrogate writing as a training camp and a test ground. They cherish the hope of becoming independent writers and launching their own writing careers online. It is the hope of progressing towards the more formal end of the spectrum that drives these invisible writers. Indeed, outsourcing often overlaps with incubation in the formal/informal dynamics (Lobato and Thomas 2015; Zhao 2019). Yet such chances for those at the bottom of the creative pyramid to climb up are slim. The success or failure of creative works goes beyond literary creation itself, since promotion plays a crucial role in elevating visibility. However, platforms often prioritize more established writers in promotion strategies. In this context, the informal practice of surrogate writing arises from and at the same time perpetuates the hierarchy among online literature writers. The experience of navigating the hierarchies and shadows is complicated by the platform politics of visibility, a point I will return to later.

Navigating platform politics of temporality

In addition to the negotiated access to the market of hierarchies and shadows, platform politics of temporality raises another challenge for writers. The serialized nature of platformization of online literature production in China means regular updates are crucial to maintaining readership. The serial format, operating in connection with platform-imposed terms regarding instalment upload and update cycle, puts writers in an inequitable temporal regime. Existing literature has well documented the broader development of time compression in contemporary societies and how that impacts workers (Epstein and Kalleberg 2004; Harvey 1989; Hochschild 1997; Rosa 2003; Sharma 2014). The increasing penetration of information and communication technologies has further complicated socio-technical temporal shifts (Castells 1996; Urry 2000; Wajcman 2008).

The lived experience of time among writers in China's online literature market highlights flexibility as more of a myth than reality. In fact, it has become common for platforms to include a clause on instalment update frequency in the contract, for example to maintain a daily update of 6,000 words. Many writers agree that a pause in update is costly. As one writer said,

> If I stop uploading new chapters for a week, the number of clicks on the book could plunge drastically. Some less tolerant platforms will terminate a contract in such circumstances. Other platforms may provide financial support. For example, if an author earns less than 500 yuan a month, then the author can apply for some allowance. An author can only have such allowance, which is around 1500 yuan, for several months of the year, usually not more than 6 months. It can be very stressful.

Furthermore, the typical length of online literature works exacerbates the challenge of platform temporality. Under the freemium model, authors are motivated to deliberately lengthen their works to increase their income. Many interviewees pointed to the tedious nature of such work, which is paradoxically perceived as a feasible measure to maximize financial prospects. As both product and process influence creator experience (Hesmondhalgh and Baker 2011), such a measure can be seen as a compromise. As a result of such strategic extension, it is common for a novel published on online literature platforms to reach several million characters. To put things in context, novels published in print usually range between 0.1 and 0.3 million Chinese characters. In this context, the extended lengths make it more challenging to adhere to regular daily updates over the long term. For many writers, it takes relentless perseverance to maintain daily updates and the completion rate over the long term, which is a crucial part of the success formula. One author mentioned a well-known writer for his capacity to stick with daily updates over a long term:

> It's not difficult to upload 10,000 words a day. What makes it challenging is to keep doing so for eight years. This is a major reason why Xuehong has so many fans.

However, to keep up with platform-imposed terms and readers' expectation has a cost in health and well-being. As one author reflected on his earlier experience:

> I cannot afford to stop uploading new instalments. When my wife was in labour, I brought my laptop with me and wrote my novel in the hospital. When I had a high fever at 40°C, I wrote about 6000 words as soon as the fever faded a bit. I'm making blood and sweat money (*xuehanqian* in Chinese, meaning money earned through arduous efforts).

Some authors who have worked in the field longer show more self-reflective recalibration of their practice, although to a limited extent. As one writer shared her experience:

> When I started three years ago, I made it my first priority to upload new instalments frequently. At one time I only slept 4 hours a day for about two to three months. Later I realised the importance of a healthy lifestyle and stopped staying up late. Still, I cannot afford to relax much.

For more successful authors, there is a strong sense of urgency to maximize productivity while they have their readers' attention. The highly risky nature of creative production evidently drives online writers to seize the moment. They have to produce works quickly and well enough in the hope of capitalizing on any indication of market popularity. As one writer put it,

> I'd rather capture the moment when I have my fans with me. Who knows if they are still there for me if I take a break?

Clearly, platformization of online literature production in China is a process entangled with politics of temporality. On one hand, the urgency to 'sync up' and the fear of failure to do so result in anxiety, frustration, insecurity, and exhaustion. On the other hand, the urgency to capture or build on current market worth creates a lock-in effect among more successful writers. As writers recalibrate to readers' time needs, platform-imposed terms, and their own entrepreneurial ethos, they do so at the expense of health and well-being, quality of work, and sense of satisfaction. In other words, they tend to internalize inequitable temporal relations through self-exploitation. This in turn throws the sustainability of their creative pursuits into question.

Countering platform politics of visibility

As aspiring writers pursue the goal of getting paid for creative labour, self-promotion and relationship building with readers and peer writers is widely recognized as an important part of skillsets. This is considered particularly important given the politics of visibility, where platforms tend to prioritize more established writers in support mechanisms as discussed earlier. In the context where clicks, subscriptions, favourites, and comments become a barometer of readers' interest and writers' commercial prospects, the instrumental value of sociality becomes evident. As Duffy (2016) points out, the instrumentality of affective relationships is a salient feature of aspirational labour. Many authors mentioned how readers' comments inform their writing. Moreover, authors are increasingly utilizing social media platforms to establish affective relationships with readers. As one author shared his experience,

> I have a WeChat public account, and I spend much time there interacting with my fans. I make sure their questions are answered, and sometimes I reveal a little bit on how the story will unfold. It's important to maintain a constant connection with my fans. I cannot rely too much on 17k (the platform where he publishes) to promote my works. On social media I can have my own channel.

Another author echoed the importance of third-party social media platforms in building audience and interacting with them:

> Commenting on the publishing platform is useful in converting readers to paying subscribers. However, I need to get to that point of reaching wide enough readers first. A separate social media platform such as WeChat is more useful here. I need my own channel to build the community.

Apart from interacting with readers, several authors mentioned the conscious efforts to connect with their circle of peers, with the hope of receiving potential validation and cross-promotion. This is reflective of the phenomenon where creative workers rely on informal networking as support in the absence of institutional or organizational support (McRobbie 2002).

Evidently, self-promotion on social media is a measure to circumvent hierarchical platform promotion mechanisms, which depend very much on metric performance and often go to big-name authors. This results in a scenario where emerging authors find it hard to access platform promotion in various forms, such as home page recommendations or editor's picks.

In the context of a highly consolidated market, writers perceive it as urgent to establish their own channels to boost attention and visibility. As Marwick (2013) insightfully points out, 'Web2.0 sites instruct wannabes in the art of entrepreneurialism, self-promotion, and careful self-editing' (p. 15). Platform politics of visibility further cultivate the entrepreneurial culture of self-promotion and community building for instrumental value.

As writers exhibit the neoliberal subjectivity of entrepreneurs and commit themselves to self-promotion on social media, the line between public and private becomes increasingly permeable. Neoliberal, market-driven values not only manifest in the literature production process but also infiltrate into non-writing time. Self-promotion thus becomes a part of life where 'work is dispersed into all areas of life and the social becomes the site for the creation of new forms of productive activity and their transformation into commodities' (Hearn 2006: 132). As entrepreneurial-minded authors garner attention and reputation on social media, self-promotion becomes 'a process of transforming and shifting cultural labor into capitalist business practices' (Banet-Weiser 2012: 8).

Negotiating platform politics of copyright

As writers seek readership, it is undeniable that readers include not only paying subscribers but also infringing content consumers. Indeed, informal consumption of cultural products has a long-standing history in China (Pang 2006; Wang and Zhu 2003; Zhao 2019; Zhao and Keane 2013). In the case of online literature, non-paying readers can easily access content for free under dedicated threads in online forums or via cloud services. The boundary between freemium business model and free riding can be shaky. By monitoring updates of original serialized content, some users manually type out the updated content and make it available in online forums with only a couple of minutes' lag. Increasingly, with the aid of optical character recognition software, infringing parties can convert original content into text and make it available online in seconds. Commercially motivated infringing parties insert advertising into their updates or put advertising on top of the threads to profit from it.

For platforms, pirate versions are regarded as the culprit of lost revenue. Industry statistics show online literature firms lose 10 billion yuan a year to piracy (*Xinhua News* 2016). This has resulted in an increasing number of copyright litigations in the field. The establishment of China Online Literature Copyright Alliance in 2016 further attests to the industry's determination to recoup the lost revenue to some extent. However, as some writers revealed, platforms essentially prioritize their own interests over authors' interests in copyright litigations. For emerging writers who have not secured solid subscription data, their claims of rights are often left unheard. If the two authors involved publish on the same site, the platform tends to pacify the original writer and extenuate the infringement matter. When the two writers work for different websites and the work proves to be of considerable market value, then the platform tends to invest significant resources in copyright litigations against the infringing writer. In other words, platform approaches to copyright infringement are contingent upon the market worth of relevant authors and creative works. This constitutes another layer of hierarchy in copyright governance.

For some authors, infringing content raises serious concerns. As one author said somewhat excitedly:

> I write thousands of words every day to earn some of the subscription fees, but readers can access my work in online forums and cloud services for free soon after my updates at the legitimate site. I'm losing a lot of money as a result.

When asked if he had taken any measures to protect copyright, the author said with obvious frustration:

> I did contact the owner of an online forum. They compromised a little and agreed to delay their update for half an hour. Can you believe it? This was the best result I got. There are so many infringing sites and it's just impossible for me to deal with all this. I simply cannot afford so much time on this.

Another author reflected on how he became disillusioned:

> It's impossible for me to spend time collecting all evidence and negotiating with them [infringing sites]. Moreover, as I understand, the compensation, if at all, is very small. It is simply not worth my time.

In the context of inequitable and ineffective platform governance, individual responses of self-reliance have developed in the attempt to mitigate risks. These derive from the consensus that copyright litigations are time- and resource-consuming, and that platforms often shift resources to big-name authors. Some authors have attempted to protect their copyright by adjusting their own creative process. One author mentioned a common practice:

> Some writers update in two steps. They deliberately publish wrong content in the first update, and then upload the right chapter in the second update. The chapter in the first update is called anti-piracy chapter. Usually the software capture updates in real time and for once only. Two-step updates with the correct content uploaded later can prevent piracy. However, if infringing parties capture the content twice or even more times, they are more likely to access the correct updates.

When asked if he used this method, he said he did not do so and explained why:

> While such a method disrupts infringing parties' plan, it disrupts reading experience for paying subscribers as well. Readers have to delete the book from their bookshelves first and then reload it to see the correct new instalments. This is very confusing for readers. When you attack the enemy, you suffer great loss yourself.

Another author recounted the experience of receiving vehement complaints from paying subscribers when he created the anti-piracy chapter:

> Many paying subscribers complained about this and said they would not read the book any more. I agree it's inconvenient, for lack of a better alternative though. My readers can complain about this to me. Who will listen to my complaint then?

The possible impact of creative problem solving on paying subscribers raises the need for writers to communicate well with readers. Some choose to insert a stand-alone chapter to notify paying subscribers about their decisions and explain why they have made such decisions. This has to be crafted carefully to gain understanding from readers. As one author put it:

> We are not selling our books, as readers can access these books for free if they want. We are in fact seeking empathy.

While some have relied on themselves in the attempt to overcome inequity in copyright governance, not all authors treat infringing parties and readers as enemies. For small-time authors, the chance to be pirated is perceived as a privilege. Some tend to adopt a more pragmatic mindset and approach infringing online forums as a site for self-promotion. As one well-known author reflected on his earlier experience:

> Once I thought we were friends. I addressed them [readers] as brothers and sisters. I thought that as long as they liked my book, I should be grateful even when they

read infringing content ... I am one of the first authors who go to online forums to chat with readers who consume infringing content. I did so despite the hints about the misalignment with publishing platforms' intention to go after piracy.

However, such affective investment and the accompanying approach to informal consumption may prove to be disappointing. Writer's tolerance of infringing consumption is not necessarily reciprocated by readers on other fronts, for example in negotiation of temporalities. The author recounted how his heart sank at two critical points in his writing career and in his life more broadly. These were the days when he failed to publish new instalments on time after experiencing a divorce. Under such circumstances, he explained to readers what he was experiencing in his life. While some readers sent condolence messages, many assaulted him with abusive language for his failure to update in time. As the author recalled:

> I still remember a private message full of abusive words, and ironically, this reader read my work at infringing sites. I felt my heart shrivel within me. I treated non-paying readers well. I even purchased my print books and sent to winners of a lucky draw on these forums. To my surprise, when I was suffering, there was no sympathy at all. What's worse, insults and curses kept coming at me. I've thought about quitting altogether since then. After all, I've been here for over 10 years. I'm exhausted. Why should I stay to bear all this?

This emotionally charged account shows how feelings and affective states 'reverberate' in and out of cyberspace (Kuntsman 2012). Affective investment, when unreciprocated, results in disappointment and self-doubt.

In addition to challenges in negotiating with infringing consumption practices, hidden risks are embedded in the contracting process with platforms from the very start. Platforms usually require authors to relinquish all copyright including subsidiary rights. This provides potent evidence of how Marxian notions of primitive accumulation (Marx 1867 [1990]) remain alive and well as digital platforms devise contracting terms in their own interest. As several authors mentioned, when digital platforms profit from print publications or mobile media distribution, they usually only receive some nominal rewards instead of a share of the total revenue. Even when there was revenue sharing, lack of transparency in third-party data and metrics raised significant doubt among authors. While authors are under constant performance monitoring, which largely determines their future prospects, they are often left in the dark about subscription data generated on mobile platforms or in-print publications. Such information asymmetry put authors at significant disadvantage. This reflects a broader phenomenon where digital platforms skew power relations via orchestration of information asymmetries (Rosenblat and Stark 2016).

As Bettig (1996) points out, copyright, when combined with the control of the distribution system, plays an important role in value extraction and capital accumulation. From this analysis, it is clear that copyright politics is manifested not only in the ultimate ownership and control of the creative output but also in terms and conditions of creative labour. As writers publish on digital platforms, they do so on terms structured by those who own the platforms and control the means of production, interaction, communication, and community building (Andrejevic 2009). Therefore, the choice to sell their labour remains coercive as it 'internalises the forms of violence and alienation that structured the terms of the choice itself' (Andrejevic 2009: 49). While knowledge sharing is crucial in improving risk literacies, hierarchies, shadows, and associated structural precarity are likely to persist among entrepreneurial-minded writers.

Conclusion

The platformization of the online literature field in China has witnessed a new generation of amateur yet increasingly professionalizing writers with commercial aspirations. While digital platforms offer an alternative pathway to seeking audience and economic returns beyond the traditional publishing system in China, the process of platformization is certainly not value-neutral. This article has (1) analysed how hierarchies, shadows, and precarity emerge in this creative labour market, which complicate the celebratory discourses about creative labour and platform empowerment; (2) explained how hierarchies, shadows, and precarity are imbricated with platform politics of access, temporality, visibility, and copyright protection; (3) revealed how aspiring writers exhibit an entrepreneurial ethos in navigating the uneven process of platformization. In doing so, this article advances knowledge about the impact of platformization of cultural production on creative labour in China.

The seemingly open alternative space architected by digital platforms outside the traditional literary production system in China should not blind us to the politics of access to market, platform support structure, and monetization possibilities. Underpinned by the tiered contracting system, the uneven access to opportunities paints a picture of sobering reality, where many have to commit to creative labour for free before they can gain access to and climb up the ladder. Meanwhile, this has motivated contracted writers to devise creative measures such as strategically extending the work length to maximize monetization possibilities. Furthermore, the politics of access is entangled with the spectrum of informality. While the market has formalized to some degree, informality persists, not only in the nature of platform labour and contracting mechanisms, but also in the unexpected shadow market of surrogate writing. The shadow market, while resulting from the hierarchy among writers, tends to solidify rather than reduce hierarchical stratification.

Concomitant with hierarchies and shadows, multiple forms of precarity manifest themselves in the process of platformization. Meanwhile, platform-mediated tiers of opportunities promote an entrepreneurial ethos among writers despite precarious conditions. Notably, quantification of consumption and production constantly informs performance metrics, which pushes writers to internalize the neoliberal ideology of the enterprising self. Moreover, inequitable temporalities resulting from market and technological structures pressure writers to calibrate their tempo and rhythm to cater to readers' time needs, comply with platform-imposed terms, and follow their own entrepreneurial drive. In other words, writers tend to internalize inequitable temporal relations through self-exploitation, often at the expense of health and well-being, quality of work, and sense of satisfaction. Furthermore, as platform politics of visibility operates in connection with tiers of access to opportunities, aspiring writers find it imperative to rely on themselves by engaging in self-promotion and pursuing instrumental sociality. In addition, writers face hidden but real risks associated with inequity in copyright governance by platforms. While some find themselves vulnerable with few counter measures available, more entrepreneurial responses range from adapting the creative process to leveraging the informal distribution sites for self-promotion.

Different layers of platform politics in access, temporality, visibility, and copyright protection do not exist in isolation. In fact, they interact with each other with real consequences for writers. Individualistic creative measures adopted by aspiring writers, however, do not necessarily constitute effective and sustainable solutions to overcome structural precarity. Notably, in the context of tiered access to opportunities and platform-mediated inequitable temporalities, few alternatives exist for entrepreneurial writers but to subscribe to platform logic. Moreover, writers' tolerance of informal consumption practices does not necessarily beget tolerance of failure to accommodate readers' time needs. In a similar vein, when writers face hidden risks in dubious contracts, information asymmetries, and inequitable platform governance, the terrain of copyright protection becomes more challenging to navigate. While knowledge sharing may help creative labourers sidestep some risks, subversive possibilities have so far been attenuated by their subscription to the platform logic.

As China's labour market is undergoing transformation with the growth of digital creative industries and platform economy, actually existing labour conditions deserve closer scrutiny. Furthermore, it is of paramount importance for understanding platform-mediated labour relations in the broader social, economic, and cultural context. The rose-tinted portrayals should not blind us to the reality of persistent hierarchies, murky shadows, and multiple forms of precarity. As creative labour assumes a prominent place in the state's political rhetoric and digital platforms' promotional narratives, the question remains as to what constitutes a more equitable and sustainable platform economy for creators, and how pathways to a better future could be created.

References

Andrejevic, M. (2009) 'Critical media studies 2.0'. *Interactions: Studies in Communication & Culture*, 1(1): 35–51.

Banet-Weiser, S. (2012) *AuthenticTM: The Politics of Ambivalence in a Brand Culture*. New York: New York University Press.

Bauman, Z. (2001) *The Individualized Society*. Cambridge: Polity Press.

Beck, U. (1992) *Risk Society*. London: Sage.

Bettig, R. (1996) *Copyrighting Culture: The Political Economy of Intellectual Property*. Boulder, CO: Westview Press.

Burgess, J. and Green, J. (2009) *YouTube: Online Video and Participatory Culture*. Cambridge, UK: Polity.

Castells, M. (1996) *The Rise of the Network Society*. Oxford: Blackwell.

Chang, D. (2009) 'Informalising labour in Asia's global factory'. *Journal of Contemporary Asia*, 39(2): 161–179.

China Daily. (2016) 'Top Chinese web-writer's income tops 100 million'. 25 March. Available at: http://europe.chinadaily.com.cn/culture/2016-03/25/content_24099404.htm/.

China Literature (2016) 'Home page'. 26 December. Available at: https://www.yuewen.com/.

Davis, D. W. and Yeh, E. Y.-y. (2017) 'Zimuzu and media industry in China'. *Media Industries Journal*, 4(1). doi: http://dx.doi.org/10.3998/mij.15031809.0004.102.

Deuze, M. (2007) *Media Work*. Cambridge: Polity.

Duffy, B. E. (2016) 'The romance of work: Gender and aspirational labour in the digital culture industries'. *Internaitonal Journal of Cultural Studies*, 19(4): 441–457.

Epstein, C. and Kalleberg, A. (eds.) (2004) *Fighting For Time: Shifting Boundaries of Work and Social Life*. New York: Russell Sage Foundation.

Florida, R. (2002). *The Rise of the Creative Class*. New York: Basic Books.

Gill, R. and Pratt, A. (2008) 'In the social factory? Immaterial labour, precariousness and cultural work'. *Theory, Culture Society*, 25(7–8): 1–30.

Harvey, D. (1989). *The Condition of Postmodernity*. Oxford: Blackwell.

Hearn, A. (2006). '"John, a 20-year-old Boston native with a great sense of humour": On the spectacularization of the "self" and the incorporation of identity in the age of reality television'. *International Journal of Media and Cultural Politics*, 2(2): 131–147.

Hesmondhalgh, D. and Baker, S. (2011) *Creative Labour: Media Work in Three Cultural Industries*. Abingdon: Routledge.

Hochschild, A. R. (1997) *The Time Bind: When Home Becomes Work and Work Becomes Home*. New York: Henry Holt.

Hockx, M. (2015) *Internet Literature in China*. New York: Columbia University Press.

Hong, Y. (2011). *Labor, Class Formation, and China's Informationized Policy of Economic Development*. Lanham, Md.: Lexington Books.

Howkins, J. (2001). *The Creative Economy: How People Make Money from Ideas*. London: Penguin.

Kalleberg, A. and Hewison, K. (2013) 'Precarious work and the challenge for Asia'. *American Behavioral Scientist*, 57(3): 271–288.

Keane, M. (2007) *Created in China: The Great New Leap Forward*. London and New York: Routledge.

Keane, M. (2013) *Creative Industries in China: Art, Design and Media*. Cambridge, UK; Malden, MA: Polity.

Kuntsman, A. (2012) 'Introduction: Affective fabrics of digital cultures'. In A. Karatzogianni and A. Kuntsman (eds.), *Digital Cultures and the Politics of Emotion: Feelings, Affect and Technological Change*. Basingstoke: Palgrave, pp. 1–20.

Latham, K. (2005) 'Shuhao (book numbers)'. In E. L. Davis (ed.), *Encyclopedia of Contemporary Chinese*. London: Sage, p. 758.

Li, W. (2008) *Creative Industries are Changing China (Chuangyi gaibian Zhongguo)*. Beijing: Xinhua Press.

Lobato, R. and Thomas, J. (2015) *The Informal Media Economy*. Cambridge: Polity Press.

McRobbie, A. (2002) 'Clubs to companies: Notes on the decline of political culture in speeded up creative worlds'. *Cultural Studies*, 16(4): 516–531.

Martinsen, J. (2006) 'The Chinese Writers' Association: What good is it?' 17 November. Available at: http://www.danwei.org/state_media/china_writers_association_what.php/.

Marwick, A. E. (2013) *Status Update: Celebrity, Publicity and Branding in the Social Media Age*. New Haven, CT: Yale University Press.

Marx, K. (1867 [1990]) *Capital: Volume 1: A Critique of Political Economy*. London: Penguin Classics.

Nieborg, D. B. and Poell, T. (2018) 'The platformization of cultural production: Theorizing the contingent cultural commodity'. *New Media & Society*, 20(11): 4275–4292.

Ouyang, Y. (2002) 'On spiritual orientation of the internet literature' [Lun wangluo wenxue de jingshen quxiang]. *Literature and Art Studies [Wenyi Yanjiu]* (5): 74–77.

Ouyang, Y. (2011) 'Chinese literature's transformation and digital existence in the new century'. *Social Sciences in China*, 32(1): 146–165.

Pang, L. (2006) *Cultural Control and Globalization in Asia: Copyright, Piracy, and Cinema*. Abingdon: Routledge.

People's Daily. (2017) 'China's online literature market valuation reaches 9 billion RMB'. 4 July. Available at: http://ip.people.com.cn/n1/2017/0414/c136655-29212128.html/.

Poell, T., Nieborg, D., and Duffy, B. E. (2021) *Platforms and Cultural Production*. London, UK: Polity.

Qiu, L. C. (2017) *Goodbye iSlave: A Manifesto for Digital Abolition*. Champaign, IL: University of Illinois Press.

Rosa, H. (2003) 'Social acceleration: Ethical and political consequences of a desynchronized high-speed society'. *Constellations*, 10(1): 3–33.

Rosenblat, A. and Stark, L. (2016) 'Algorithmic labor and information asymmetries: A case study of Uber's drivers'. *International Journal of Communication*, 10: 3758–3784.

Ross, A. (2009) *Nice Work If You Can Get It: Life and Labor in Precarious Times*. New York: New York University Press.

Sharma, S. (2014) *In the Meantime: Temporality and Cultural Politics*. Durham, NC: Duke University Press.

Sohu.com. (2017) 'AliResearch forecast: Platform economy will be the new world where 50% of China's labour force will realise self-employment'. Available at: http://www.sohu.com/a/125898191_494931/.

Sun, W. N. (2014). *Subaltern China: Rural Migrants, Media, and Cultural Practices*. Lanham: Rowman & Littlefield.

Swider, S. (2016) *Building China: Informal Work and the New Precariat*. Ithaca: Cornell University Press.

Urry, J. (2000) *Sociology Beyond Societies: Mobilities for the Twenty-First Century*. London: Routledge.

Wajcman, J. (2008) 'Life in the fast lane? Towards a sociology of technology and time'. *The British Journal of Sociology*, 59(1): 59–77.

Wang, J. (2004). 'The global reach of a new discourse: How far can "creative industries" travel?' *International Journal of Cultural Studies*, 7(1): 9–19.

Wang, S. and Zhu, J. J. H. (2003) 'Mapping film piracy in China'. *Theory, Culture Society*, 20(4): 97–125.

Wu, Q., Zhang, H., Li, Z., and Liu, K. (2019) 'Labor control in the gig economy: Evidence from Uber in China'. *Journal of Industrial Relations*, 61(4): 574–596.

Xiang, R. and Montgomery, L. (2012) 'Chinese online literature: Creative consumers and evolving business models'. *Arts Marketing*, 2(2): 118–130.

Xinhua News (2016) 'Online literature subject to flash piracy, costing the industry a yearly loss of 10billion yuan'. 27 April. Available at: http://news.xinhuanet.com/tech/2016-04/27/c_128935773.htm/.

Zhang, L. and Fung, A. (2013) 'The myth of "shanzhai" culture and the paradox of digital democracy in China'. *Inter-Asia Cultural Studies*, 14(3): 401–416.

Zhao, E. J. (2011) 'Social network market: Storytelling on a Web 2.0 original literature site'. *Convergence*, 17(1): 85–99.

Zhao, E. J. (2017) 'Writing on the assembly line: Informal labour in the formalised online literature market in China'. *New Media & Society*, 19(8): 1236–1252.

Zhao, E. J. (2019) *Digital China's Informal Circuits: Platforms, Labour and Governance*. Abingdon, Oxon; New York, NY: Routledge.

Zhao, E. J. and Keane, M. (2013) 'Between formal and informal: The shakeout in China's online video industry'. *Media, Culture Society*, 35(6): 724–741.

9
Making Sense of Inequalities at Work

The Micropolitics of Everyday Negotiation among Non-Regular Workers in Japan

Shinji Kojima

Introduction

Many industrialized capitalist countries are seeing an increase in workers who suffer from precarious employment arrangements that are typically characterized by job insecurity, low pay, and a weak benefits package (Kalleberg 2011; Shin 2010; Standing 2011). In Japan, the number of non-regular workers is close to reaching 40 per cent, and they suffer from the typical characteristics of precarious work (Osawa, Kim, and Kingston 2013; Sato 2013). Japanese employers often preach the virtue of unity and harmony by likening the company to a family, yet merciless divisions based on gender and employment status run through many workplaces (Gottfried 2014, 2015; Miura 2012). While we know much about the history of neoliberal labour policymaking that contributed to the institutionalization of precarious work (e.g. Hamaguchi 2011; Imai 2021), we know relatively little about how workers interpret and negotiate their daily work experiences. This chapter examines the ways in which neoliberal employment institutions and culture both shape the way non-regular workers understand how they are treated at work. I raise the question, given the gendered, neoliberal structural arrangements of the Japanese employment system, how is precarious work experienced and its meanings negotiated by female non-regular employees?

Scholars have argued that neoliberalism is both a legal–institutional and cultural means to create a market where the entrepreneurial selves are promoted to engage in competitive commercial transactions with minimal regulations (Harvey 2005; Mudge 2008). The state takes an interventionist approach (Gilbert 2013; Howell 2020) in privatizing institutions, liberalizing trade, and deregulating the economy. This structural rearrangement of the economy creates social fragmentation and deepens existing inequalities.

Therefore, the state's elites must win legitimation from its citizens and get them to believe that 'individualized competition in the marketplace [is] the only effective or legitimate mechanism for the distribution of rewards' (Gilbert 2013: 11). This form of consent does not necessarily have to be positively enthusiastic in nature; it may well be 'passive'. This chapter employs the concept of 'disaffected consent' (Gilbert 2015), defined as a particular 'structure of feeling', characterized by 'a profound dissatisfaction with both the consequences and the ideological premises of the neoliberal project; on the other hand, it involves a general acquiescence with that project, a degree of deference to its relative legitimacy in the absence of any convincing alternative, and a belief that it cannot be effectively challenged' (Gilbert 2015: 29). Using data from semi-structured interviews of female non-regular workers, I show how disaffected consent is shaped in the process of negotiating the meanings of precarious employment and the legitimacy in the treatment they receive.

For my interviewees, making sense of their low pay and differential treatment vis-à-vis the regular employees is a difficult process. They are engaged in a mental struggle of searching for a point of compromise between strong feelings of dissatisfaction on the one hand, and self-doubt in the legitimacy of demanding better treatment on the other. The negotiation is about striking an emotional balance between yearning for a better job and the awareness of the lack of better alternatives. It also involves engaging in informal struggles to correct the disparity in treatment but subsequently finding employment practices unalterable. In this way, the affective responses to precarious working conditions take the form of 'disaffected consent'.

Background

The Japanese employment system has historically been characterized by lifetime employment, a seniority-based wage structure, and enterprise unionism, in which employment is guaranteed until retirement, raises are assured based on seniority, and workplace unions serve to secure these conditions for regular employees in exchange for deference to managerial demands. These employment practices helped corporations to achieve internal flexibility. They allowed management to freely rotate, relocate, and transfer its regular workers while maintaining employment security. Such internal flexibility was in tandem with the use of non-regular workers that served to achieve external flexibility. Non-regular workers were primarily hired to reduce labour costs but also to achieve flexibility to hire and fire according to short-term needs. This Japanese way of achieving flexibility has created a dual labour market (Gordon 2017; Imai and Sato 2011), and the corporate management's response to economic recession and the intensifying global competition exacerbated the use of non-regular workers (Genda 2001).

The Confucian ideal of a family was reflected in the employment institutions. As breadwinners, male workers predominantly enjoyed regular employment status in exchange for long work hours and unrefusable transfers and job rotations. Female workers were chiefly relegated to non-regular employment status with wages determined by the local labour market, assuming a primary role to be played in managing the home. The distribution of employment statuses by gender and the large pay gap between them have made life precarious for many female non-regular employees. Non-regular workers constituted 37 per cent of the working population in 2020, of which 68 per cent are women. Even though female job seekers are increasingly landing permanent positions, 54 per cent of female employees are still non-regular workers (Ministry of Internal Affairs and Communication 2021).

Regarding the pay gap, average lifetime earnings significantly diverge by gender and employment status as shown in Table 9.1.[1]

Studies also show that female non-regular employees receive anywhere between 27 per dent and 44 per cent less wages than regular employees, controlling for variables such as work hours, education, years of service, age, and workplace (Kawaguchi 2018). Statistics that compare the hourly wages of part-time workers show that they earn 40 per cent less than regular workers receive, compared to 27 per cent in the UK (Japan Institute for Labour Policy and Training 2019). Such pay gaps cause non-regular workers to live an economically precarious life. As noted in the following section,

Table 9.1 Average lifetime earnings by gender and employment status

		Lifetime Earnings (Million JPY)	%
Men	Regular	272	100
	Non-Regular	154	57
Women	Regular	215	79
	Non-Regular	122	45

(*Source*: Japan Institute for Labour Policy and Training 2020)

the non-regular employees' wages are barely enough to cover their monthly expenses, let alone to save enough for a comfortable life after retirement. It is in this structural, economic context that the female non-regular employees negotiate the meanings of their treatment and work experiences.

Data and method

This study is based on semi-structured interviews conducted with 13 female employees between April and May 2017 and February and March 2021. All 13 interviewees have either worked for or are currently employed by the same company, which is a public-interest corporation located in a western Japanese prefecture. The workplace broadly used five employment categories for hiring clerical staff. Compensation differed significantly by employment status, as shown in Table 9.2.[2]

Regular A and B employees were hired on an open-ended contract. Regular A was the core workforce, the typical '*seishain*' (regular employee) in a Japanese workplace who enjoyed a seniority-based wage. They were subject to routine annual performance assessment, but their wages and bonus pay were hardly affected by it; bonus pay was a total of five months' worth of pay per annum stipulated in the workplace regulation. They periodically rotated across teams and were also subject to transfers across workplaces in different prefectures. They were on a managerial track where some were selectively promoted to managerial positions. They were responsible for overseeing tasks assigned to a team and for making decisions before the team executed tasks. This employment category was a mixture of both sexes, but all other

Table 9.2 Employment categories and remuneration

	Contract	Monthly Wage JPY	Bonus Payment	Pay Rise	Allowances	Pay Gap
Regular A	Open-ended	Seniority	5 months	Annual	Multiple	100%
Regular B	Open-ended	250,000	3 months	No	Multiple	94%
Non-Reg. A	Fixed Term	230,000	3 months	No	Commutation, Overtime & Night Shift Allowances, Paid Leaves	87%
Non-Reg. B	Fixed Term	160,000	3 months	No		61%
Non-Reg. C	Fixed Term	130,000	None	No		42%

categories were predominantly women. Regular B employees were the '*genteigata seishain*' (translated as 'limited regular employee'), who were employed on an open-ended contract but hired locally and exempt from workplace transfers. The corporation hired them for particular skill sets such as their native-level English ability and expected them to execute work without the direction and supervision of Regular A employees.

Non-regular A employees were also hired for their English ability. Part of the assigned duties involved operating in both Japanese and English, thus requiring the applicant to have a working level of both languages. Non-regular B employees were hired to undertake a range of routine clerical tasks. The exact nature of the tasks depended on to which office and team the employee was assigned. Job advertisements for the post usually required basic PC software skills. Non-regular C employees were hired to play an assistant role to other clerical employees, such as making Xerox copies and mailing out documents. While all other employees were paid a monthly wage, Non-Regular C employees were paid by the hour.

The non-regular employees' annual income before tax was approximately JPY 3.7 million, 2.6 million, and 1.8 million for Non-Regular A, B, and C respectively, by taking into account the commutation allowance of JPY20,000/month. To place their income into the national context, Non-Regular B employees earned a little over half of the nation's average income, and Non-Regular C employees earned a little over the nation's poverty line. The pay gap was calculated in reference to Regular A employees' starting wage at the age of 22, which amounted to approximately JPY 4.2 million plus a long list of allowances. Thus, the pay gap shows the smallest possible value for each employment category, which grows as workers age.[3]

Table 9.3 is the list of interviewees. All were female workers with an age range between late 20s and mid 40s. Some had an associate's degree from a two-year college, but the majority were 'local elites' who graduated from four-year national universities in the region. Two of the interviewees had a master's degree. All but one interviewee were ethnically Japanese and held a Japanese nationality. 'Years of service' shows the cumulative years of employment at the corporation. Those exceeding five years shows that the corporation has rehired the same non-regular worker after the six-month 'cooling off' period.[4]

All interviews were semi-structured and conducted in Japanese except for one interviewee (Mary) who was a native English speaker. Interviews in Japanese were translated into English by the author for quoting purposes. Each interview lasted between 90 minutes and two hours. A few of the interviewees were introduced by personal acquaintances, and others were accessed through snowball sampling. All names are pseudonyms.

Table 9.3 List of interviewees

	Employment Category	Age	Academic Credential	Marital Status	Years of Service
Ami	Nonregular B	Early 30s	Bachelor	Married	5 years
Hiroko	Nonregular C	Mid 40s	Bachelor	Single	2 years
Kei	Nonregular A	Early 30s	Associate	Single	3 years
Kyoko	Nonregular B	Mid 40s	Associate	Single	15 years
Mai	Nonregular B	Early 30s	Bachelor	Single	8 years
Mana	Nonregular B	Early 40s	Associate	Single	7 years
Nao	Nonregular A	Late 20s	Bachelor	Single	2 years
Rieko	Nonregular B	Late 30s	Associate	Married	4 years
Sae	Nonregular A	Mid 40s	Master	Married	4 years
Saki	Nonregular B	Mid 40s	Bachelor	Single	12 years
Mary	Nonregular A	Late 20s	Bachelor	Married	2.5 years
Waka	Nonregular A	Mid 30s	Master	Single	2 years
Yumi	Regular A	Mid 30s	Bachelor	Single	12 years

The transcribed interview data were systematically coded to identify patterns (Glaser and Strauss 1967).

Negotiating resentment and the legitimacy of asking for more

Nearly all interviewees were dissatisfied with the treatment they received. The female non-regular workers found their compensation scheme to be frustratingly low, especially in comparison to what the regular workers received. However, even though they felt disappointed, they were ambivalent and unsure about the legitimacy of the unequal treatment. Their resentment was simultaneously limited and constrained by the reservations they had about the question of merit as well as differences in job duties. Some found themselves partly to blame for their non-regular employment status. Others schematically separated the regular employees based on ability, thereby reducing the issue of structural inequality to an individual worker's problem.

Differences in job assignments and self-reservations about ability

Sae is in her mid-40s with a master's degree in international relations. She is married to a full-time working husband with two children. She has been working at the current job for four years as a Non-Regular A employee. When asked about her feelings about the pay gap vis-à-vis the regular workers, she replied, 'I'm not convinced.' In responding to my request for elaboration, she said, 'It's not that I've agreed. But it's also that I think "Maybe that's the way it is"', or *shōganai* in Japanese, which was commonly repeated by the interviewees. Sae assists her clients to apply for national grants and to use them according to regulations, which in her view requires specialized knowledge and skills. Observing daily what the Regular A employees do, she feels they are doing the job because the job comes with the position, not because they possess any special ability that she does not possess. However, she is also aware that she is not entirely doing the same job assigned to Regular A employees. Sae explained, '...[T]here are jobs that only the [regular employees] do. And I don't exactly know for sure what or how much of it.' It is partly this awareness that job assignments do not neatly overlap with her own that trumps her sense of legitimacy in demanding better treatment. When she is restricted to the job she is assigned to do, it is the restricted nature of her job per se that disempowers her to demand more parity in treatment. She stated with a tone of resignation, 'If I'm told, "The compensation is what you are currently worth", I have to submit and think to myself, "Maybe so". But it's hard. I know what [the regular employees] receive.' When Sae is aware that there are tasks that only the regular workers are assigned to do, even though she is confident anyone can do it if given sufficient years on the job, she is shouldering the burden of proof that she deserves it when her task is limited to what she is assigned to do. In this situation, proving one's ability and asking for more is something hard to do.

In contrast, Kei, who is in her late 30s, was relatively new to the job at the time of interview. It is the English language ability she acquired from studying abroad that enabled her to secure a Non-regular A position. Her assessment of the Regular A employee's performance on the team was quite negative. In her eyes, a regular employee who was fresh on the team lacked the knowledge about the team's tasks. It was a seasoned Non-Regular B employee who practically managed the team. After telling stories of numerous instances that were signs of a lack of ability, she said, 'I don't think [Regular A] is doing much of a difficult job.' When discussing her feelings on the remuneration vis-à-vis the regular employees, she said, 'I knew the conditions coming in, but I've been working on the current position for only one and a half years, and I'm not really confident about my own performance.' After a pause, she stated, 'So yeah, it's not that I think, "I deserve more". I'm rather still new to the job, and my mind is more focused on getting myself used to the job.' Kei's case illustrates how the question of the ability of regular employees boomeranged back to the non-regular workers' self-assessment.

When a better compensation package is not institutionalized for non-regular workers, they undergo a process of searching for legitimate reasons for this, which turns into a self-reflective project where confidence comes into play. Self-confidence is affective, subjective, and amorphous in nature. For self-reserved individuals like Kei, a lack of self-confidence may serve to reduce the legitimacy in claiming oneself as deserving better treatment.

Legitimacy trumped by self-blame

In negotiating the resentment from differential treatment and the legitimacy in demanding better treatment, some of the interviewees were haunted by a sense of self-blame. Even when the female non-regular workers were confident in their performance, they reluctantly acquiesced to the large pay gap after finding themselves partly to blame for their current status.

Mana is a Non-Regular B employee who has spent a total of seven years in three different sections in the same office. Like many, Mana had her own story to tell about 'bad' regular employees. In telling such a story, she in turn affirmed her own ability. 'I have spent years in the office, so I naturally knew how things worked and how to get things done, better than [the regular employee].' She told me how she had to supervise the agency temporaries on the team because the Regular A employee who was fresh out of college did not know how to handle their work. When asked about the pay gap in this context of having had to do the job assigned to regular employees, Mana said, 'I know the pay gap, it's huge. But what can you do about it? I would have no words if someone says to me, "If you don't like it, you should have taken the recruitment exam for new graduates." What can I say to that? I can't complain.' Mana felt the kind of job she does, the sheer volume of her duties, and her ability to execute them could hardly be justified by her low pay. She also felt some regular workers were undeserving of good pay. Yet, when it came to making sense of the differences in treatment, she found it hard to formulate a clear sense of injustice. In the search for an explanation of the statutory difference, she found a part of the answer in herself. She blamed her past self for not having chosen to apply for and secure a permanent position upon graduating from college. This structure of feeling, of finding oneself responsible for one's own predicament, constitutes a significant part of the neoliberal hegemonic project (Harvey 2005). When Mana finds herself at fault for something that cannot be undone, this leads to reluctantly giving in to the differential treatment as something beyond one's control.

Nao is another example of a non-regular employee who felt a tinge of self-blame in acquiescing to the bad treatment. She is a Non-Regular A employee in her late twenties who earned a bachelor's degree from a national university. When asked her thoughts about the pay difference with the regular employees, she replied, 'I'm unhappy, that's for sure.' She said her pay is 'too little, if I look at what they do compared to what I do'. Similar to other interviewees, she then went on to tell stories about how there were just too many regular employees who 'either could not or did not work'. In response to my affirmation that she is unhappy with the pay in comparison to these regular employees, she answered, 'Yes. But the thing is, I am interested in working at [this particular workplace], not anywhere else. So I didn't take the recruitment exam for a regular position. I knew the pay was good, but I didn't because there was a possibility of being assigned to a different workplace. So if I'm told, "Then that's your fault", I cannot retort. Do you know what I mean?' In the case of Nao, the difference in treatment was already negotiated at the point of entry to the workplace. She had weighed the choice between applying to a permanent position that paid well but with the risk of being transferred to a different workplace, or opting to work at the workplace of her choosing but for lesser pay as a non-regular employee. The awareness that she chose the latter served to silence her discontent.

The politics of 'good perms' and 'bad perms'

As has been seen, many of the interviewees had their own stories to tell about incompetent regular employees who failed to perform up to expectations. However, the common stories about 'bad perms' were sometimes carefully followed by an acknowledgement of regular employees who were great at their jobs. In the eyes of some interviewees, the regular employees were differentiated between the 'good perms' and the 'bad perms', and this schematic separation led to reducing the pay gap to an issue of the individual worker's problem rather than a systemic issue of statutory discrimination.

Ami graduated from a national four-year college and is married to a full-time working husband with two children. She has spent five years serving her position as a Non-Regular B employee. In common with others, she worked with a Regular A employee who was 'clueless' about what she was doing. Ami said many on her team had 'given up on her' and were crossing their fingers that she'd be transferred to a different team at the next round of rotation. Given the incompetence, she said 'it was faster and better that I did [the job]. At the end, I took the job and did it myself.' Such uncommon instances of assuming the regular employee's job made her question the legitimacy of the pay gap. She confessed that during breaks and lunch hours, the non-regular employees shared complaints with each other. After expressing disgust, however, Ami stated, 'But if they're doing their job, like X and Y (both regular employees), it's okay.' I asked Ami what was so great about those regular workers that justified the pay. She replied, 'When they were done with their tasks, they'd come over, and check how I am doing, and helped out when necessary. They would ask what I was so busy with, and try to find ways to redistribute the tasks more evenly among the team members.' In her view, there were regular workers who competently fulfilled the roles they were expected to serve, which led Ami to agree to what they received. Such schematic division between the 'deserving' and the 'undeserving' regular employees shifted attention away from the structural inequality based on employment status to individual competence.

After sharing her troublesome experience with a particular Regular B employee who failed to demonstrate her worth, Nao also mentioned, 'But I do appreciate other regular employees. They do work worth their pay.' Accordingly, the compensation was appropriate for some, commensurate with her subjective assessment of merit, while inappropriate and unacceptable for others. The distress about their own pay often invited them to narrate stories of regular workers who underperformed, but then was followed by a recognition of regular employees who worked well. This pattern of schematic distinction made their critique of the pay gap nuanced and ambivalent; nuanced and ambivalent because the affective response to the unequal treatment was unclear in their minds as to whether the sense of illegitimacy was about the individual or the structural inequality in pay.

The limited nature of their critique is partly shaped by the culture of patriarchy dominant in Japanese society. Japanese are socialized, through the institutions of family and formal education, to appreciate their position in a group according to the roles and responsibilities s/he fulfils in maintaining harmony. These roles and responsibilities are hierarchically ordered, and those who undertake paternalistic roles and responsibilities enjoy privileged access to material and cultural resources. As a way to maintain group harmony, Japanese society has historically agreed to reward seniors and male figures for fulfilling the higher order responsibilities assigned to them (Cave 2004; Eng 2006). Such cultural practices significantly overshadow the way non-regular workers understand and interpret the legitimacy of the pay gap between the regular workers who perform well. The majority of the non-regular workers were quite sure about the illegitimacy of the pay gap between them and the 'bad' regular workers. However, when it came to the regular workers who competently fulfilled their responsibilities, the criticism lost its momentum.

Yearning for a better job, but where is the alternative?

Another form of disaffected consent is shaped by the negotiation between the unsatisfactory treatment at the current job and the lack of a better employment opportunity beyond what they currently enjoy. The non-regular workers suffered from the awareness of the bleak employment prospects in the local Japanese labour market. They had firsthand experience of 'bad regular jobs', that is, permanent positions that provided low pay, irregular and long work hours, or unpaid overtime. Others had been hopping between non-regular positions that paid less than the current job. It is the structural shortage of a good job and affirming personal experiences that result in reluctantly acquiescing to the current remuneration. Others who were married recognized that regular employment was incompatible with child-rearing. Because permanent positions were subject to long work hours and workplace transfers, they had given up their work careers in exchange for fulfilling gendered responsibilities in the private sphere.

Mai is a Non-Regular B employee in her mid-30s. She secured a permanent job as a cameraman at a local photo studio after graduating from a national four-year college. Her first job forced her to work irregular hours, including weekend shifts. The job was busy and made her frequently skip lunch. Her job had nothing to do with what she studied in college (economics), but she was made to take customers with little training. Dealing with unhappy customers was the most difficult part of the job, giving her much mental stress. She left the job and was then employed by the current workplace. She worked the full five year maximum as a fixed-term employee, followed by a non-regular position as a member of the clerical staff at a local hospital. It was during this time that she received a phone call from the current workplace asking if she was interested in coming back. She agreed and returned to the current workplace again as a non-regular worker. When asked about her thoughts on the remuneration, she stated, 'It's true we don't get a pay raise here, not a single dime. But at least the pay is higher than other jobs. We have a three month's bonus payment, holidays are relatively longer, and paid leave is easy to take. In that sense, I thought it was good. Quite a few of my friends are working without bonus payment.' Mai's statement indicates that non-regular workers evaluate their remuneration with a particular reference point, which is the jobs they have experienced as well as those available in the local labor market.

Kyoko, a Non-Regular B employee, is another example who has returned to the workplace multiple times, six times to be exact. She re-entered the workplace in various forms of non-regular employment, including on a fixed-term contract, as an agency temporary, and as an employee of a subcontractor used by the corporation. Kyoko entered a life in precarity after leaving the permanent job she secured after graduation. Her first job was a pink-collar clerical position on an open-ended contract. Thanks to the economic bubble at the time, the position allowed her to live comfortably with eight months' worth of bonus pay per annum. Once she left the permanent job and began searching for work locally, all she could find were bad permanent jobs and non-regular jobs. Her second job was an agency temporary position that paid by the hour without commutation allowance. Other jobs included a full-time *pāto* position that made her work over 40 hours a week for the minimum wage, a non-regular position subcontracted out by the prefectural government without commutation allowance or bonus pay but with unpaid overtime. Savings from her first job have long gone dry. The fortune of being able to live with her parents, not employment, served as a safety net. Kyoko says, '[O]f course I'm unhappy with the pay' at the current workplace. However, she finds herself coming back to the workplace because 'It's close to my home. And it's easy to take a leave. We get bonus pay too. Compared to other workplaces, it's better if you think about it.' Given the absence of an alternative, she found herself helpless except to accept the bad treatment as relatively good.

Saki is a Non-Regular B employee in her mid-40s who had returned to the workplace three times and worked for a total of 13 years. After graduating from a national university, she found a permanent clerical job at a local construction company. Ever since she left the company, she had worked a series of non-regular jobs. In response to my question about her thoughts on the large pay gap, she commented, 'I'm not 100% happy, but I have to concede. Here in [name of prefecture], if you have this much holiday, it's on the better side. So, I'm like, oh well, what can I do (*shōganai*).' Saki had previously worked as a non-regular clerical staff member at the local public job-placement office *Harōwāku*, ('Hello Work'), so she is well aware of the kind of work available to local job seekers. 'There are plenty of permanent jobs out there, but that's only if you don't choose.' The permanent jobs available are mostly posted by SMEs with bad remuneration. When I asked if she thinks the current job is relatively better than other jobs, she responded with a resigned smile, 'Yes, I do. That's why I keep on coming back.'

The non-regular workers are placed in a structural bind that squeezes them to passively acquiesce to a treatment that is difficult to accept. Wages have remained stagnant for decades, and the regional minimum wage is rising too slowly, especially for rural residents. The labour shortage plaguing the Japanese workplaces has not resulted in a significant rise in wages (Genda 2017). Studies have identified possible causes to this puzzle, such as the oversupply of services resulting in the suppression of wages (Abe 2017), and the arbitrary use of justifications to legitimize the statutory discrimination against non-regular workers, including differences in job duties, responsibilities, and skills (Arita 2017). Especially in the rural regions where there are relatively few large corporations, permanent positions do not necessarily mean better treatment. The compensation for non-regular employment positions is pegged to the local minimum wage, which in turn serves to create low-paying non-regular jobs in the rural regions. The disaffected consent observed among the interviewees can only be understood in the context of these structural constraints.

Ami's case demonstrates another form of a reluctant compromise, that is, between a permanent position that demands long work hours with less flexibility in taking days off, and a non-regular position that is precarious but allows more time for child-rearing. In her words, 'I know the pay is better here compared to other clerical jobs available, so, yeah, what can I say (again, *shikata ga nai* in Japanese)? But in my case, I have a working husband, so it's not that I have to earn a whole lot, so the situation is a bit different. I have children, so if I take into consideration that child-rearing is my priority, it's alright.' The disaffected consent, that is, reluctantly giving in even though she wishes for better treatment, is shaped in this case by the compromise she made for the pay in exchange for the liberty to spend time raising children. This form of consent is uniquely gendered. Japanese employment practices hardly allow an employee to have both a permanent position that provides a life security wage and sufficient time for parental care. Ami is a 'labour market adjuster' if applied to Brinton and Oh's (2019) analytical distinction. While maintaining full-time employment, Ami has adjusted her employment according to her gendered role in the private sphere by choosing a non-regular employment, which allows her to go home at 5pm sharp. The awareness of her life's priority served to cause her to reluctantly settle for the pay she finds unsatisfactory.

Sae is another example of a non-regular employee making a gendered compromise. As noted earlier, she has a full-time working husband and two children. She stated, 'I would go work somewhere else if I was single.' She meant this in the double sense that the current pay does not allow her to live a decent life without a full-time working partner, as well as affirming the fact that she had made a compromise in letting go of her career long ago when she decided to leave her first job upon marriage. As noted earlier, she is unhappy with the pay she receives in return for the job she does. However, she finds her anxiety eased 'because my husband is working', and she finds childrearing to be possible only because the non-regular position exempts her from long work hours. She confessed, 'I would have to think twice even if I were to be offered a permanent position here.' This shows how gender dynamics play a role in the micro-level interpretation of the macro-structural employment practices in creating disaffected consent.

Struggling to cross the employment caste

The third form of disaffected consent observed among the interviewees is the feeling of helplessness in finding the unequal treatment unalterable. At the workplace under study, there were no institutionalized routes for promotion, as no such clause was to be found in the workplace regulations. The workplace union excluded non-regular workers from membership, thereby providing no formal occasions to negotiate for better treatment. Given these constraints, some have resisted and struggled informally in an attempt to correct the caste-like system of employment (Morioka 2015). Some have in fact voiced concerns over doing jobs that were in the regular workers' area of responsibility. Some have requested an institutionalized route for promotion to a Regular A position. However, these attempts have failed to change the employment practices. Such experiences of having resisted but to no avail reaffirmed the awareness that the system cannot be effectively challenged (Gilbert 2015) and is here to stay, contributing to the prevalence of disaffected consent.

Rieko is a Non-Regular B employee in her late 30s with over four years of experience. She was never able to find the pay gap acceptable. She was confident that she gave 100 per cent to the assigned tasks. She was also aware that she was doing jobs that were the Regular A employee's responsibility. One day she was requested by an assistant to the section chief to train a Regular A employee who had just been assigned to lead her team. 'I thought to myself, "What? *I'm* supposed to train her?" She's a regular employee in charge of managing the team, and that's why she's being paid so much more. I'm a mere 160,000 yen employee, and *I* was being asked to care for a 300,000 yen employee.' The Regular A employee concerned tended to cherry-pick jobs and leave the rest to the non-regular employees. Noticing the non-regular employees taking over tasks assigned to the regular employee, the section chief came over to Rieko and told her to 'leave it for [the Regular A employee], have her do it'. Although Rieko felt uncomfortable telling the regular employee, she finally decided to politely ask the Regular A to change her ways and manage the overall tasks assigned to the team. When I asked if the regular employee changed the way she worked, Rieko replied, 'No, she didn't. She said she understood but didn't change after all.' In an interview with the Regular A employee concerned, Yumi affirmed that the separation of jobs by employment category is ambiguous and muddled in practice. Rieko finally got fed up and decided to leave the workplace. 'I thought to myself, I should quit if I'm going to complain like this every day. After that, leaving the workplace was a quick decision.' Unlike others, Rieko was fortunate to land a non-regular position with the possibility of promotion to regular employee status.

Saki also engaged in informal resistance. Having a total of 13 years of experience at three different offices is akin to Regular A employees rotating positions. Her academic qualifications did not differ significantly from the regular employees either. When I asked her what she thought about not enjoying any pay raise despite having years of experience at multiple offices, she stated, 'I wish I had a pay raise, but that's the way it goes (*shōganai*). It just makes me weary to put my energy into thinking about things that aren't going to change.' During a night out among the office staff, she informally asked the section chief if the corporation was willing to convert the non-regular staff into permanent employees. The corporation is chronically short on staff. She suggested it was a win-win situation for both to retain the non-regular staff by creating more permanent positions. I asked what the section chief responded. Saki stated, 'He said this is a big corporation, and unless the head office in [prefecture's name] changes the hiring system, there isn't much we can do.' In answering what she felt about the response, she stated, 'All I was able to say was, "Oh I see".' She took a stand but hit a brick wall, which contributed to the formation of a disaffected consent, as represented by her use of the word *shōganai*. Gilbert (2015) states that 'the point of neoliberal ideology is not to convince us that Hayek was right; it is to console us that the [calamities] produced by neoliberal government is natural, because "that's what life is really like"(15).' The phrase *shōganai* is almost a synonym for 'that's what life is really like'. The experience of raising one's voice and failing to see change reaffirmed the existence of a rigid employment caste system and finding oneself helpless in the face of it.

Exceptions: Dissatisfaction without consent and consent without dissatisfaction

While the majority of interviewees showed some form of disaffected consent, there were exceptions to the general pattern. Mary harboured dissatisfaction without any signs of consent. She was unhappy with the treatment, period. On the other hand, Waka was positively satisfied with the remuneration without any negative feelings.

Dissatisfaction with consent

Mary is a trilingual foreigner in her late twenties hired as a Non-Regular A employee. She holds a bachelor's degree from a globally ranked university abroad. Observing what her team members did and how they performed, she stated in English, 'I don't feel like I'm less competent than any [regular worker]. When it comes to efficiency, productivity, speed of learning, I wouldn't say I'm worse off than any of them. The only difference is that I didn't take the exam to be a [regular staff].' In her view, she equally contributed ideas on how to improve the presence of the corporation on social media. The only difference between her and the regular employee on the team was that the latter was responsible for making the final decision, which was essentially nodding to what the team had already discussed. Her frustration was not trumped by the fact that she had not taken the exam for regular employees, but was exacerbated by the significant pay gap when the duties did not differ significantly. She stated, 'A lot of the resentment is coming from not knowing when our work and responsibilities and duties aren't that different, what is the reason for the difference in that big pay gap?'

Mary was not only unhappy with the pay gap but also with not receiving any pay raise. She stated, 'Maybe I shouldn't compare it to outside of Japan, but in other countries, you can negotiate. After say two years on the job, I have managed to for example raise the number of Facebook followers from 300 to 1,500, you know, times five! You can say, "I think I deserve a pay raise" and negotiate with your employer, but here it's no! You never get to benefit from it.' Her sense of injustice is rooted in having a unique reference point different from the other Japanese non-regular employees. Mary's reference point is not confined to the norms of the Japanese workplace. Her normative standard was the employment practices abroad where pay is negotiable by performance, which made it difficult for her to accept the treatment as inevitable. She often discusses her treatment with her husband as well as her friends, all from Europe working in Japan. Having a reference point outside of Japan that treats its workers based on performance rather than status served to dissuade her from consenting to the treatment she received.

Having an income-earning partner did not persuade her to settle with the current treatment either. She had not internalized the gendered norm of paying less for women on a non-regular job with the assumption of having a male breadwinner. She stated, 'It's very unfair. Why should I need a husband if I want to be just by myself all my life? Why should I have to be a wife or a mother? If I think that way, does that mean that I have to get a permanent position?' Mary was unwilling to concede to the differential pay based on employment status or marital status. She firmly believed workers should be treated based on the job and their performance. She was so frustrated with the treatment that she once informally asked the section chief, 'So in essence, what is the difference between a regular staff and an irregular staff?' And the answer she received was short and vague, that the regular staff 'should take responsibility'. This unsatisfactory response reinforced her sense of injustice. She stated, 'It's like if you're unhappy with the terms of conditions you can leave any time.' Finding herself powerless to change the Japanese employment system, she is determined to leave the workplace as soon as she can.

Consent without dissatisfaction

Waka is equally as academically gifted as Mary. She graduated from a top-ranked high school in her region and earned a master's degree in fine arts. After several years of working in the field of art as a regular employee, she suffered from depression. She confessed that the industry is particularly notorious for the ill management of its workers. Creators work around the clock without much distinction between night and day, work days and holidays. Consequently, those working in the industry were also prone to working irregular hours. The staff were asked to do a variety of tasks on demand. The irregular work hours and the sheer amount of work took a toll on her mental health. She left the job, received treatment, and after some stints in other workplaces, she began working at the current workplace.

In response to my question about her thoughts on the remuneration and the pay gaps, she stated, 'My initial impression was, "I get paid so much?!" Compared to my previous job, the work load here had reduced to about 1/3 (laughter). And the wage had gone up. So for me, comparatively speaking, life got so much easier.' She is aware of what the Regular A employees receive. But she used the word 'curious' to express her thoughts about the pay gap. 'I feel curious. I just wonder about it. But it's also curious to me why I receive what I'm receiving now.' How a job or work performance corresponds to what quantity of money remains a mystery to her.

Waka was positively happy and content with the remuneration when others were dissatisfied and reluctantly settled for the remuneration. The divergence stems from her purposive choice of not working as a permanent employee. She is confident she could manage the Regular A employee's job if she had to but is aware of her tendency to overwork herself. She is intentionally reserving herself from giving full effort to the job by working as a non-regular employee. When I asked her what makes an ideal form of work, she answered, 'It's health. I work to be healthy. That's my number one priority.' In reference to her previous job that was too awful, she feels, 'I made the right choice to be here.' She also manages an art-related NPO, in which she invests about half of her mind and energy. The regularity of work hours suits her interest and purpose to work.

One point of concern was financial well-being. After all, her pay was insufficient by far to save enough for a comfortable life after retirement. Her side business brought her little income; she was in it for the love of art. Finance was the source of dissatisfaction shared by the majority of interviewees. Then why is Waka able to ponder on the difficult question of how labour can be justifiably converted into money without being concerned about her future? When I pointed to a government statistic that projected 20 million yen as the required amount of savings to sustain a decent life after retirement, she responded, 'I think those numbers are a lie!' She elaborated, 'I don't think my life would be hard if I don't have money. I think I'd be happier if I had the life skills to survive even as a homeless person.' After admitting to the extremity of her example, she commented, 'But I think life's choice is wider if I have the ability to survive with only cold running water.' A salaried life is only one of the many choices of lifestyle in her view. I felt her statement was a different way for her to say she is confident of surviving without being dependent on employment by a corporation.

Conclusion

This study showed how disaffected consent is not only a Western European phenomenon but can also be found at work in an East Asian society like Japan. The female non-regular workers were dissatisfied with the low pay as well as the pay gap. However, they reluctantly gave in to the differential treatments. When differences in employment status were translated into differences in job duties and responsibilities (Arita 2017), the non-regular employees had a hard time refuting the large disparity in pay. Given the prevalence of bad jobs in the local labour market, they had no choice but to accept the bad treatment as relatively good. Some gave in to the bad treatment in exchange for prioritizing child-rearing. Others blamed their past selves for not choosing and winning a permanent position as fresh recruits. When the workplace excluded the non-regular employees from union membership, they engaged in informal means of protest, only to reaffirm that the employment practices were unalterable. As a result, the sense of helplessness and inevitability dominated their minds, as represented by the frequent usage of the term *shōganai* in describing their feelings. The workers felt resigned and helpless in believing that the arrangements were here to stay and not much could be done about it. This study has contributed to existing studies that examine the cultural dimensions of the neoliberal world of work as well as those that focus on the agency of non-regular workers (e.g. Fu 2011; Kojima 2015; Rydzik and Anitha 2020).

The findings from this study have implications on how non-regular workers' working conditions can be improved. The state is now forced to deal with the consequences of its neoliberal labour policymaking for the past decades, given the labour shortage and the stagnant economic growth. It is in this context that the Work Style Reform was launched by the Abe government in 2016 (Kojima, North, and Weathers 2017; Vogel 2018). Labour laws were revised to institutionalize the equal pay for equal work (EPEW) principle to correct the pay gap between regular and non-regular workers. The EPEW legislation went into effect in April 2020 for large corporations and in April 2021 for SMEs. It is too soon to judge the impact of the new regulations, but the findings from this study can provide some insights.

The workplace under study is a large corporation, thus subject to the EPEW regulations since April 2020. However, the corporation has made little changes to the base wage or bonus pay for its non-regular employees. At the time of this writing, Kyoko has returned to the workplace for the seventh time as a non-regular employee, with no changes to the pay scheme. The non-regular workers continue to enjoy no pay raise, severance pay, or housing allowance. The only changes were made to benefits and allowances, such as to paid leave, and this change was made by reducing the amount of paid leave for entry-level Regular A employees to match the non-regular employees during the first five years of employment.

The new regulations also place a heavy burden on the workers to proactively engage the employer to close the pay gap. The employer is now obligated to explain the reasons behind the differences in treatment upon hire. If the worker concerned is not convinced, s/he can now seek an out-of-court settlement, such as taking the issue to the local labour bureau for mediation. However, studies have shown that such 'reactive enforcement', i.e. enforcement in response to voicing workers, fails in practice because vulnerable workers have limited knowledge on changes in regulations and little incentives to voice their opinions because of the high cost in doing so (e.g. Alexander and Prasad 2014). This study suggests that when workers suffer from disaffected consent, they are unlikely to 'voice' (Hirschman 1970). As evidence of this, all non-regular employees I interviewed in 2021 were unwilling to officially confront the employer, even when I shared a copy of model questions for inquiry drafted by a labor lawyers' association. To close the pay gap, the state should consider creating tougher laws to ensure enforcement, such as heavily fining the noncomplying employers as well as mobilizing labor inspection officers to raise the likelihood of being caught for non-compliance.

Notes

1. The statistic assumes the worker with a minimum of a college degree and has continuously worked until the age of 60. The statistic for non-regular workers assumes the worker has continuously worked full time as a non-regular employee after graduating from college until the age of 60.
2. Wages are approximated based on a hypothetical regular work week, assuming 40 hours of work per week without overtime. The titles of employment categories are modified to assure anonymity, but the numbers are accurate enough to reflect the pay gap. The actual pay gap is larger due to longer work hours for regular workers. In addition to the three categories of non-regular employees, the corporation used agency temporaries as well as a subcontractor that also used a variety of non-regular employees.
3. In the third year of employment, the wage gap grew to 80%, 57%, and 39% for Non-Regular A, B, and C employees respectively. In the fifth year, 72%, 50%, and 35% respectively. The growing gap in compensation is due to seniority wage only enjoyed by Regular A employees.
4. The Labor Contract Act limits the duration of a fixed-term contract to a maximum of five years. A permanent position must be offered to the worker concerned if the management wishes to use the worker beyond the five-year limit. However, this regulation is accompanied by a derogation clause that enables the employer to use the same contact worker beyond the five-year limit by having a six-month "cooling off" period in between the five-year stints.

References

Abe, M. (2017) 'Kisei o Kanwa shitemo Chingin wa Agaranai: Basu Untenshu no Jirei kara'. In Y. Genda (ed.), *Hitodebusoku nanoni Naze Chingin wa Agaranainoka*. Tokyo: Keio Gijuku Daigaku Shuppankai.

Alexander, C. S. and Prasad, A. (2014) 'Bottom up workplace law enforcement: An empirical analysis'. *Indiana Law Journal*, 89: 1069–1131.

Arita, S. (2017) 'Shakaigaku kara Kangaeru Hiseikikoyō no Teichingin to sono Hen'yō'. In Y. Genda (ed.), *Hitodebusoku nanoni Naze Chingin wa Agaranainoka*. Tokyo: Keio Gijuku Daigaku Shuppankai, pp. 251–266.

Brinton, M. and Eunsil, O. (2019) 'Babies, work, or both? Highly educated women's employment and fertility in East Asia'. *American Journal of Sociology*, 125(1): 105–140.

Cave, P. (2004) 'Bukatsudō: The educational role of Japanese school clubs'. *The Journal of Japanese Studies*, 30(2): 383–415.

Eng, K. (2006) *Kōkōyakyū: High School Baseball*. PBS.

Fu, H. (2011) *An Emerging Non-Regular Labour Force in Japan: The Dignity of Dispatched Workers*. London: Routledge.

Genda, Y. (2001) *Shigoto no naka no Aimai na Fuan: Yureru Jakunen no Genzai*. Tokyo: Chuo Koronsha.

Genda, Y. (2017) *Hitodebusoku nanoni Naze Chingin wa Agaranainoka*. Tokyo: Keio Gijuku Daigaku Shuppankai.

Gilbert, J. (2013) 'What kind of thing is "neoliberalism"?' *New Formation: A Journal of Culture/Theory/Politics*, 80–81: 7–22.

Gilbert, J. (2015) 'Disaffected consent: That post-democratic feeling. Can we turn dissatisfaction into resistance?" *Surroundings: A Journal of Politics and Culture*, 60: 29–41.

Glaser, B. and Strauss, A. (1967) *The Discovery of Grounded Theory: Strategies for Qualitative Research*. Chicago: Aldine Publishing.

Gordon, A. (2017) 'New and enduring dual structures of employment in Japan: The rise of nonregular Labor, 1980s-2010s'. *Social Science Japan Journal*, 20(1): 9-36.

Gottfried, H. (2014) 'Precarious work in Japan: Old forms, new risks?' *Journal of Contemporary Asia*, 44(3): 464–478.

Gottfried, H. (2015) *The Reproductive Bargain: Deciphering the Enigma of Japanese Capitalism*. Leiden: Brill.

Hamaguchi, K. (2011) *Nihon no Koyō to Rōdōhō* (Employment and Labour Law in Japan). Tokyo: Nikkei Publishing.

Harvey, D. (2005) *A Brief History of Neoliberalism*. Oxford: Oxford University Press.

Hirschman, A. O. (1970) *Exit, Voice, and Loyalty: Responses to Decline in Firms, Organizations, and States*. Cambridge: Harvard University Press.

Howell, C. (2021) 'Rethinking the role of the state in employment relations for a neoliberal era'. *ILR Review*, 74(3): 739–772.

Imai, J. (2021) *Koyōkankei to Shakai Fubyōdō: Sangyōteki Shitizunshippu Keisei Tenkai to shiteno Kōzō Hendō* (Employment Relations and Social Inequalities: Social Structural Changes Shaped by the Development of Industrial Citizenship). Tokyo: Yūhikaku.

Imai, J. and Sato, Y. (2011) 'Regular and non-regular employment as an additional duality in Japanese labor market: Institutional perspectives on career mobility'. In Y. Sato and J. Imai (eds.), *Japan's New Inequality: Intersection of Employment Reforms and Welfare Arrangements*. Melbourne: Trans Pacific Press, pp. 1–31.

Japan Institute for Labour Policy and Training (2019) *Dētabukku Kokusai Rōdō Hikaku 2019 nenban* (Databook of International Labour Statistics 2016). Tokyo: JILPT.

Japan Institute for Labour Policy and Training (2020) *Yūsufuru Rōdōtōkei 2020* (Useful Labor Statistics 2020). Tokyo: JILPT.

Kalleberg, A. L. (2011) *Good Jobs, Bad Jobs: The Rise of Polarized and Precarious Employment Systems in the United States, 1970s to 2000s*. New York: Russell Sage Foundation.

Kawaguchi, D. (2018) 'Koyōkeitaikan Chinginsa no Jisshōbunseki'. *Nihon Rōdōkenkyū Zasshi*, 701: 4–16.

Kojima, S. (2015) "Why do temp workers work as hard as they do? The commitment and suffering of factory temp workers in Japan'. *The Sociological Quarterly*, 56(2): 355–385.

Kojima, S., North, S. and Weathers, C. (2017) 'Abe Shinzo's campaign to reform the Japanese way of work'. *The Asia-Pacific Journal Japan Focus*, 15(23): 1–17.

Ministry of Internal Affairs and Communication. (2021) 'Rōdōryoku Chōsa Shōsai Shukei' (Labor Force Survey, Detailed Aggregate Data).

Miura, M. (2012) *Welfare through Work: Conservative Ideas, Partisan Dynamics, and Social Protection in Japan*. Ithaca: Cornell University Press.

Morioka, K. (2015). *Koyō Mibun Shakai* (Employment Caste Society). Tokyo: Iwanami Shinsho.

Mudge, S. L. (2008) 'What is neo-liberalism?' *Socio-Economic Review*, 6: 703–731.

Osawa, M., Kim, M. J., and Kingston, J. (2013) 'Precarious Work in Japan'. *American Behavioral Scientist*, 57(3): 309–334.

Rydzik, A. and Anitha, S. (2020) 'Conceptualizing agency of migrant women workers: Resilience, reworking and resistance'. *Work, Employment and Society*, 34(5): 883–899.

Sato, Y. (2013) 'Seiki Koyo to Hiseiki Koyo: Nihon ni okeru Kakusa Mondai'. In Y. Sato and Kimura, T. (eds.), *Fubyodo Seisei Mekanizumu no Kaimei: Kakusa, Kaiso, Kosei*. Tokyo: Mineruva Shobo, pp. 15–34.

Shin, K.-Y. (2010) 'Globalisation and the working class in South Korea: Contestation, fragmentation and renewal'. *Journal of Contemporary Asia*, 40(2): 211–229.

Standing, G. (2011) *The Precariat: The New Dangerous Class*. New York: Bloomsbury Academic.

Vogel, S. K. (2018) 'Japan's labor regime in transition: Rethinking work for a shrinking nation'. *The Journal of Japanese Studies*, 44(2): 257–292.

10
'I'm Not a *Real* Freeter'

Aspiration and Non-Regular Labour in Japan

Emma E. Cook

Introduction

'I guess I am a freeter', 27-year-old Nobu-san said hesitantly in 2007. 'Personally, I don't like labelling people and "freeter" is a label. If I had to label myself, I would say "artist" ... My image of freeters is of people who work in a convenience store, that's my image ... [A] part-time worker who works 100% [full time].'[1] This quote doesn't convey how uncomfortable Nobu was when saying this. Generally a relaxed and laid-back person with quick answers, he took time to deeply consider my question of whether he considered himself a freeter—one type of non-regular worker—before answering. His discomfort speaks to the precarious social stakes embedded in the label of freeter, which is significantly mediated by socio-cultural ideas of gender norms related to employment embedded in both the definition of the employment category and the lived experience of it. But what actually *is* a 'freeter'?

In 2007 the Ministry of Health, Labour and Welfare defined freeters as people aged between 15 and 34 who were directly employed on a contract (not as a full-time employee, *seishain*) by a company or enterprise, and were not a student or—if female—married (MHLW 2007). Freeters are considered different from temporary workers (*haken*) because although temps are hired via an agency (Fu 2012) and day labourers are hired by the day (Gill 2001), freeters are hired directly by companies on a short-term contract (e.g. six months), often defined as part time.[2] As of 2014, government statistics suggest there were 1.79 million freeters: 730,000 between the ages of 15 and 24, and 1.06 million aged between 25 and 34 (Cabinet Office 2016). In the last decade their number has been decreasing: since 2017 this figure has dropped to 1.52 million and in 2019 it dropped to 1.38 million.[3] Whilst it used to be the case that many more women worked as freeters than men the numbers in recent years illustrate it has become almost equal within the freeter category

Emma E. Cook, *'I'm Not a* Real *Freeter'*. In: *Temporary and Gig Economy Workers in China and Japan*. Edited by Huiyan Fu, Oxford University Press. © Oxford University Press (2023). DOI: 10.1093/oso/9780192849694.003.0011

(Statistics Bureau 2018). It should be clearly noted, however, that the term 'freeter' remains a bit of a slippery category, often subsumed into the general category of non-regular employee (*hiseiki shain*). It is perhaps better understood as denoting a particular cultural category of labourer within a bracket defined as 'youth employment' and which is used to categorize not only type of work (part-time), but also worker motivations: such as being 'free' and pursuing dreams; being unsure what to do; working part time as a stop gap while retraining, as well as those youth who have been unable to find alternatives due to a lack of education or chances (see for example, Hori 2021; Kosugi 2021).

Despite increasing numbers of men moving into the non-regular labour market over the past thirty years, it does, however, remain overall primarily a female sphere. For example, within the non-regular employment sphere itself women constituted 73.7 per cent of all part-time workers (broadly defined) in 2000, though this decreased slightly to 69.8 per cent in 2015 (JILPT 2017a: 36). Women's position as part-time labourers is linked to pre- and post-war policies that provided the employment sector with more flexibility and a buffer zone (Gordon 2017) and was premised on culturally mediated gender norms (see also Chapter 2, this volume). In the post-war period (middle-class) women were socio-culturally positioned primarily as homemakers undertaking supplementary part-time work (therefore comprising a flexible labour force that could be cut as companies needed), and men were positioned as the main breadwinners working in the core 'regular' labour market. This positionality and division of labour was encouraged and reinforced via a patriarchal family system, a gendered employment system split into a primarily male career-track (*sōgōshoku*) and primarily female general (non-career) track (*ippanshoku*) jobs from the 1980s, and state policy such as social welfare policies and tax breaks on marital income, which relied and built upon the heteronormative family structure (Miura 2012; Osawa 2011). However, the gradual increase in male non-regular employees points to significant shifts within working practices, ideals, and opportunities. As of 2015, male non-regular employees (of all types) constituted 21.9 per cent of the workforce, up from 7.4 per cent in 1985 (JILPT 2014, 2017a; Osawa 2011). Mary Brinton (2010) has described this movement of men into the non-regular sector as representing the 'de-gendering of irregular employment in post-industrial Japan' (2010: 30). Given that it remains, however, a significantly female sphere, the movement of men into this arena has notable gendered repercussions—one of which is that such work is often considered, in the social imagination, to be problematic and inappropriate labour for men to do and potentially contributes to the feminization of men in such work (see also, Vera-Sanso 2016).

Within the government definition of freeter outlined here it is clear that labour expectations for men and women are conceived of differently: if women are *married* and working directly for a company in the part-time labour market they are not categorized as freeters, yet men (and single women) are. This difference was also reflected in *how* people engaged with the freeter label. In general, the female freeters I worked with understood it as a labour category that was not particularly linked to negative judgements about their character, whereas for men the label was intimately linked to how their characters were perceived—as adults and as men—in wider society. The label is perhaps less socially burdensome for women in part because their labour in the non-regular sector has been understood as 'normal' practice in the post-war and post-bubble periods (Macnaughtan 2006). Part-time labour and character were thus interlinked for men in ways that were felt and experienced as problematic and uncomfortable (see Cook 2013, 2014, 2016).

In this chapter, drawing on ethnographic fieldwork since 2006,[4] I illustrate the various ways that the male freeters I worked with attempted to distance themselves from this employee category, primarily because of the social ramifications and character critiques that male non-regular employment engenders.[5] In their attempts to prove themselves as responsible men, most drew on alternative labour aspirations and framed freeterhood as just one step on their journey to achieving their labour or lifestyle goals. By mobilizing narratives of *ganbaru* (trying one's best) and *gaman* (endurance) these men sought to locate themselves within acceptable discourses of hard work, sacrifice, and striving that are also present in the social imagination of full-time labour and which bridge older Fordist ideas of labour and current neoliberal discourses. Other men drew parallels between themselves and full-time workers by highlighting the number of hours they worked, or how they were financially independent of their families, or financially responsible for others. Full-time 'regular' labour was an ever-present expectation that they framed their narratives around and against in various ways. A much smaller number of people claimed the label of freeter for themselves, but they argued for a reframing of how freeter labour—and labour in general—should be understood. Although these men were not active in freeter protests or unions their desire to rethink and reshape labour practices and attitudes corresponds with a small but insistent call for change (Cassegård 2013; O'Day 2013; O'Day 2015; PAFF 2005). It is important to note, however, that men's understandings of the label of freeter and its link to themselves were not static, but also shifted over the years and as their situations changed. I have consequently selected and cite cases of men that I have worked with over an extended period of time to illustrate these fluctuations as their lives and labour status have changed.[6]

Problematic (male) freeters

The categorization of 'freeter' has been strongly embedded in both neoliberal ideology and labour deregulation from the 1990s onwards in Japan. Indeed, the term was initially created in the late 1980s' bubble economy by the head of an employment magazine who sought to make part-time jobs appear cool and desirable. They did this by drawing on ideas of entrepreneurialism, self-determination, individualism, and aspiration, and even went so far as to produce a film titled *Freeter* (Smith 2006). 'Freeter' jobs at the time were envisaged to be short term and for young people who were chasing their dreams. However, with the implosion of the bubble economy at the beginning of the 1990s, an extended recessionary period, and increasing employment deregulation, such non-regular (and precarious) jobs have become an increasing feature of the employment landscape, for men as well as for women. We can see this as a precursor to the gradual emergence of the gig economy that has burgeoned in other post-industrial societies such as the UK and elsewhere, and has in recent years begun to emerge in Japan. For example, since 2012 there has been a gradual rise in 'nomad workers' who do not need a fixed space in which to work, such as freelance programmers, designers, and writers who are working with, and relying on, internet technologies and social media in co-working spaces and cafes as they move from gig to gig (Matsushita 2016). Matsushita (2016: 42) argues that, 'The nomad boom of 2012 was . . . supported by . . . aspirations for jobs in which people could utilize their time and location more freely' (see also, Honda 2013; Tachibana 2012). More recently we can see an expansion of the gig economy to other industries in Japan, such as in deliveries with the start of UberEats in Tokyo in 2016 (Pascaline 2016). In this set-up, workers are essentially self-employed delivery drivers, known as 'Delivery Partners', who are encouraged to 'earn on your own schedule' as independent contractors (see also Millward 2017).[7] The initial 1980s' framing of freeters to pursue flexible working can thus be seen as Japan's first step to an increasing and broader cross-section of the post-war population, not only working-class individuals with limited employment opportunities engaging in insecure employment.[8]

Dardot and Laval (2013: 7) have argued that contemporary capitalism's rationality—in the West and beyond—is the 'existential norm' of neoliberalism. It is a form of governmentality that 'is based on a *global normative framework* which, in the name of liberty and relying on the leeway afforded individuals, orientates their conduct, choices and practices in a new way'. They argue that:

> Neo-liberalism is … productive of certain kinds of social relations, certain ways of living, certain subjectivities. … Neo-liberalism defines a certain existential norm … This norm enjoins everyone to live in a world of generalised competition; it calls upon wage-earning classes and populations to engage in economic struggle against one another; it aligns social relations with the model of the market; it promotes the justification of ever greater inequalities; it even transforms the individual, now called on to conceive and conduct him- or herself as an enterprise. For more than a third of a century, this existential norm has presided over public policy, governed global economic relations, transformed society, and reshaped subjectivity.
>
> (Dardot and Laval 2013: 3)

In Japan, whilst neoliberal capitalism is now a dominant feature of the employment landscape, it exists alongside post-war gendered socio-cultural norms of labour that were rooted in Fordism. Therefore, whilst there is an increasing 'emphasis on self-making and self-management, on the neoliberal self as an entrepreneurial self' (Cornwall 2016: 10), many of the male freeters I worked with felt they had to navigate neoliberal employment realities alongside socio-cultural gender norms positioning them as future breadwinners which no longer necessarily represented their employment realities and consequent opportunities. Men therefore drew on neoliberal discourses of self-making while at the same time thinking about how they would attempt to move into the core regular employment sector by their late twenties at the latest in order to mitigate against the possibility of moving into a state of potentially permanent precariousness.

Non-regular work is a precarious social location along a number of registers: wages are paid hourly and are typically low, there are usually no annual bonuses, sick pay, or paid holidays, and no real protection against unfair firing. Precarious work conditions are the norm for non-regular labourers who are used when needed and potentially discarded when not.[9] There is also a temporal dimension to this precarity. Companies have historically not considered non-regular work experience to have value and have hesitated to employ long-term freeters. Remaining in the non-regular job market for too long can therefore become a precarity trap that minimizes the possibility of finding full-time opportunities (Allison 2013; Brinton 2010; Ishiguro 2008;

Kosugi 2008). Most of the men I worked with were conflicted and nervous as they aged because of this, and some struggled with what they felt they should do to maximize their chances of finding more socially acceptable work contracts as they aged. This dilemma continues because the Japanese employment market remains primarily split into a core (regular) workforce with status, benefits, and a recognizable social contract,[10] and a peripheral non-regular labour market that is typically characterized by fluid and unstable labour conditions.[11]

In addition to the lived realities of low wages and precarious labour conditions, non-regular workers—especially *male* non-regular workers—were subject to critiques of their character for being in such work. As I have written about elsewhere, two prevailing views dominated social and media discourse in the early and mid-2000s: they were either considered to be victims of changing employment norms in the wake of deregulation (Allison 2013; Anon 2013b; Brinton 2010; Genda 2005; Hirano 2005; Otake 2002; Tarōmaru 2006, 2009) or they were thought of as lazy good-for-nothings who were prioritizing their desires, job-hopping, and consequently shirking their social responsibilities and contributing to dragging down productivity (Anon 2003a, 2003b; Kageyama 2005; Kitazume 2005; Parry 2006).[12] More than a media/moral panic, (male) freeters at the time epitomized national fears about Japan's economic and employment health amid demographic decline (Driscoll 2007).

Today, freeters—and the non-regular labour market more generally—are often viewed by policymakers as a problem that needs to be solved. There have, for example, been programmes put forth to convert part-time jobs into full-time positions, and the Ministry of Health, Labour and Welfare have offered private companies subsidies to offer trial employment for freeters (Anon 2006a, 2006b, 2008a, 2008b, 2013a; JILPT 2016, 2017b; Ogino 2015; Toivonen 2008, 2013). In November 2015 the MHLW uploaded a 16 minute anime to YouTube aimed at freeters titled '*Bokura no ashita ~ furītā no genjō ni kansuru wakamono e no shūchi kōhō jigyō*' (Our Tomorrow—Public Relations Project for Young People about the Current Situation of Freeters) in which they introduced the experiences of a male character who had quit university before graduating, and a female character who had failed at job hunting and anticipated becoming a freeter.[13] Through the drama they introduced two initiatives being run through Hello Work, the government's Employment Service Centre: 1). 'Youth Hello Work' (*Wakamono Harō Wāku*) aimed at job hunters under the age of 35, and 2). 'New Graduate Support Hello Work' (*Shinsotsu Ouen Harō Wāku*) aimed at graduates of universities, junior colleges, technical colleges, and vocational schools.[14] An 8-page manga pamphlet of the video and information was also published under the title: 'Full-time employee? Freeter? What's the difference?? For those who are worried about their future course' (MHLW 2015). More recently, the Abe government also proposed 'equal pay for equal work', which became effective from 1 April 2020 with the aim of reducing 'irrational gaps' between regular and non-regular (fixed-term/part-time) workers (MHLW 2019). In addition, an increasing number of companies have begun programmes to promote non-regular employees into regular contracts after two or three years of work, as well as introducing the category of 'limited regular employee' or 'area-limited regular employee', which consists of open-ended contracts that do not require employees to move locations, but are more stable than non-regular positions (Ogino 2015). Despite these initiatives and discourses, however, seniority and salaried regular contracts continue to be privileged in terms of benefits and in social status (Harding 2016). Such a division between regular and non-regular employment continues to reinforce moral, political, and economic injunctions to work in particular ways, as well as maintaining social and economic inequality for those unable to work in the regular employment sector.

Day-to-day representations of non-regular workers also focus on the moral and social imperative for men to work in regular salaried positions, rather than on the precarity or inequality that is embedded in such positions. A good example of this is the 2010 television drama 'Freeter, buys a house' (*Freeter, ie o kau*) which aired with high ratings on Fuji Television (Perkins 2014). The drama begins by highlighting the issues of the protagonist's character: he's too picky, selfish, and immature, and his behaviour negatively impacts his family—especially his mother. Over the course of its ten episodes, however, the drama highlights the protagonist's gradual rehabilitation and growth into responsible male adulthood through efforts at work. The focus is thus on character growth through labour and the eventual positioning of a man looking after his family. This is a typical normative trope of adult manhood that male freeters are often, as a result of their labour practices and alleged problematic character, not able (or find it difficult) to embody. This drama thus highlights one of the dominant discourses about male freeters—a picky, selfish, immature youth who will (or should) grow into appropriate manhood through his labour practices. Such a framing suggests that being a freeter is a selfish choice, which is of course, an oversimplified representation of freeters' lives and future potentialities. It also positions 'freeters' as middle-class men with university degrees, rather than illustrating the diversity of backgrounds that men in such employment come from.[15] The drama effectively ignores the often very real structural constraints of employment opportunities, class, and educational capital that limit people's ability to move into the regular employment sphere.

The categorization as freeter thus locates people into particular social, moral, class, and temporal positionings, and many of the freeters I worked with consequently had conflicting feelings about the label. This was especially so for those whose parents were in the middle class and who had attended university. Working as a freeter after growing up with such social and cultural capital was thought to be wasteful (*mottainai*).[16] However, even those who grew up with less social and cultural capital and fewer opportunities were socially expected to try to find stable employment, albeit in small (non-elite) companies. Such expectations are strongly linked to normative ideas of masculinities and adulthood that position men primarily as breadwinners of future families.[17] Working in non-regular labour jeopardizes their ability to fulfil such positioning and is therefore considered socially problematic in wider (middle-class) discourse. The negative discourses about male freeters are a clear representation of the conflict and contradiction that exists between post-war social ideas of male labour that were rooted in post-war Fordist labour practices, and contemporary neoliberal practices that emerged out of increased deregulation since the 1990s. The categorization of freeter can thus be read as a problematic bridge between older labour norms, practices, and ideals, and the realities of labour practices in the neoliberal present.

I'm not a *real* freeter because. . .

I turn now to some of the narratives that emerged about the freeter category during fieldwork. For many of the individuals I worked with, future-oriented aspiration and achievement were mobilized and narrated as a way to distance themselves and their labour from 'real' freeters. Whilst some men have achieved what they set out to do and have been able to move into and maintain a stable labour environment as they have aged, others have dipped in and out of freeterhood, leading to complex and at times contradictory positioning with regards to socio-culturally gendered discourses of non-regular labour and freeterhood, as the narratives that follow illustrate.

'I'm working towards a goal . . .'

Eiji was a 32-year-old university graduate who had achieved the main labour aspiration of his twenties, but had then been unable to sustain it.[18]

After working full time after university for four years, he resigned and attended a one-year vocational college course that trained individuals to become chefs, baristas, and sommeliers. He aspired to be a self-made man doing work that he loved on his own terms. After graduating from the vocational course he set up his own café specializing in home-style dishes (*katei ryōri*) and was able to sustain the business for three years before reluctantly deciding that it was fundamentally not profitable enough to continue. When we met in 2014 he was working long hours as a part-time barista in a speciality coffee shop run by a well-respected visiting lecturer at the vocational college he had studied at. He expressed embarrassment about his labour status, his failure to sustain his café, and his precarious labour positioning, mentioning a few times his age of 32 (Cook 2017). It wasn't a position he ever really imagined himself to end up in—part time at 32—and he lamented his inability to marry due to his labour status. In musing about freeters he clearly differentiated himself from 'regular' (*futsū na*) freeters because of his previous labour experiences and the kind of specialist skills he was learning:

> If you look just at my contract you could call me a freeter. But I'm not really. I'm working part-time at the moment, but it is to learn more deeply about coffee: how to roast it, the complexity of taste and temperature. Atmospheric conditions really affect the beans so how and when you grind it, the amount you put in etc. all depends on temperature and humidity—it is quite complicated.

For Eiji, his seriousness and the focus he displayed when discussing the skills and techniques he was learning while working part time emerged from his previous culinary endeavours and labour experiences. He understood his part-time position to be temporary—a kind of training period that he hoped would lead to achieving a permanent (regular) labour status: his labour goal at the time, and which he succeeded at in 2019.

Takeshi also illustrates the ups and downs of labour aspirations, freeterhood, and how individuals may end up dipping into and out of the non-regular labour market. When we first met in 2003 Takeshi was a self-proclaimed freeter who, since graduating from university three years previously, was focused on surfing and saving money to travel. His aim at the time was to work in a way that facilitated his desire to see the world, and he was highly critical of Japan's working environment which he considered to be inhuman (*hiningen teki na*). In 2006 he felt the following about work:

> I like working, but only working is not good . . . I want time for myself. Working is not life . . . I think that the way of thinking about work in Japan is crazy. Working

is natural, but working very hard is normal in Japan. People think working hard is beautiful... I don't think so. I think work is the way to get money. We need money to live. How can I say... work is for our life, but in Japan life is for working. I think it's strange. My friends go to work at eight in the morning and come home at about ten in the evening. It's too much (*yarisugi!*). I feel really envious (*hontō ni urayamashī*) when I think about how people work in Europe. They can take two or three weeks off when they choose to go on holiday. If I did that I would be fired.[19]

At the time, his aspirations were to become an Amway entrepreneur because he wanted to be able to make a living whilst also having some control over his work environment.[20] After consistently bad sales, however, Takeshi accepted a full-time contract at a factory he had been working at part time because it provided more stability. This move was largely prompted by hitting his late twenties and becoming concerned about his future and his desirability to women who he thought found his insecure labour status off-putting (see Cook 2014, 2016). He continued, however, to spend his evenings and days off trying to sell Amway products in an attempt to become a self-sufficient entrepreneur. After it became clear, however, that he wasn't going to make a success of Amway he moved from his factory job (which had clearly defined hours and limited overtime) to being a contract salesman (*keiyaku shain*) for a beer maker.

The Great East Japan Earthquake of March 2011, however, made him reassess his labour and lifestyle and he quit his position when it was time to renew the contract in order to volunteer more in areas hit by the tsunami and to do some travelling, something he had been unable to do because of a limited ability to take time off in his contract position. In 2013 he continued to have a similar take on work as in 2007:

We work so much in our lives that I think it's important to do something that you find enjoyable or meaningful. I think work is really important, but it should not be everything. If I was asked to choose what was more important, work or family, I would choose family... and the same for friends and relationships. Work should not be our whole lives.[21]

At the time, he really wanted to give himself a year to travel, however, he felt unable to because of the way the employment market works:

People often move jobs these days. You can't depend on a company anymore, you have to make your own path, have skills (*sukiru ha hitsuyō*). If you stay in one company for a long time and then lose your job no one else will hire you, you're useless. So, although I am a bit worried about the future, I think working styles are changing... Well, but... I am worried about my position though. To be honest, last year I wanted to travel for the whole year, but having a year blank on your resume is really bad (*hontō ni yabai*) and companies won't even look at you, so that's why I just travelled for two months and then worked again.[22]

Despite his aim to join the regular labour market, in a meeting in August 2016, Takeshi remained working on a contract and was increasingly concerned about his positionality. At 38 years of age he was in a remarkably precarious position earning low wages and living with his parents again. Because of his previous resume and his age he is potentially considered to be less malleable, and a risky hire with a tendency to move on (Brinton 2010). For Takeshi, however, he sees his resume to be a reflection of a changing labour market. He argued that it is the type of *intention* a person has—for example, to travel, to surf, to do something unrelated to labour—that marks an individual as a freeter. If someone in a part-time position was attempting to achieve a goal related to labour they were not, he thought, a freeter. Thus, for Takeshi, a freeter was someone young whose aim was to enjoy life outside of work, where work was not the goal or aspiration. In his youth he unequivocally felt he was a freeter; however, he no longer considers himself to be one because of his strong intention to work in the regular labour market and his age. He had a strong desire to mitigate the negative social connotations of being in non-regular employment in his late thirties, and was concerned that his labour continued to make him an unattractive potential marriage partner.

'I work full-time hours'

Not all men drew primarily on labour aspirations to differentiate themselves from 'regular' freeters. Others drew more on the number of hours they worked and how they lived independently to differentiate themselves. Some also mentioned labour goals but made this less of a focus in discussions. For example, in 2007 vocational school graduate Koji was 33 years old and had been working on and off part time at a cinema for around five years after quitting a full-time regular job that he had come to really dislike. The cinema job was his second job: during the day he worked in the basement food floor of a local department store. He consistently distanced himself personally from the label of freeter, but understood that others would categorize himself as one:

> For me, a freeter is someone who lives with their parents, sometimes works and goes out and plays. I think that Japanese society has a bad image of freeters, but

because I have worked with freeters I do not have any bad image. In some ways I am a freeter. People would describe me as one. But I think I work regularly (*futsū ni*) so I don't think I really am. My contract is not full-time, but I work full-time hours... If we look just at the contract we can say I am a freeter. But I don't feel like it. If I was not working at all, or was only working a few shifts a week then maybe I would think I was definitely a freeter, but I am working properly, can pay for my food and rent and am living my life independently. I don't live with my parents or get money from anyone... I'm an adult (*ichininmae ni natta*).[23]

Koji makes a direct link in his narrative to freeters not being conceived as adults. For him, if you are an adult—understood here as being responsible and financially independent—then you cannot be a real freeter. Although Koji worked only a few shifts a week at the cinema, his hours at the department store consisted of five days' work at around eight to nine hours per shift. The amount of work he did differentiated him, he thought, from freeters who were working fewer hours and were more focused on enjoying themselves outside of work. Age was also a critical part of his feeling that he was not a real freeter: his image was that of younger people, typically in their early twenties, not of men in their early thirties. He therefore positioned himself as being linked to, but different from, regular freeters. Koji also stressed his desire to attain a full-time permanent contract at the department store. Whilst many men narrated labour goals that were more creative or entrepreneurial, Koji's aspiration was to work on a regular contract. As such, he was keen to show himself as being serious, responsible, and worthy of gaining this type of status to his employers and was aware that as he aged it was becoming more difficult to be taken on as a full-time employee. In 2014, Koji made the move to contract employee (*keiyaku shain*) and he continued to aspire to gaining a regular (*seishain*) position.

'I'm responsible for others'

For a minority of others, family responsibilities were argued to differentiate them from regular freeters. Vocational school graduate Masaru, 24 years old, for example, got married when he was 21 after his wife became pregnant.[24] In 2014 Masaru was a barista working as a regular employee (*seishain*) and his wife worked part time. His salary was not very high, but he enjoyed his work and between them they were able to remain financially afloat. In early 2015 they had a second child and Masaru quit his regular job to work at a restaurant for a higher hourly wage that would enable him to earn more. He hoped that after a few months they would give him a regular position.

This didn't, however, come to pass. He consequently began reworking at the coffee shop on weekends, thereby holding down two non-regular jobs. Over the year he gradually looked more drawn and exhausted. Despite his labour fitting the government definition, at no point did he consider himself to be a freeter. In 2015, being a father and husband clearly differentiated him, but financial responsibility was also a part of it as well:

> My contracts at the moment are part-time. I'm what is called a non-regular worker. But I work every day, and now I have taken a second job I am working a lot of hours every day. I have a family and children to support. So I am not a freeter. I think freeters have no responsibility except for themselves. I used to be a freeter when I was younger, but I'm not anymore.

Thus, for Masaru, having responsibilities for others—and embodying a dominant socio-cultural ideal of male adulthood of being financially responsible for a family—moves a person out of the freeter category regardless of whether their labour meets the definition. He retained hope that one day he could open his own café but was realistic that at the present moment this was not possible. Indeed, it took all his and his wife's efforts to remain financially afloat each month. Although he worked in the non-regular sphere, he primarily understood himself as doing what needed to be done for his family, and thus he felt he was not a freeter.[25] We can see in all the narratives thus far that despite the official definition the category of freeter is less about the type of non-regular *contract* and more about an understanding about the *type* of person doing such work.

'Yes, I am a freeter!'

A minority of men claimed the freeter label for themselves. A couple did this because of their long history of non-regular labour, a couple of others claimed it for themselves as a result of deep dissatisfaction with ways of working in Japan and their conflicted history of regular employment. For these men, claiming freeterhood was also about reframing how they thought freeter labour should be understood in wider society. For example, Hideo was a 37-year-old man who had graduated from a top university and gone on to have a twelve-year career in the civil service. Long unhappy in his job, he finally decided to quit when he was 34 to pursue his goal of being a self-made entrepreneur. Reflecting on freeter labour he mused:

> I think it is healthy to work 'as you like'. Working for a company is stressful and it can make people feel ill. So I think it is better to work freely as a freeter... I am definitely

a freeter—I work as much and whenever I like. My work is piecemeal (*barabara*) ... Japanese society only looks at freeters from an economic perspective. But as many companies go bankrupt there is no guarantee of employment even as a regular worker. I think that it is better to work more freely ... I think it is not fair that society suggests that freeters are bad (*yokunai*). This makes people feel that they are doing something wrong and I think that that is not right.[26]

He understood himself as a freeter because his work was not secure and not consistent. It should be noted, however, that he, like some of the other men discussed in this chapter, also framed his freeter labour as a means to achieving a different labour goal: to become a self-made entrepreneur. He strongly stressed, however, that the wider discourse of freeters was fundamentally unfair. For him, being able to work freely was not a shirking of social responsibility, but rather an act of self-responsibility. He was looking after his mental and physical health through seeking balance and meaning in his life and work. Of course, he was initially more financially able to do this because of substantial savings, living with his parents, and significant educational and residual social capital to draw on.[27] His desire for balance and for not blaming freeters for their labour practices is something that freeter organizations and precarity activists have also called for. For example, PAFF (Part-time Arbeiter Freeter Foreign Worker), a network of non-regular workers, have argued that:

Human beings are more than labour power. Life should be something richer, with things like talking and laughing with friends, watching movies, reading books, listening to music, traveling and loving. Such things are not necessarily earned by labour ... We freeters are forced by our cheap wages to work long hours to feed ourselves. And you have the stomach to tell us to work more!

(PAFF 2005, cited in Cassegård 2013: 100)

Cassegård (2013) argues that at the heart of PAFF is the idea that they are defending the reasonableness of not working to the limits of endurance—that a simpler life: of 'simply living' and getting by—should be possible. In discussing freeter protests, he suggests that,

Protests are not just directed at neoliberal deregulation, but also at the tendency to put the blame for young people's precarious situation on their own idleness or unwillingness to lead a conventional life. Against such arguments, activists usually emphasize that the problem has social, not individual, causes. They point out that many freeters do not wish for anything else but regular work, that they are not lazy and that working hours of freeters are often as long as or longer than those of regular employees.

(Cassegård 2013: 99)[28]

For PAFF the solution is to reject the 'work-centrist conviction' operating in wider society: to push for more acceptance of alternative ways of living and working. Hideo agrees with such a stance, but he also simultaneously draws on neoliberal discourses when arguing that his freelance work is an act of self-responsibility.

Aspiration, achievement, and freeterhood

Although the freeters I worked with were not engaging in these protest movements or labour unions, their desire to distance themselves from the label of freeter and, for many, their determination to draw on alternative labour aspirations, was both a desire to work in ways that made sense to them as well as a distancing strategy that was a response to the negative social discourses that suggested that (male) non-regular workers were lazy and not working in an appropriate manner. Many argued that life was—or should be—about more than work. Yet, in navigating socio-cultural ideas of labour and manhood, most framed their aspirations *in* labour. They grappled with normative ideas of work in Japan that draw on post-war Fordist labour practices that expect men to work long hours as regular employees in companies, along with the realities of a deregulated labour market that draws on neoliberal ideas of self-responsibility and individual blame for people who have either chosen not to, or are unable to, access the core labour market. Most men, in their attempts to navigate, make sense of, and adapt to post-Fordist neoliberal capitalism and labour realities, drew on neoliberal ideas of entrepreneurial selfhood and self-responsibility and sought to carve out a work-lifestyle that had individual meaning. Their narratives often suggested a desire to escape from post-war normative demands of labour and capitalism. Yet whilst they positioned themselves within normative neoliberal logics, most simultaneously felt the need to find full-time positions as they aged lest they remain in precarious positions in perpetuity. The benefits of flexibility waned as they aged and as the social and financial repercussions of remaining overly long in the non-regular labour market came to pass.

Han (2015: 8–9) has argued that increasing deregulation in post-industrial societies today is replacing disciplinary regimes with regimes of achievement:

> Prohibitions, commandments, and the law are replaced by projects, initiatives, and motivation. Disciplinary society is still governed by *no*. Its negativity produces madmen and criminals. In contrast, achievement society creates depressives and losers.

For Han the institutional separation of normal/abnormal is no longer relevant. Instead, achievement is the name of the game. What we can see in the social discourses of freeters, however, are two understandings of the institution of work that span ideas of both disciplinary and achievement societies—it is neither one nor the other in post-industrial Japan, but both. Moreover, the focus on achievement is itself a disciplinary mode of being. Cornwall (2016) has argued that deregulation, in the form of neoliberalism, has marketized the social and that 'it is precisely the ways in which neoliberalism engages the production of accountable, entrepreneurial subjectivities that makes it so insidious and pervasive, and that invite consideration of neoliberalism as governmentality' (2016: 8). This suggests that the very pervasiveness of what Han (2015) has called an 'achievement-subjectivity' is actually a form of governmentality. Its pervasiveness engenders a disciplinary mode of being that demands achievement and relies on the notion of self-responsibility in the process.[29] The negative discourses that suggest that freeters' characters are suspect because of their non-normative work styles is clearly embedded in Han's (2015) disciplinary society: there are 'normal' (and normative) ways of working and 'abnormal ways'. Freeter labour is typically considered abnormal and undesirable for men. Male freeters, in attempts to deal with their precarious social positioning and concerns over their futures as a result of this social positioning therefore draw on ideals that Han would argue epitomize an achievement society: they narrate labour aspirations, initiatives, and motivation to do something different—to achieve something related to labour—whilst at the same time negotiating disciplinary expectations of what they 'should' be doing as they age. There is not, therefore, a clear divide from a disciplinary to achievement society but rather a crossover of different ideals operating at the level of social discourse, with such discourses being navigated at the level of the subject in various ways in the messy reality of daily life.

Concluding remarks

In this chapter I have argued that many male freeters I worked with were conflicted and felt ambiguous about the label of 'freeter' because of the persistent problematic characterization of men in non-regular labour. As a consequence, they described themselves through the language of aspirations and goals, embedding themselves within the remit of neoliberal discourses of achievement, despite many of them individually protesting the 'work-centrism' that is implicit in understandings of regular labour practices in Japan.

With the negativity that has surrounded the label of freeter, discourses of (labour) achievement have become coercive and almost compulsory. To not proclaim some goal that involved ultimately moving out of freeter labour was to potentially be read—socially and economically—as a loser, unless it was invoked in a political vein. Hideo, for example, appropriated the label when he declared himself a freeter and, much like the narratives of PAFF, argued in a positive vein that freeter labour could and should be understood as a symbol of a life that included more than work: that a life worth living was one in which meaning and balance in life were dominant. He argued against discourses that framed freeters as people who were too lazy to work full time. Takeshi likewise drew on similar discourses, proclaiming a desire to not live and work like a robot. Yet both of these men also stressed in their narratives their aspirations of becoming self-made entrepreneurs in control of their labour—a status that transcends that of the non-regular labour market that freeters are embedded in and instead shifts them to the terrain of self-employment with greater social status and, potentially, a middle-class location rather than the low social status and working-class/potential underclass positionality that represents the lived reality of much freeter labour. However, as Japan diversifies non-regular labour into new forms, along with a gradual burgeoning of a gig economy with the expansion of 'nomad workers', and the expansion of companies like UberEats into urban areas (Pascaline 2016), it is likely we will see a further expansion of precarious working conditions, such as that being discussed now in other post-industrial countries. For example, whilst companies like Uber and others stress the independence, entrepreneurialism, and freedom that supposedly comes with being self-employed and working as independent contractors, the reality that has emerged in the UK, for example, is one of significant precarity and exploitation, with many feeling compelled to work all the time regardless of sickness so they don't get fined for missing shifts (Booth 2018a, 2018b; Mason 2018).

For men I have worked with in Japan, elaborations of how they were different (or not) from images of freeters was often related to how they ended up in non-regular labour, their previous work experiences, and the amount of educational and social capital they had. Most university graduates were focused on narrating and achieving labour goals, although this fluctuated over the life course in various ways as their situations changed. Many of the vocational school and high school graduates were more focused on describing their sense of responsibility in other ways: by narrating financial independence from kin, by living alone, or by looking after family. These men also had goals and aspirations but focused less on these than on how they were already responsible men. This directly feeds into post-war patriarchal family ideals, with men positioned as the pillar of the household (the *daikokubashira*) and the primary breadwinner responsible for the financial well-being of the family and household. This ideal continues to underpin the regular (core) employment system and its benefits packages, as well as state and welfare policy, and company and social attitudes. Given that this gendered ideology remains so insidious in much of the social, institutional, and employment frameworks, it is unsurprising that most of the men I worked with consistently drew on narratives of responsibility for others whilst at the same time juggling neoliberal ideals embedded in the non-regular employment sphere.

In following these men's lives (some since 2006, others since 2010 and 2013) it seems that, on the micro-level, the benefits of flexibility remain beneficial only as long as men are young and are thus not yet expected to work in a particular 'proper' way.[30] By upholding the social and moral stance that men should be 'responsible workers' through full-time salaried labour in the core labour market, ideologies of male labour and linkages to men's characters continue to be reinforced to the detriment of people who are outside this core labour market. Many male non-regular workers are thus between a rock and a hard place: in unstable, low-paid, precarious work on the one hand, and social expectations on men to continue to be a full-time regular worker who is the main breadwinner on the other. This is exacerbated by women's unstable position in the employment market, their over-representation in the non-regular labour market, and continuing difficulties for women to work full time while raising children (Macnaughtan 2015). For men in non-regular work who wish to continue creative endeavours and also create families there consequently needs to be a delinking (or at least weakening) of the persistent connection between labour and adult masculinities, social recognition that men can be productive citizens even if their labour is in the non-regular sector, and an expansion of well-paid regular work for women so that couples have more flexibility in the ways they organize—and finance—their households. At present, many men who remain in the non-regular labour market as they age become a precariat underclass effectively stuck in non-regular positions, with limited social capital and, for many, difficulties in marrying. Unless there is considerable change in social and company attitudes to non-regular labour, employment benefits, tax breaks for dependents, and social welfare policy, it is hard to see how any benefits that *might* exist in greater flexibility will be beneficial to a wider range of people, nor whether such flexibility would even be a desirable move to advocate for, given the exploitation, uncertainty, and precarity that has emerged with the expansion of non-regular employment and gig economies in other post-industrial societies.

Acknowledgements

This chapter develops further some of the arguments found in Chapter 2 of *Reconstructing Adult Masculinities: Part-time Work in Contemporary Japan*. London and New York: Routledge. Research was supported by a Japan Foundation Japanese Studies Fellowship (2006), a Meiji Jingu Studentship (2008), a Federation for Women Graduates Main Foundation Grant (2007), and a JSPS Postdoctoral Fellowship (2010, grant number: PE09533). Thanks go to my interlocuters for their time and generosity, and to Huiyan Fu for her comments on this chapter during the revision process.

Notes

1. Cited in Cook (2016): 48.
2. Part time in Japan is an ambiguous labour category with different definitions. The part-time labour law (*pāto taimu rōdō-hō*)—enacted in 1993—defined it as working less than 35 hours a week (Broadbent 2003). However, when the law was revised in 2007, the definition of part time was that of employees whose hours of work were shorter than the working hours of regular employees (*tsūjō no rōdōsha*) within the company (Assmann and Maslow 2010; Ministry of Justice 2009). Part-time work is also typically characterized by wages paid by the hour rather than monthly (Kawaguchi 2013), as well as the existence of a fixed-term contract which has to be renewed at regular intervals. Open-ended part-time contracts do exist and depending on the company non-regular workers may also be 'covered under public insurance systems including workers' compensation, unemployment, healthcare and retirement pension' (Asao 2011: 1). There is significant variety of classification of non-regular employment contract type in government statistics, and in practice this can also vary from company to company (see Asao 2011: 1–2). In an effort to clarify non-regular and regular employees' work, the 'Part-Time Employment Act' was amended in 2014 with the 'Act on Improvement in Management of Employment of Part-Time Workers'. This Act stipulates that if a part-timer's work is the same as a regular employee's with the same amount of responsibility, and if it is expected that the part-timer's job will change within the company or they will be relocated, they should be re-categorized as a 'Deemed Regular Employee' instead, even if their contract was originally a fixed-term contract (Anderson, Mōri, and Tomotsune 2014). Of course, whether this leads to part-time workers being re-categorized is dependent on company practice and their understanding of what constitutes the same amount of responsibility, etc. With regards to social insurance, there have, however, been recent changes. Since 1 October 2016, social insurance payments have been expanded to part-time employees if they meet the following conditions: if they are contracted to work more than 20 hours a week; earn more than 88,000 yen a month; are expected to be employed for more than one year on a continual basis; are not a student, and are employed by a company with more than 501 employees (MHLW 2016). Since 1 April 2020 revisions have been made to the Part-Time Employment Act, Labor Contract Act, and the Worker Dispatching Act with the aim

to reduce 'irrational gaps' between the treatment of regular and non-regular workers. Non-regular workers who are doing effectively the same duties—and scope of duties—as regular employees are now supposed to be treated as regular employees.

3. The 2017 figures don't split freeters into age brackets, but do show us that they comprised 700,000 men and 820,000 women (Statistics Bureau 2018). Whilst numbers of freeters aged 15–34—in the 'young to early-prime-age bracket' (JILPT 2017b: 4)—have been gradually decreasing as a result of a number of 'freeter measures', numbers of non-regular workers in the 'mid-prime-age bracket' between the ages of 35 and 44, who are doing similar jobs, were on the rise (JILPT 2017b: 1–22). Since 2019 overall freeter numbers dropped to 1.38 million, with 790,000 between the ages of 25 and 34 and 590,000 between 15 and 24. Those between 35 and 44 (who technically are no longer covered by the category 'freeter') have dropped from 570,000 to 530,000. In this recent publication they do not, however, provide a breakdown of freeter numbers by gender (MHLW 2021).

4. In 2006 I began fieldwork in Hamamatsu city focusing on male freeters' lives and their masculinities. I conducted nine months of ethnographic fieldwork in a multiplex cinema where I worked part time and engaged in participant-observation while working alongside freeters, part-time married workers, students, and full-time managers. In addition, I participated in meetings and events at a non-profit organization (NPO) that worked to help freeters and people who were not in employment, education, or training (NEETS) into employment. During this time period I also conducted semi-structured interviews with male and female freeters, with follow-up interviews in the summer of 2009, and throughout 2010–2011 in Hamamatsu and Tokyo whilst on a postdoctoral fellowship at Waseda University, and in the summer of 2013 (see Cook 2016). Between 2013 and 2016, I also conducted research with male and female non-regular workers in the service sector in Hokkaido (see Cook 2017). In total I interviewed 67 male freeters and 42 female freeters. This paper draws on narratives from across these different fieldsites and time frames. For a more in-depth discussion of research methods see Cook (2016: 18–22).

5. Female freeter experiences can be found in Cook (2016: 144–167). See also Chapter 9, this volume for a discussion of women's experiences of non-regular labour.

6. This chapter was initially written in 2017 and updated in 2018 and in 2021 before publication. As I write the final edits the Covid-19 pandemic continues to rage on around the world. Some of the men I worked with between 2006 and 2016 have remained in non-regular work and the pandemic has hit some of them hard. For example, one man works primarily as a tour guide and has consequently had no work since Covid-19 shut down the international tourism industry. Others in the service sector have also been struggling with reduced shifts and lower wages. I have refrained from positing an in-depth analysis of how this has changed their relationship to the category of 'freeter' and non-regular labour because the pandemic is ongoing. For an exploration of freelance workers' struggles during the pandemic, see Uno and O'Day (2020).

7. In 2018, the Uber website stated: '[E]arn good money . . . You'll make money by bringing people the things they love. Between deliveries, it's just you. So bump your favorite tunes and enjoy cruising around your city.' When re-checking this quote in 2021 it became apparent that the reference to earning 'good money' has been changed to 'Make money . . .' (https://www.uber.com/a/signup/drive/deliver/?70307t=). In 2018, UberEats Japan also stated on their English page: 'Deliver with Uber in Japan[:] No boss. Flexible schedule. Quick pay. . . . Between picking up and dropping off deliveries, it's just you

and the road—relax and enjoy cruising around town.' In 2021 this has been edited to 'Your vehicle, your time. Weekly payments. Enjoy your city . . . Between picking up and dropping off deliveries, it's just you and the road—relax and enjoy cruising around town.' (https://www.uber.com/en-JP/drive/delivery/). Meanwhile, on their Japanese page and unchanged since I checked in 2018 they suggest: 'Just by placing an application online you can work when you like and it's possible to earn an income on a weekly basis (*apuri wo onrain ni suru dake de suki na toki ni kadō deki, shū tani de shūnyū wo eru koto ga kanō desu*)' (https://www.uber.com/ja-JP/drive/delivery/).

8. A 2017 JILPT report suggests there has been a recovery trend of youth employment (those between 15 and 24) over the previous decade, with youth unemployment dropping from 10 per cent in 2003 to 3.8 per cent in 2019. Moreover, the total number of freeters (between the ages of 15 and 34) dropped to 1.38 million freeters, though with working conditions of non-regular employees worsening compared to that of regular employees (Hori 2021). The 'Japan Revitalization Strategy' had the aim of reducing the number of freeters to 1.24 million yen by 2020 by helping freeters move into regular employment and improving job matching (JILPT 2017b).

9. Passet (2003: 160) has argued in his study of the employment system that as of the late 1990s and early 2000s 'a considerable share of marginal workers also has long employment tenure'; however, this doesn't necessarily make the work less precarious as they remain an adjustable buffer for companies, nor does it change the fact that they generally earn lower wages and don't share the same benefits that regular (*seishain*) workers receive, though it remains to be seen if this will change with recent amendments to the Part-Time Employment Act (MHLW 2019). Where I did fieldwork, non-regular contracts were renewed every six months and employees were always aware that their renewal was dependent on their cooperation and performance at work as well as the financial needs of the company.

10. Although typically understood as a lifetime contract, it is not necessarily so. Companies can and do restructure and lay off regular employees and it is also possible to fire employees as North (2016) clearly explains (see also Foote 1996; Upham 2011; Yamakawa 2011). In recent years 'Limited regular employment' (*gentei seiki koyou*) has emerged as a possible middle ground between regular and non-regular employment. The work location is limited (there are no transfers), work content is defined, and work hours are fixed (there is no, or limited, overtime). While it can potentially be considered more secure than non-regular work, it has also been argued that it could lead to regular employees being 'downgraded' to the limited regular category. This category of worker is also potentially more vulnerable to being made redundant than regular employees if companies deem it economically necessary (Gordon 2017; North 2014).

11. This is not just a characteristic of the Japanese employment market but can be seen across other post-industrial economies, for example in Europe (see for example, Booth, Francesconi, and Frank 2002; Pedaci 2010).

12. More recently, however, it has been argued that it is the regular salaried employee who is dragging down economic productivity, and that what Japan needs to do is make the job market liquid by creating more flexible contracts with pay based on productivity, as well as creating more movement at the mid-career level. This would, the argument goes, dismantle the core/peripheral model of employment (Lewis 2016).

13. https://youtu.be/6FIegzNFek4. As of November 13th, 2022 the video has been viewed 1,921,740 times.
14. See https://www.mhlw.go.jp/stf/seisakunitsuite/bunya/0000181329.html for descriptions of Youth Hello Work and https://www.mhlw.go.jp/stf/seisakunitsuite/bunya/0000132220.html for New Graduate Support Hello Work.
15. As of 2017, approximately 60 per cent of male freeters had a junior high or high school diploma, 16.9 per cent had graduated from vocational colleges or two-year colleges, and 21.8 per cent had a university degree. For women, approximately 54 per cent had junior high/high school diplomas, 28.8 per cent had vocational or two-year college diplomas, and 16 per cent had a university degree. Since 1982 the figures of those with university education has been gradually increasing: from 12.2 per cent to 21.8 per cent in 2017 for men, and from 9.3 per cent to 16 per cent in 2017 for women (Hori 2021).
16. Bourdieu (1984) has argued that there are different types of capital which locate us within the social order and form the foundation of social life. The three primary types of capital are: economic (e.g. wages, property, investment assets); social (e.g. connections, networks, alliances); and cultural (e.g. education, cultural goods, bodily and mind dispositions).
17. Vera-Sanso (2016) argues that strong ideologies of men as primary providers reduces ideological possibilities of masculinities to just one: that of the breadwinner model of masculinity. However, economic and employment changes make this an increasingly unattainable aspiration for many men. In the context of South India, Vera-Sanso suggests that men in economically disadvantaged positions often experience 'progressive feminization' as they age and are unable to achieve the demands of the breadwinner model of masculinity, instead being supported by the women in their households. For the men I have worked with, the majority of those who are still working in the non-regular labour sector remain unmarried and are therefore not experiencing feminization within the household as a result of women's capacity to provide and their inability to materially provide (Cook 2014). Instead they appear to be largely locked out of family creation—something Allison (2012) has dubbed 'ordinary refugeeism' from the heteronormative home and family—and therefore in a state of stasis in relation to this particular ideology of masculinity. Many attempt to carve out alternative, and at times ambiguous, narratives of masculinity and labour-meaning for themselves (see Cook 2016).
18. The case of Eiji is also discussed in Cook (2017).
19. Cited in Cook (2016: 63).
20. Amway is short for American Way, a network marketing business (see http://www.amway.co.jp/).
21. Cited in Cook (2016: 70).
22. Cited in Cook (2016: 96–97).
23. Cited in Cook (2016: 50).
24. The case of Masaru has been discussed in Cook (2017).
25. A year or so after our conversations about freeters and masculinity he and his wife divorced, and in 2018 he quit his jobs and left the city to return alone to the familial farm.
26. Cited in Cook (2016: 48).
27. The Covid-19 pandemic has, however, hit Hideo hard as his main income stream in recent years has come from tourism-related work, which has entirely dried up. In a recent

online conversation in 2021 he confided that he had not had a salary for the past year, and while living with his parents has helped him considerably, he was anxious and worried about what the future holds.
28. Precarity activists like Karin Amamiya have called for all those whose lives are hard—financially and mentally—to head out to the streets to protest. Railing against the culture of overwork and labour exploitation, precarity activists demand that people just be allowed to live a decent life 'without dying from overwork, without becoming homeless, without committing suicide' (Amamiya 2007: 282, cited in Cassegård 2013: 96).
29. This process is also temporal. Munia (2016) has argued that the nature of work today collapses time. From his fieldwork in a Japanese company that hires foreigners to provide telephone support for international customers, he traces company practices in hiring and in day-to-day running that exploit workers and coerce work to be done outside of work hours at home. Although in their recruitment the company makes no mention of requiring extra work, they strongly push a discourse of being a team player, rather than being a selfish individual. In doing so, they extract work on weekends and on holidays from home with no extra hours being paid, despite promising paid overtime in the hiring process. Exploitation is therefore cloaked in the rhetoric of being a team player. Munia argues, along the lines of Graeber (2013), that technology is forcing people to work more, not less, by collapsing distinctions between work-life and private-life, and that such discourses are embedded in what Han (2015: 8) has called the 'achievement society'. We can see an even heightened version of this collapse between work-life/private-life occurring during the Covid-19 pandemic.
30. Auer and Cazes (2003) have argued that, because of a general perception of youth as a temporary state, young people have consequently been seen as temporarily 'outside' the labour market in precarious positions before transitioning into something more stable. Of course, for some youth this may be the case, for others the relationship to precarious labour is more complex, fluid, and embedded in class dynamics and educational and social capital (MacDonald 2009).

References

Allison, A. (2012) 'Ordinary refugees: Social precarity and soul in 21st century Japan'. *Anthropological Quarterly*, 85(2): 345–370.

Allison, A. (2013) *Precarious Japan*. Durham and London: Duke University Press.

Amamiya, K. (2007) *Ikisasero! Nanminka suru wakamonotachi (Let us Live! The Refugeeization of Young People)*. Tokyo: Ōta shuppan.

Anderson Mori & Tomotsune (2014) 'Amendment to the Part-Time Employment Act of Japan'. *Labor and Employment Law Bulletin* June 2014 (35). Available at: https://www.amt-law.com/en/pdf/bulletins7_pdf/LELB35.pdf/.

Anon. (2003a) 'Government sees "freeters" as early warning sign'. *The Japan Times*, 31 May. Available at: http://search.japantimes.co.jp/cgi-bin/nb20030531b4.html/. Accessed April 2011.

Anon. (2003b) 'White Paper says "freeters" are a drag on productivity'. *The Asahi Shimbun*, 31 May. Available at: http://www.freerepublic.com/focus/f-news/921072/posts/. Accessed: April 2008.

Anon. (2006a) 'Panel mulls hiring 100 "freeters" in civil service'. *The Japan Times*, 16 May. Available at: http://search.japantimes.co.jp/cgi-bin/nn20060516b7.html/. Accessed: June 2008.

Anon. (2006b) 'Support clubs to make "old freeters" into full-timers'. *The Japan Times*, 24 August. Available at: http://search.japantimes.co.jp/mail/nn20060824b2.html/. Accessed: June 2008.

Anon. (2008a) 'New plan aims to reduce "freeters" by 110,000'. *The Japan Times*, 23 April. Available at: http://search.japantimes.co.jp/cgi-bin/nb20080423a3.html/. Accessed: April 2008.

Anon. (2008b) 'Subsidies to make "freeters" full-timers'. *The Japan Times*, 22 October. Available at: http://search.japantimes.co.jp/cgi-bin/nb20081022a2.html/. Accessed: April 2011.

Anon. (2013a) 'Furītā Shiken Koyō he no Shōreikin, Minkan Shōkai mo Taishō ni Kōrōshō' (Ministry of Health Labour and Welfare decides subsidies for trial employment of freeters, opens to private companies), 11 April. Available at: http://www.nikkei.com/article/DGXNASFS1002A_Q3A410C1PP8000/. Accessed: October 2013.

Anon. (2013b) 'Toboshii Shokugyō Kunren—Furītā Shien Kyūmu (Hatarakenai Wakamono no Kiken)' (Meagre vocational training: Freeter support urgently needed (crisis of young people unable to work). *Nihon Keizai Shinbun* (Morning Editions), 16 January, 5. Accessed 16 January2013. Print Edition.

Asao, Y. (2011) 'Overview of non-regular employment in Japan'. *JILPT Report*, 10 (2011): 1–42.

Assmann, S. and Maslow, S. (2010) 'Dispatched and displaced: Rethinking employment and welfare protection in Japan'. *The Asia-Pacific Journal*, 8(15), 3. Available at: http://www.japanfocus.org/-sebastian-maslow/3342/.

Auer, P. and Cazes, S. (2003) 'The resilience of the long-term employment relationship'. In P. Auer and S. Cazes (eds.), *Employment Stability in an Era of Flexibility: Evidence from Industrialized Countries*. Geneva: International Labour Organization, pp. 22–58.

Booth, A. L., Francesconi, M., and Frank, J. (2002) 'Temporary jobs: Stepping stones or dead ends?' *Economic Journal*, 112: 189–213.

Booth, R. (2018a) '700,000 gig workers paid below national minimum wage'. *The Guardian*, 7 February. Available at: https://www.theguardian.com/business/2018/feb/07/death-dpd-courier-don-lane-tragedy-business-secretary?CMP=Share_iOSApp_Other/. Accessed: 22 February 2018.

Booth, R. (2018b) 'Gig economy workers angry at lack of bogus self-employment curbs'. *The Guardian*, 7 February. Available at: https://www.theguardian.com/business/2018/feb/07/gig-economy-workers-angry-at-lack-of-bogus-self-employment-curbs/. Accessed: 22 February 2018.

Bourdieu, P. (1984) *Distinction: A Social Critique of the Judgement of Taste* (Translated by Richard Nice). London: Routledge & Kegan Paul.

Brinton, M. C. (2010) *Lost in Transition: Youth, Work, and Instability in Postindustrial Japan*. Cambridge: Cambridge University Press.

Broadbent, K. (2003) *Women's Employment in Japan: The Experience of Part-Time Workers*. London: RoutledgeCurzon.

Cabinet Office (2016) '2016 Children and Youth White Paper (Full Edition)' (Heisei 27 nen do kodomo / wakamono hakusho zentaiban). Available at: http://www8.cao.go.jp/youth/whitepaper/h27honpen/index.html/. Accessed: 22 February 2018.

Cassegård, C. (2013) *Youth Movements, Trauma and Alternative Space in Contemporary Japan*. Leiden, Boston: Koninklijke Brill.

Cook, E. E. (2013) 'Expectations of failure: Maturity and masculinity for freeters in contemporary Japan'. *Social Science Japan Journal*, 16(1): 29–43.

Cook, E. E. (2014) 'Intimate expectations and practices: Freeter relationships and marriage in contemporary Japan'. *Asian Anthropology*, 13(1): 36–51.

Cook, E. E. (2016) *Reconstructing Adult Masculinities: Part-time Work in Contemporary Japan*. London and New York: Routledge.

Cook, E. E. (2017) 'Aspirational labour, performativity and masculinities in the making'. *Intersections: Gender and Sexuality in Asia and the Pacific*, 41. Available at: http://intersections.anu.edu.au/issue41/cook.html/.

Cornwall, A. (2016) 'Introduction: Masculinities under neoliberalism'. In Andrea Cornwall, Frank G. Karioris, and Nancy Lindisfarne (eds.), *Masculinities Under Neoliberalism*. London: Zed Books, pp. 1–28.

Dardot, P. and Laval, C. (2013) *The New Way of the World: On Neoliberal Society*. London: Verso.

Driscoll, M. (2007) 'Debt and denunciation in post-bubble Japan: On the two freeters'. *Cultural Critique*, 65: 164–187.

Foote, D. H. (1996) 'Judicial creation of norms in Japanese labor law: Activism in the service of stability?' *UCLA Law Review*, 43: 635–709.

Fu, H. (2012) *An Emerging Non-Regular Labour Force in Japan: The Dignity of Dispatched Workers*. Abingdon: Routledge.

Genda, Y. (2005) *A Nagging Sense of Job Insecurity: The New Reality Facing Japanese Youth* (Translated by Jean Hoff. 1st English ed.) Tokyo, Japan: International House of Japan.

Gill, T. (2001) *Men of Uncertainty: The Social Organization of Day Laborers in Contemporary Japan*. Albany: State University of New York Press.

Gordon, A. (2017) 'New and enduring dual structures of employment in Japan: The rise of non-regular labor, 1980s–2010s'. *Social Science Japan Journal*, 20(1): 9–36.

Graeber, D. (2013) 'On the phenomenon of bullshit jobs'. *Strike Magazine*, 17 August. Available at: http://strikemag.org/bullshit-jobs/. Accessed: 19 November 2016.

Han, B. C. (2015) *The Burnout Society* (Translated by Erik Butler). Stanford: Stanford University Press.

Harding, R. (2016) 'Shinzo Abe fears wrath of the salaryman on labour reform'. *The Financial Times*, 12 October. Available at: https://www.ft.com/content/5e3114be-902a-11e6-8df8-d3778b55a923/. Accessed: 19 November 2016.

Hirano, K. (2005) 'Freeters: Free by name, nature: Exploitative corporate culture breeds nomadic workers'. *The Japan Times*, 29 January. Available at: http://www.japantimes.co.jp/text/nn20050129f1.html/. Accessed: May 2008.

Honda, N. (2013) *Nomado raifu: Suki na basho ni sunde jiyū ni hataraku tame ni, yatte okubeki koto (Nomad Life: What to Do in Order to Live in a Place you Like and Work Freely)*. Tokyo: Asahi Shimbun Publications.

Hori, Y. (2021) 'Changing consciousness and reality of part-time workers: An interview survey with a view to the impact of the spread of Covid-19' (Henka suru furītā no ishiki to jittai—shingata korona kansen-shō kakudai no eikyō o shiya ni ireta intabyū chōsa kara). Japan Institute of Labor Policy and Training (JILPT) Survey research results, materials (chōsa kenkyū seika, shiryō shirīzu). Available at: https://www.jil.go.jp/institute/siryo/2021/documents/237.pdf/.

Ishiguro, K. (2008) 'Japanese employment in transformation: The growing number of non-regular workers'. *Electronic Journal of Contemporary Japanese Studies* Article 10 (December). Available at: http://www.japanesestudies.org.uk/articles/2008/Ishiguro.html/.

JILPT. (2014) 'Labor situation in Japan and its analysis: General overview 2013/2014'. (The Japan Institute for Labour Policy and Training). Available at: http://www.jil.go.jp/english/lsj/general/2013-2014.html/.

JILPT. (2016) 'Japanese working life profile 2015/2016: Labor Statistics'. Available at: http://www.jil.go.jp/english/jwl/2015-2016/all.pdf.

JILPT. (2017a) Japanese working life profile 2016/2017. Available at: http://www.jil.go.jp/english/jwl/2016-2017/all.pdf.

JILPT. (2017b) 'Labor situation in Japan and its analysis: Detailed exposition 2016/2017'. (The Japan Institute for Labour Policy and Training). Available at: http://www.jil.go.jp/english/lsj/detailed/2016-2017.html/.

Kageyama, Y. (2005) 'Job-hopping "freeters" growing in ranks in Japa—and authorities are worried'. *Post-Gazette Now*, 18 July. Available at: http://www.postgazette.com/pg/05199/536823.stm/. Accessed: May 2008.

Kawaguchi, D. (2013) 'Introduction to wage statistics in Japan'. *Japan Labor Review*, 10(4): 24–33.

Kitazume, T. (2005) 'Weak work ethic holding back a generation of freeters'. *Japan Times*, 26 July. Accessed 26 July 2005. Print Edition.

Kosugi, R. (2008) *Escape from Work: Freelancing Youth and the Challenge to Corporate Japan* (Translated by Ross Mouer). Melbourne: Trans Pacific Press.

Kosugi, R. (2021) 'From the perspective of career development and vocational ability development: Freeters in 2020 and Freeters in 1999' (Kyaria keisei shokugyō nōryoku keisei no shiten kara: 2020 nen no furītā to 1999 nen no furītā). In Yukie Hori (ed.), *Changing Consciousness and Reality of Part-Time Workers: An Interview Survey with a View to the Impact of the Spread of Covid-19 (Henka suru furītā no ishiki to jittai — shingata korona kansen-shō kakudai no eikyō o shiya ni ireta intabyū chōsa kara)*. Japan Institute of Labor Policy and Training (JILPT), pp. 15–26.

Lewis, L. (2016) 'The curse of the salaryman'. *The Financial Times*, 3 May. Available at: https://www.ft.com/content/d1a6aa18-1045-11e6-91da-096d89bd2173/. Accessed: 19 November 2016.

MacDonald, R. (2009) 'Precarious work: Risk, choice and poverty traps'. In Andy Furlong (ed.), *Handbook of Youth and Young Adulthood: New Perspectives and Agendas*. London and New York: Routledge, pp. 167–175

Macnaughtan, H. (2006) *Women and Work in Postwar Japan*. London and New York: Routledge.

Macnaughtan, H. (2015) 'Womenomics for Japan: Is the Abe policy for gendered employment viable in an era of precarity?' *The Asia-Pacific Journal*, 13(12): 1–10. Available at: http://www.japanfocus.org/-Helen-Macnaughtan/4302/article.html#/.

Mason, R. (2017) 'May says she will help gig economy workers but fails to pledge new laws'. *The Guardian*, 11 July. Available at: https://www.theguardian.com/business/2017/jul/11/theresa-may-help-gig-economy-workers-rights-no-legislation/. Accessed: 22 February 2018.

Matsushita, K. (2016) 'Mediated workplaces and work styles as second offline'. In Hidenori Tomita (ed.), *The Post-Mobile Society: From the Smart/Mobile to Second Offline*. London and New York: Routledge, pp. 37–46.

Millward, S. (2017) 'They want to turn Japan's job-for-life workers into giggers'. *TechInAsia*, 26 July. Available at: https://www.techinasia.com/japan-gig-economy-zehitomo-funding. Accessed: 24 February 2018.

Ministry of Health, Labour and Welfare (MHLW) (2007) 'White Paper: Work-Life Balance and Employment Systems'. Available at: http://www.mhlw.go.jp/wp/hakusyo/roudou/07/index.html. Accessed: February 2010.

Ministry of Health, Labour and Welfare (MHLW) (2015) 'Seishain? Furītā? Nani ga chigau no?? Shōrai no shinro ni tsuite nayande iru kata e ~' (Full-time employee? Freeter? What's the difference?? For those who are worried about their future career). https://www.mhlw.go.jp/file/06-Seisakujouhou-11600000-Shokugyouanteikyoku/0000105821.pdf. Accessed: November 2022.

Ministry of Health, Labour and Welfare (MHLW) (2016) 'Heisei 28nen 10 gatsu kara kōsei nenkin hoken kenkō hoken no kanyū taishō ga hirgarimasu!' (Shakai hoken no tekiyō kakudai) (From October 2016 the target to join welfare pension insurance and health insurance expands! Expansion of adoption of social insurance). http://www.mhlw.go.jp/stf/seisakunitsuite/bunya/2810tekiyoukakudai. Accessed: 24 November.

Ministry of Health, Labour and Welfare (MHLW) (2019) 'Ensuring fair treatment of workers irrespective of their employment types' (Revision of the Part-time Employment Act, Labor Contract Act and the Worker Dispatching Act). Available at: https://www.mhlw.go.jp/english/policy/employ-labour/fixed-term-workers/dl/201904koyo.pdf. Accessed: 3 May 2021.

Ministry of Health, Labour and Welfare (MHLW) (2021) 'Future employment of young people, 7th study group materials' (Dai 7-kai kongo no jakunenmono koyō ni kansuru kenkyūkai shiryō). https://www.mhlw.go.jp/stf/shingi/other-syokunou_130000.html. Accessed: 24 April 2021.

Ministry of Justice (2009) 'Tanjikan Rōdōsha no koyō kanri no kaizen Inado ni kan suru hōritsu: Heisei 19 nen hōritsu dai 72 gō' (Act on Improvement, etc. of Employment Management for Part-Time Workers: Amendment Act No. 72 of 2007). http://www.japaneselawtranslation.go.jp/law/detail/?id=84&vm=04&re=01/. Accessed: 24 November 2016.

Miura, M. (2012) *Welfare Through Work: Conservative Ideas, Partisan Dynamics, and Social Protection in Japan*. Ithaca and London: Cornell University Press.

Munia, R. (2016) 'Discussing idleness in the achievement society: Work and youth in Japan'. *East Asian Anthropological Association* Conference Presentation, Hokkaido University, 16 October 2016.

North, S. (2014) 'Limited regular employment and the reform of Japan's division of labor'. *The Asia-Pacific Journal*, 12(15): 1–22. Available at: https://apjjf.org/2014/12/15/Scott-North/4106/article.html/.

North, S. and Morioka, R. (2016) 'Hope found in lives lost: Karoshi and the pursuit of worker rights in Japan'. *Contemporary Japan*, 28(1): 59–80.

O'Day, R. (2013) 'Japanese irregular workers in protest: Freeters, precarity and the re-articulation of class'. PhD Thesis, Department of Anthropology, The University of British Columbia.

O'Day, R. (2015) 'Differentiating SEALDs from freeters, and precariats: The politics of youth movements in contemporary Japan'. *The Asia-Pacific Journal: Japan Focus*, 13(37): 1–9. Available at: http://apjjf.org/-Robin-O_Day/4376/.

Ogino, N. (2015) 'JILPT research eye: Sign of change in employment portfolio'. *JILPT Research Eye*, 24 March. Available at: http://www.jil.go.jp/english/researcheye/bn/RE006.html/.

Osawa, M. (2011) 'Gender-equality and the revitalization of Japan's society and economy under globalization'. *World Development Report: Gender Equality and Development Background Paper* 2011: 2–21.

Otake, T. (2002) 'Are "freeters" result of slump, source of next one?' *The Japan Times*, 5 February 2002. Available at; http://search.japantimes.co.jp/cgi-bin/nn20020205b6.html/. Accessed: April 2008.

PAFF (2005) 'Wakamono no Ningenryoku o Takamenai Hikokumin Sengen' (The unpatriotic movement for not raising the human ability of the young). Available at: http://freeter-union.org/resource/statement_20051026.html/. Accessed: 4 November 2016.

Parry, R. L. (2006) 'A nation lives in fear of the neets and freeters'. *The Times*, 2 November 2006. Available at: http://business.timesonline.co.uk/tol/business/markets/japan/article622158.ece/. Accessed 27 June 2011.

Pascaline, M. (2016) 'UberEATS: Uber to launch food delivery service in Japan'. *International Business Times*, 28 September. Available at: http://www.ibtimes.com/ubereats-uber-launch-food-delivery-service-japan-2422954/. Accessed: 22 February 2018.

Passet, O. (2003) 'Stability and change: Japan's employment system under pressure'. In Peter Auer and Sandrine Cazes (eds.), *Employment Stability in an Age of Flexibility: Evidence from Industrialized Countries*. Geneva: International Labour Office, pp. 159–217.

Pedaci, M. (2010) 'The flexibility trap: Temporary jobs and precarity as a disciplinary mechanism'. *WorkingUSA: The Journal of Labor and Society*, 13(2): 245–262.

Perkins, C. (2014) 'Part-timer, buy a house: Middle-class precarity, sentimentality and learning the meaning of work.' In Kristina Iwata-Weickgenannt and Roman Rosenbaum (eds.), *Visions of Precarity in Japanese Popular Culture and Literature*. London and New York: Routledge, pp. 64–85.

Smith, C. (2006) 'After affluence: *Freeters* and the limits of new middle-class Japan.' PhD Thesis, Department of Anthropology, Yale University.

Statistics Bureau, Japan (2018) 'Rōdōryoku chōsa (shōsai shūkei). Heisei 29 nen do (2017) heikin (sokuhō)' (Labour Force Survey (Detailed Total) 2017 Averages (preliminary report). Available at: http://www.stat.go.jp/data/roudou/sokuhou/nen/dt/pdf/index1.pdf/. Accessed 22 February 2018.

Tachibana, T. (2012) *Nomad Worker toiu Ikikata (Way of Life Called Nomad Worker)*. Tokyo: Toyokeizai Shinpousha.

Tarōmaru, H. (ed.) (2006) *Furītā to Nīto no Shakai Gaku (Sociology of Freeters and NEETs)*: Shakai Shisōsha.

Tarōmaru, H. (2009) *Jyakunen Hiseiki Koyō no Shakaigaku: Kaisō, Jendā, Gurobaruka (The Sociology of Irregular Youth Employment: Class, Gender, Globalization)*. Osaka: Osaka Daigaku Shuppankai.

Toivonen, T. (2008) 'Introducing the youth independence camp: How a new social policy is reconfiguring the public-private boundaries of social provision in Japan'. *SocioLogos (ソシオロゴス)*, 32: 40–57.

Toivonen, T. (2013) *Japan's Emerging Youth Policy: Getting Young Adults Back to Work*. Abingdon: Routledge.

Uno, S. and O'Day, R. (2020) 'Japanese freelance workers struggle during the COVID-19 pandemic: Social media, critique, and political resistance'. *The Asia-Pacific Journal: Japan Focus*, 18(18): 1–16. Available at: https://apjjf.org/2020/18/Uno-ODay.html/.

Upham, F. (2011) 'Stealth activism: Norm formation by Japanese courts'. *University of Washington Law Review*, 88: 1493–1505.

Vera-Sanso, P. (2016) 'Taking the long view: Attaining and sustaining masculinity across the life course in South India'. In Andrea Cornwall, Frank G Karioris, and Nancy Lindisfarne (eds.), *Masculinities Under Neoliberalism*. London: Zed Books, pp. 80–98.

Yamakawa, R. (2011) 'From security to mobility? Changing aspects of Japanese dismissal law'. In Daniel H. Foote (ed.), *Law in Japan: A Turning Point*. Seattle: University of Washington Press, pp. 483–520.

Index

Note: Tables and figures are indicated by an italic *t* and *f* following the page number.

Abe, Shinzo
   Covid-19 pandemic and school closures 85
   emergence of gig work 64–65
   equal pay for equal work principles 60–61, 214, 224–225
   labour market and gender policies 48–49
   social compromise 59–64, 68–69
   Work-Style Reforms 61–62, 64, 214
ACFTU 10–11, 43 n.7
   organizing around precarity 93, 95, 112–113
      1978–1990 96–99
      1990–2002 99–100
      2002–2012 102, 106
      2012–present 108, 110–112
achievement discourses 232–234
agricultural sector, China 159–160, 169
   organizing around precarity 96
   pre-reform era (1949–1978) 30–32*f*
   reform era (1979–2007) 33–34
All-China Federation of Trade Unions *see* ACFTU
All Japan Metal and Information Machinery Workers' Union *see* JMITU/JMIU
amakudari 11–12
Amway 227
anthropology
   British ('social') *vs* American ('cultural') 5–6
   holism 4–6
   rural migrants, China 25
   symbolic 5–6
area limited regular employee category, Japan 223–224
Asian Financial Crisis (AFC, 1997–1998) 52–53
aspiration and freeterhood, Japan 225–230, 232, 234–235

authors *see* online literature platforms, China

Baidu 178–179
Beijing
   hukou 40
   Olympics 43 n.8
   organizing around precarity 100, 106–108, 111–112
   rural migrant women 155, 159, 160–162, 166, 167–168
Beijing Migrant Women's Club 100–101
bonuses
   China 97
   Japan
      freeters 222–223
      gender pay gap 199–200, 199*t*, 206–207, 214

Cabacula Union 58–59
Calbee 77
caring services sector, Japan 57
Cassegård, C. 231
censorship, China
   online literature platforms 178
   organizing around precarity 110–113
children/childcare
   China, labour NGOs 103, 109–110
   Japan 57, 235
      Covid-19 pandemic 74–76, 81–82, 85–86
      gender pay gap 208–209, 213–214
China Labour Bulletin (CLB) 101, 111–112
China Literature 178–180
China Online Literature Copyright Alliance 186–187
China Writers' Association (CWA) 177–178
Chinese Communist Party (CCP)
   industrial relations 10–11
   organizing around precarity 93

1978–1990 96–99
1990–2002 99–100
2012–present 108–110
pre-reform era (1949–1978) 30–33
reform era (1979–2007) 35–36
regulation era (2008–present) 37–38
Chinese Magic Fantasy Union 178
Chinese Working Women's
 Network 100–101
civil service, Japan 63
closed shop agreements *see* union shop
 agreements, Japan
Cloudary 178–179
commune system, China 96
Communist Party *see* Chinese Communist
 Party (CCP)
Confucianism
 China 2–3, 8, 14–15, 41–42
  guanxi 36
  hukou 8–9
  pre-reform era (1949–1978) 30–33
  reform era (1979–2007) 35–36
  regulation era (2008–present) 39–40
 family 11–12
 harmony 10–11, 39–42
 Japan 2–3, 8, 14–15, 198
  women's familial roles 9–10
construction sector, China
 organizing around precarity 94–95, 97,
  106, 110–111
 rural migrant women 166
Contract Law (China, 2008) 102, 112
contracts
 China
  Labour Contract Law 27–28, 37–38
  online literature platforms 180–183,
   189–192
  organizing around precarity 93–95,
   97–98, 102, 107–108, 112
  rural migrants *vs* urban
   workers 27–28f, 29–30
 Japan 56–57
  Covid-19 pandemic 149
  freeters 223–224, 227, 228
  Labour Contract Act 215 n.4, 236 n.2
  part-time work 236 n.2
  trade unions 118, 128
copyright 179, 186–192
corporate social responsibility (CSR),
 China 103–104

corruption, China 35–36, 99
Covid-19 pandemic 1–2, 18
 China, rural migrants 24–25, 27
 Japan 48–49
  freeters 237 n.6, 239 n.27
  labour market dualism 149
  teleworking 74–89
  women 66–69
 work *vs* private life, collapse of 240 n.29
creative industries, China 175–176
 see also online literature platforms, China
crony capitalism 10–11, 36–37
Crystal Group 145
cultural production *see* online literature
 platforms, China
Cultural Revolution (1966–1976) 32–33
culture 4–8, 17–18, 196
 China 2–4, 25, 41
  and institutions 4–5, 7–8, 41–42
  Confucianism 2–3, 8–33, 41–42
  holism 4–5, 18
  pre-reform era (1949–1978) 30–31
  regulation era (2008–present) 38–39
  rural migrants 25
 Japan 2–4, 14–15
  business 76–77, 80, 87–89
  Confucianism 2–3, 8, 9–11, 14–15
  gender 51–52, 60, 62–63, 149, 219–220
  holism 4–5, 18
  and institutions 4–5, 7–8
  patriarchy 205–206
  trade unions 13–14, 120, 133

dagongmei 156–157, 163, 164–165, 168, 170
Dardot, P. 221–222
decentralization, China 38–39
Deliveroo 111
Democracy Movement, China 98–99
demographics 3–4
 China 31, 40
 Japan 80
Deng Xiaoping
 'get rich' slogan 35–36
 'open-door' economic reforms 8–9,
  33–34, 99
 organizing around precarity 97
Didi Chuxing 27
digital divide, Japan 76–77, 83–84, 88–89
digital technology
 China 27

digital technology (*Continued*)
    online literature platforms 175–192
    organizing around precarity 106, 112–113
    Japan 49
        emergence of gig work 64–65
        nomad workers 80–81, 83, 221, 234
        teleworking 74–89
        working hours 240 n.29
disabled people, Japan 77
discourse analysis 5–6
discrimination
    China, rural migrants 29–30, 105–106
    Japan 208
        gender 51–52, 63–64, 204
        trade unions 141, 149–150, 151 n.11
Domei 119–120
domestic violence, Japan 85–87
double dispatching 145
Durkheim, E. 5–6

Edogawa 120–121
education
    China, rural migrants 12–13, 29–30, 37–38
    women 156, 161, 163
    Japan
        freeters 218–219, 223–226, 228, 229–231, 234–235, 238 n.12, 239 n.15
        gender pay gap 198–199, 203–207, 210, 212
        trade unions 128
elderly people, Japan
    care 57, 85
    Covid-19 pandemic 74
    increased labour market participation 65
Ele.me 111
employment contracts *see* contracts
Employment Security Law (Japan) 151 n.14
England, industrialization 28–29
Equal Employment Opportunity Law (Japan, 1986) 51
equal pay for equal work principle, Japan
    Abe administration 60–61, 214, 224–225
    teleworking 78
    trade unions 125
European Union
    Covid-19 pandemic 74
    trade unions 133–134

family 17–18
    China
        organizing around precarity 94
        patriarchy 154–155
        rural migrant women 154–155, 159–161, 164, 166–167, 169–170
    Japan
        Abe administration 62
        company likened to family 196
        Confucianism 11–12
        Covid-19 pandemic and teleworking 74–76, 78–83, 85–86
        freeters 225, 227, 228–230, 234–235
        gender divide 9–10, 14–15, 51–52
        gender pay gap 206–209, 211–214
        patriarchy 205–206, 219–220
        trade unions 133
    see also children/childcare
foreign-owned enterprises (FOEs), China 26–30
    organizing around precarity 99–100
    reform era (1979–2007) 34–35
    women 29–30
foreign workers, Japan 58
France, wages 56*f*
Free Labour Union of China, Preparatory Committee 100
freemium business model 178, 180, 183, 186
Freeter (film) 221
'Freeter buys a house' (television drama) 224–225
Freeter Zenpan Roudou Kumiai 58
freeters, Japan 218–221, 233–235
    achievement discourses 232–234
    aspiration 225–230, 232, 234–235
    narratives 225–232
    problematic (male) 221–225
Fujitsu 77, 80
Fullcast 142–143
furlough, Japan 74

Gang of Four 97
gender
    China 155
    identity 157
    Japan 48–49, 68
        Abe administration 62–65
        Covid-19 pandemic 74, 84
        culture 149

emergence of gig work 64–65
freeters 218–235
Suga administration 63–64
teleworking 78, 85
trade unions 13–14, 118–119, 133–134, 138–139, 141, 144–145
see also women
Gender Equality Bureau, Japan 63
Georgia, Colour Revolution 108–109
Germany
Covid-19 pandemic 83–84
teleworking and productivity 79
wages 54–56f
global financial crisis 66–67, 145
globalization 2, 7–8, 154
China 101
Japan 52
Goodwill 142–143, 145
Great Leap Forward (1958–1960) 31, 96
Great Recession 138–139
grievances *see* labour unrest and grievances
Guangzhou 106–107
guanxi 36–41
industrial relations 10–11
rural migrant women 159, 161, 163, 169

Haken Union 138, 141–143, 145, 146–148t, 149–150
Hakenmura 13–14
Hamamatsu 237 n.4
Han, B. C. 232–233
Han Dongfang 101
Hann, C. 6–7
Harvey, D. 6–7
health insurance, China 27–28f
Hebei 155, 161–162, 164–166, 168
Hello Work 223–224
Henan 155
High Professional System, Japan 61–62
Hitachi 74–75, 77
Hokkaido 237 n.4
holism 4–8, 18
Honda 101, 104–105, 111
Hong Kong
labour NGOs 12–13, 101, 103–105, 109
support for Zhili Handicraft fire victims 100–101
Hongxiu 178
hours worked *see* working hours
household registration, China *see hukou*

Hu Jintao
harmony 39–40
organizing around precarity 101–107, 112–113
hukou 8–9, 14–15, 24–25, 27–30, 40–42
organizing around precarity 96
pre-reform era (1949–1978) 30–33
reform era (1979–2007) 33–34
regulation era (2008–present) 40
women 156, 159, 161, 169, 170
hybrid working, Japan 76, 80, 81–83, 88–89

identity negotiation, Chinese rural migrant women 155–171
Improvement in Management of Employment of Part-Time Workers Act (Japan, 2014) 236 n.2
Independent Trade Union (UK) 110–111
India, 'progressive feminization' of ageing men 239 n.17
individualism 4–8, 18
industrial relations
China 10–11, 14–15
Japan 11–15, 118–119, 121, 130–134
industrialization
China 31, 34, 154
England 28–29
Industry Federation of Express Delivery 111–112
information technology *see* digital technology
internet *see* digital technology
interns, China 29–30, 38, 98, 102, 106
iron rice bowl 26, 30–32
China Writers' Association 177–178
organizing around precarity 95–97, 100, 112
reform era (1979–2007) 34–35

Japan Community Union Federation (JCUF) 142, 149–150
Japan Federation of Service and Distribution Workers Union (JSD) 147
Japan Metal, Manufacturing, Information and Telecommunication Workers' Union *see* JMITU/JMIU
Japan Revitalization Strategy 238 n.8
Japan Trade Union Confederation *see* Rengo
JASICS 109
JCUF 142, 149–150

Index

Jichiroren 119, 125–128
   membership data 123*t*
Jinjiang 178
Jinzai Sabisu General Union *see* JSGU
JMITU/JMIU 150 n.7
   challenges 119, 125–128
   inclusive responses 138–141, 143–144, 146–148*t*
   membership data 123*t*
JSD 147
JSGU 138–139, 141, 144–147, 148*t*, 148–149, 150 n.7

Keidanren, 62
keiretsu groups 49–50, 52–53
Koizumi, Junichiro 52–54
Koyo Sealing Technology 128, 140–141, 143–144
Kyrgyzstan, Colour Revolution 108–109

Labour Contract Act (Japan) 215 n.4, 236 n.2
Labour Contract Law (China, 2008, amended 2013) 27–28, 37–38
labour contracts *see* contracts
Labour Disputes Mediation and Arbitration Law (China, 2008) 38
Labour Law (China)
   1950 99–100
   1994 99–100, 112
labour NGOs, China 12–15, 41–42, 93, 95
   1990–2002 100–101
   2002–2012 101–107, 112
   2012–present 107–112
Labour Standards Law (Japan) 61–62
labour unions *see* trade unions
labour unrest and grievances
   China 12–13, 37–38, 37*f*, 38–39
      organizing around precarity 94–101, 104–105, 109, 111–112
   Japan 13–14, 49, 58
      Abe administration 59, 68
      Cabacula Union 59
      trade unions 120–121, 140–142, 146–147, 149–150
Laval, C. 221–222
leave benefits, Japan
   Covid-19 pandemic 67–68, 67*f*, 86
   freeters 222–223
   trade unions 124, 149–150
   women 206–207, 214
Lehman Brothers 88, 126–127
Liberal Democratic Party of Japan (LDP) 63–65
liminality 18, 157
limited regular employee category, Japan 223–224, 238 n.10
linguistic turn 41–42
literature platforms *see* online literature platforms, China

Manpower Japan 144–145
manufacturing sector
   China 28–29
      organizing around precarity 97, 106, 110–111
      pre-reform era (1949–1978) 30–32
      rural migrant women 154–155, 157, 163–164, 170
   Japan
      keiretsu groups 50
      trade unions 138–140, 143–144
Maoism 30–31, 43 n.10
   vs Confucianism 32–33
   Mao's death 97
   neo- 109
   organizing around precarity 93
   and reform era (1979–2007) 36
   and regulation era (2008–present) 37–38
   rural workers 8–9
market socialism, China 35–36
marketization, China 10–11, 35–36, 41–42
Maruko Horn Company 128
Marxism
   China 25, 41–42, 43 n.10
      pre-reform era (1949–1978) 30–31
      reform era (1979–2007) 35–36
   primitive accumulation 189–190
Mauss, M. 4–5
men *see* gender
migrant workers *see* rural migrants, China
minimum wage, Japan 207–208
Ministry of Civil Affairs, China 106–109
Ministry of Health, Labour and Welfare (MHLW), Japan
   emergence of gig work 65–66
   freeters 218–219, 223–224
Ministry of Internal Affairs and Communications (MIC), Japan 66–67

Ministry of Labour, Japan 86
Ministry of Public Security, China 108–109
Mio, Sugita 64
Mizuho Research 77
modernity, and Chinese rural migrant women 157–162, 164–165, 168
modernization 154
  China 8–9, 41, 155
    reform era (1979–2007) 33–34
    regulation era (2008–present) 39–40
  technology 27
Mori, Yoshiro 63

Nanohana Union 58
National Confederation of Trade Unions *see* Zenroren
National Security Law (Hong Kong) 109
neoliberalism 2, 6–8, 17–18, 196–197, 210
  China 7–8, 41, 175
    global context 35–36
    online literature platforms 181, 186, 191
    organizing around precarity 94
    rural migrants 8–9
    suzhi 34
  existential norm 221–222
  as governmentality 233
  Japan 7–8, 48–49, 68, 214
    Abe administration 60–61
    contestation 58
    freeters 220–221, 225, 231–235
    gender 222
    gender pay gap 203, 213–214
    policies and reforms 52–57, 53*t*
    trade unions 133–134
  and precariousness 43 n.11
neo-Maoism 109
New Graduate Support Hello Work 223–224
Nichia Corporation 144
Nikkeiren 49
Ninomiya, Makoto 145–146
Nippon Thompson 143–144
nomad workers, Japan 80–81, 83, 221, 234
non-governmental organizations (NGOs)
  China 108–109
    see also labour NGOs, China
  Japan 121–122
Nonini, D. M. 36
non-profit organizations (NPOs), Japan 58

Olympic Games
  Beijing 43 n.8
  Tokyo 63
online literature platforms, China 175–177, 190–192
  access 180–182
  copyright 186–190
  evolution 177–180
  temporality 182–184
  visibility 185–186
'open-door' economic reforms, China 8–9, 24–25, 33–34, 97, 99
Opinions on Building Harmonious Labour Relations (China, 2015) 38
organizing around precarity in China 93–95, 112–113
  1978–1990 95–99
  1990–2002 99–101
  2002–2012 101–107
  2012–present 107–112
Overseas NGOs Law (China, 2016) 108–109
overtime, Japan 240 n.29
  Abe administration 61–62
  Covid-19 pandemic and teleworking 78–79, 87–88
  gender pay gap 206–207
  limited regular employment 238 n.10
overwork
  Chinese online literature platforms 184, 191, 214
  Japan 61–62, 87–88, 213, 240 n.28

Part-time Arbeiter Freeter Foreign Worker (PAFF) 231–232, 234
Part-Time Employment Act (Japan, 1993, revised 2007) 128, 236 n.2, 238 n.9
Pasona 144–145
paternalism
  China 41
    industrial relations 10–11
    pre-reform era (1949–1978) 30–33
    regulation era (2008–present) 38–40
  Japan 205–206
    trade unions 133
patriarchy
  China, rural migrant women 154–155, 161, 164–168, 170
  Japan 9–10, 88–89, 205–206
    family 219–220

patriarchy (*Continued*)
    freeters 234–235
    trade unions 133
pay *see* wages
peasants *see* rural migrants, China
pensions, China 27–28f, 161
Perfect World 178–179
petitions *see* labour unrest and grievances
piece-rate work, China 97–98, 110–111
piracy, Chinese online literature
    platforms 186–190
privacy issues, Japan
    teleworking 81–82
    vs rural life 83
private-owned enterprises (POEs),
    China 26–30, 34–35
privatization 6, 196–197
    China 33–34, 36
productivity
    China
        online literature platforms 183–184
        teleworking 78–79
    Japan
        freeters 223
        teleworking 77–79, 84, 88–89
        trade unions 139–140, 145, 146–147
Promotion of Female Participation and
    Career Advancement in the
    Workplace Act (Japan)
    2015 62
    2019 62
Promotion of Gender Equality in the
    Political Field Act (Japan, 2018) 62
Protection of Women Workers' Rights Law
    (China, 1991) 99–100
protests
    China 39–40
        Tiananmen Square 98–99
    Japan
        freeters 220–221, 231, 232–233
        gender pay gap 213–214
    see also labour unrest and grievances
Provisional Regulations on Labour Dispatch
    (China, 2014) 38
publishing houses, China 177–178, 190

Qidian 178–181

race to the bottom 6
rallies *see* labour unrest and grievances

remuneration
    Chinese online literature
        platforms 178–181, 183–214
    see also bonuses; wages
Rengo 118–125, 127–133, 142, 143–145,
    148–149
    membership data 123t
retail sector
    China 166–168
    Japan
        trade unions 138–140, 147
        women 50
        working hours 121
retirement, China 42 n.2
rural areas
    China
        migrants *see* rural migrants, China
        organizing around precarity 96
    Japan
        teleworking 80–83
        women's employment prospects 208
rural migrants, China 3–4, 8–9, 14–15,
    17–18, 24–30, 40–42
    industrial relations 10–11
    labour unrest 12–13
    organizing around precarity 96–101, 104,
        105–110
    pre-reform era (1949–1978) 30–32, 34
    reform era (1979–2007) 33–38
    regulation era (2008–present) 37–40
    women 154–171

salaries *see* wages
Seikyororen 119, 126, 127–130, 132
    membership data 123t
Sekine, Shuichiro 142
self-employment
    China 26–27, 176
        organizing around precarity 106
        rural migrant women 166
    digital technology 3–4
    Japan, freeters 221, 234
    misclassification 2
    UK 234
seniority wage system, Japan 49–52,
    197–200, 215 n.3
service sector
    China 28–30
        organizing around precarity 106–110,
        112–113

reform era (1979–2007) 34–35
rural migrant women 154–155, 166
Japan
  caring 57
  Covid-19 pandemic 85, 237 n.6
  freeters 237 n.6
  women 51, 57
sexual harassment/crimes, Japan 58, 86–87, 124
Shanda Interactive Entertainment 178–179
Shanda Literature 178–179
Shanghai 40
Shantou 155, 164, 167
Shenzhen
  organizing around precarity 100–101, 106–110
  rural migrant women 157, 164
Shu Pu Association for the Protection of the Rights of Laid-Off Workers 100
Social Insurance Law (China, 2011) 102, 104–105
social media
  China
    online literature platforms 185–186
    organizing around precarity 110–113
  Japan, nomad workers 221
social security
  China 34–35, 40
    online literature platforms 181
    organizing around precarity 94, 102
    rural migrant women 156
  Japan 49–50, 54
    Covid-19 pandemic 67–68, 86, 88
    freeters 235
    gender 219–220
    part-time work 236 n.2
    trade unions 128
    women 48, 67–68, 85–86
Social Security Law (China, 2011) 38
Sohyo 119–120
South Korea
  trade unions 137
  women 24, 29–30, 40–41
Special Economic Zones (SEZs), China 97, 112
state-owned enterprises (SOEs), China 26–28
  industrial relations 10–11
  labour unrest 12–13

organizing around precarity 95–96, 100, 102, 104–105, 112
pre-reform era (1949–1978) 30–31
reform era (1979–2007) 34–35
women 29–30
strikes *see* labour unrest and grievances
student interns, China 29–30, 38, 98, 102, 106
Suga, Yoshihide
  gender bias 63–64, 68–69
  digitalization agency 76–77
suicides, Japan 85–88
Suntory 80
supervision, and teleworking
  Germany 79
  Japan 81, 84
surrogate writing 181–182, 191
suzhi 34–36, 41
  rural migrant women 155–156, 159–160, 163, 166, 169
Sweden, wages 54–56*f*

Tangjia Sanshao 179–180
taxation, Japan
  freeters 235
  gender 48, 51, 60, 62, 68, 85–86, 219–220
  trade unions 125
Telecommunication Workers' Union 150 n.9
teleworking
  China 78–79
  Japan 74–89, 149–150
Tencent 178–179
textile sector, China 154–155, 164, 167
Tokyo
  Covid-19 pandemic and teleworking 75–76, 82, 88–89
  freeters 237 n.4
  Haken Union 141–142
  Olympics 63
  UberEats 221
Tokyo Managers Union 120–121
Tokyo Union 142
total social phenomenon 2–8, 14–15
Toyota 140–141
Trade Union Law (China, 1992) 99–100
trade unions
  China 10–11, 38–40, 43 n.7
    labour unrest 12–13

trade unions (*Continued*)
    organizing around precarity
        93, 106–107, 109, 112–113
    EU 133–134
    international 101, 103–104
    Japan 11–12, 49, 53–54, 58, 197–198
        challenges 118–134
        fragmented voice 131–132, 131*f*, 132–133
        gender pay gap 209, 213–214
        High Professional System 61–62
        inclusive responses 137–150
        labour unrest 13–14
        working hours 61–62
    liberal democracies 95
    neoliberalism 6–7
    South Korea 137
    UK 110–111
training
    Chinese online literature platforms 182
    Japan
        Covid-19 pandemic's repercussions 83–84
        freeters 218–219, 226
        remote methods 81
trust-based working-time arrangements (TBW) 79
Tsushin Rose 150 n.9
Tsushin Sangyo 134 n.2

UA Zensen
    challenges 119, 121–125, 127, 128–132
    formation 151 n.15
    inclusive responses 138, 144–145
    membership data 123*t*
Uber 1–2, 27, 221, 234
UI Zensen 119, 122–124, 138, 144–145, 147
Ukraine, Colour Revolution 108–109
underemployment, China 96, 100
unemployment
    China 98, 100
    Japan 11–12
        Covid-19 pandemic 66–67, 85–86
        trends 66–67, 66*f*
        women 85–86
        young people 238 n.8
union shop agreements, Japan 119–121, 132
    JSGU 145–146
    Rengo 122–124, 130
    Zenroren 127–128

unions *see* trade unions
United Kingdom
    creative industries discourse 175
    food-delivery workers 111
    gig economy 221
    Independent Trade Union 110–111
    industrialization 28–29
    pay gap 198–199
    self-employment 234
    wages 56*f*
United Nations, funding of Chinese labour NGOs 108–109
United States
    Covid-19 pandemic 74, 83–84
    opposition to China's Contract Law 102
    teleworking and productivity 78–79
    wages 54–56*f*
urbanization, China 31, 154, 155, 170
    reform era (1979–2007) 33–34
    regulation era (2008–present) 40
U-turn phenomenon, Japan 82

wages
    China
        organizing around precarity 94, 97, 104–105, 109, 110–112
        pre-reform era (1949–1978) 30–32
        reform era (1979–2007) 34–35
        rural migrant women 164–165, 167
    country comparison 56*f*
    Japan 57
        Abe administration 61
        Covid-19 pandemic 67–68, 86
        emergence of gig work 65
        freeters 222–223, 228, 229–231, 237 n.6
        vs job security 53–54
        part-time work 236 n.2
        seniority wage system 49–52, 197–200, 215 n.3
        trade unions 122, 124, 125, 128, 133, 141, 142–143, 145–146
        trends 54
        women 48, 51, 56, 57*f*, 68, 197, 198–209, 198*t*, 199*t*, 209–215
    UK 198–199
WeChat 111, 185
welfare corporatism, Japan 11–12
welfare state *see* social security
Wen Jiabao 101–107, 112–113

wholesale sector, Japan 50
women
  China 29–30
    organizing around precarity 100–101, 109–110
    pre-reform era (1949–1978) 31–32
    reform era (1979–2007) 34–35
    rural migrants 154–171
  Japan 17–18, 24, 29–30, 40–41, 48–49
    Abe administration 59–60, 62–63, 68–69
    caregiving role 57, 59, 60, 68
    caste-like employment system 209–210
    consent without dissatisfaction 211–213
    Covid-19 pandemic 66–68, 74, 84–89
    culture 3–4, 9–12, 14–15
    disaffected consent 196–210, 213–215
    dissatisfaction without consent 211–212
    dualism in labour market 50–51, 53–54, 57
    emergence of gig work 65–66, 68–69
    employee by type 55*t*
    employment prospects 206–209
    freeters 218–220, 235
    good *vs* bad regular workers 204–206
    self-blame 203–204
    self-reservations about ability 201–203
    sexual harassment of/crimes against 58, 86–87, 124
    teleworking 78, 85
    trade unions 13–14, 58–59, 133
    wages 48, 50, 51, 56, 57*f*, 68, 197, 198–209, 198*t*, 199*t*, 209–215
  South Korea 24, 29–30, 40–41
Women's Union Tokyo 58, 120–121
Womenomics 62
work–life balance, Japan
  teleworking 74–75, 78, 81–82
  women 67–68
Work-Style Reforms, Japan 61–62, 64, 214
Worker Dispatch Law (WDL, Japan, 1986 and amendments) 50, 52–54, 53*t*, 61, 140, 150 n.2, n.6, 236 n.2
  Crystal Group's non-compliance with 145
  double dispatching 151 n.14
  Rengo *vs* JSGU 148–149
worker grievances *see* labour unrest and grievances

working conditions 7
  China
    organizing around precarity 94, 96–98, 100, 104, 109, 112–113
    rural migrants 12–13, 17–18, 29–30, 165
  Japan 214
    Abe administration 61–62
    freeters 234, 238 n.8
    Haken Union 141–143
    rural migrants 17–18
    trade unions 118, 121, 122, 124–128, 131–132
    women 60
working hours
  China
    organizing around precarity 94, 98
    rural migrant women 166
  Japan 215 n.2, 226, 240 n.29
    Abe administration 61–62
    Covid-19 pandemic 149
    freeters 220–221, 225–226, 228–229, 231, 232
    gender pay gap 206–209, 212
    limited regular employment 238 n.10
    teleworking 77–78, 87–88
    trade unions 121–122, 130, 132
    trust-based working-time arrangements (TBW) 79
  see also overwork
World Trade Organization (WTO) 101
writers *see* online literature platforms, China

Xi Jinping 93, 104, 106–112
Xiaoxiang 178

young people
  China
    pre-reform era (1949–1978) 31–32
    regulation era (2008–present) 37–38
    rural migrants 12–13, 29–30, 160–161, 164–165, 168, 169
  Japan
    freeters 218–235
    increased labour market participation 65
    teleworking 81–83
    trade unions 13–14, 144
Youth Hello Work 223–224

Yu Yuan shoe factory 104–105
Yuewen Group *see* China Literature

Zenkoku Yunion (JCUF) 142, 149–150
Zenroren 118–121, 125–133, 143, 144
Zenryoku 119–120
Zensen Domei 151 n.13
Zhang Shanguang 100
Zhang Wei 179–180
Zhili Handicraft 100–101
Zongheng 178
Zoom burnout 86